California Thrill Sports

by Erik Fair

ISBN 0-935701-32-X

51495

9 780935 701326

California Thrill Sports

Foghorn Press
555 De Haro Street
The Boiler Room #220
San Francisco, CA 94107
(415) 241-9550

California Thrill Sports

by Erik Fair

Foghorn Press Inc.

Credits

Managing Editor.....Ann-Marie Brown
Copy Editor.............Nina Schuyler
Maps and Icons.......Luke Thrasher
Book Design............Ann-Marie Brown
and Denis Wright

Photo Credits

Front cover
Gary Duncan bungee jumps from Total Rebound's crane—and photographs himself with a camera strapped to his arm

Photo Insert (in order of pages)

1) Larry Prosor (Tahoe rock climber)
2) Morton Beebe (bungee jumper)
3) Joe Aldendifer (parasailing boat)
   Bob Gaines (woman rock climbing)
   Larry Prosor (paragliding over trees)
4) John Heiney (skydiver)
5) Willard Nordby (sea kayaker)
   Larry Prosor (whitewater kayaker)
   Larry Prosor (balloon)
6) Larry Prosor (river rafting)
   John Heiney (hang gliding over cliffs)
7) John Heiney (hang giding over water)
8) Joe Aldendifer (beginner paragliding)
   Larry Prosor (bungee jumping)

This book is affectionately dedicated
to anyone who ever said (or thought):

"Gee, I've always wanted to try that!"

TABLE OF CONTENTS

ADVISORY

No thrill sports are without risk, and injuries and death can and do occur in thrill sports, even to trained participants using proper equipment. No one should participate in any of the activities in this book unless they recognize and personally assume the associated risks.

Regarding the resource guides at the end of each chapter: We have made every effort to include changes that occurred between research and publication. Please be aware, however, that new outfitters constantly open businesses, others go out of business, and still others change ownership or programs. As such, always call to confirm—to your own satisfaction—the competence and suitability of any thrill sport provider that you are considering using. If you uncover information or have experiences that conflict with the information in this book, please let us know so that we can stay current.

NOTE FROM THE AUTHOR

By most objective standards I was a burned-out middle-aged loser. Two jettisoned careers, one botched marriage, and the breakup of a 10-year relationship deposited me in my mid-forties—dazed, confused and without much net worth.

During the exuberant years of my twenties, I had been a social worker. Troubled families, disturbed children, abusive parents, even hard-core prisoners came and went. Finally, I snapped. I bought a hang gliding business, of all things, and broke my momma's heart.

Over the next eight years I parlayed my passion for flying into a modest level of fame and fortune. I became a medium cheese in the small but enthusiastic world of hang gliding. But gradually, painfully, the passion drained from my soul. Desire and confidence went along with it. When I realized—after nearly 10 years of teaching and flying—that I was *afraid* of hang gliding, I sold the business to my partner.

With no marketable skills that I cared to use, I set out to become a full-time writer. I knew I had raw talent. I also knew that I faced long odds. A writer—especially a passionless middle-aged writer just starting out—has the same chance of success as a burger joint in Chinatown.

For a year and a half, I struggled with moderate success. One day I was presented with an opportunity to write an article about adventure sports. The good news was that if I did the article I could pay the rent. The bad news was that, to do it right, I'd have to take a ride 300 feet in the air on a parasail—and I was still afraid of flying.

But—hey—a man has got to pay his rent. So I went for it.

My ten minute "ride of passage" in a parasail fired me up. Afterwards I felt GREAT!—better than I had felt in years.

Over the next six months the passion from two lost careers seeped back into my heart. The social worker in me ached to write a book about the therapeutic and rejuvenational value of thrill sports. The hang gliding instructor agreed to get involved as long as the book was done right—factually, with a healthy dose of wide-eyed exuberance and a *relentless commitment to the principles of safety and personal responsibility.*

I wrote the book. Foghorn Press published it. It's in your hands. If you have half as much fun reading it as I had writing it, you're in for a great time.

—Erik Fair, March 1992

INTRODUCTION

WHO YOU CALLIN' A THRILL SPORT?!

- Bungee jumping and skydiving?
- Whitewater rafting and kayaking?
- Parasailing and paragliding?
- Hot air ballooning and hang gliding?
- Rock climbing?

What exactly do these "crazy" sports—these hairball activities—have in common? What are they doing lumped together in the same book?

First, let's agree that every one of the adventures listed above shares the following characteristics:

•Each offers a unique blend of real and perceived risk.

•Each gives you a highly personal encounter with the natural environment—a new kind of involvement with earth, water or air.

•Each has the power to produce altered states of consciousness, or—at the very least—do funny things to your perceptions of the world.

•Each allows you to play with gravity in strange new ways.

•Each requires a healthy measure of personal responsibility to be done safely.

•Each requires competent professional supervision, guidance or instruction at the introductory level—assuming, of course, that maximum safety and great fun are your first two priorities.

•Finally, and most importantly, each can be thoroughly enjoyed in your dreams as well as in real life—and it helps your enjoyment when you know enough to separate fact from fiction.

Admit it. It's a whole lot of fun when you get that dreamy look in your eyes and think: "Wow, I've always wanted to try that..." In some respects, fantasizing about a thrilling adventure is even more fun than actually going out and doing it.

Doing it, you see, takes a little bit of work. At the very least, you have to take great care to choose a safe, competent, state-of-the-art provider. With some thrill sports, you also have to bring concentration, focus, self-awareness and a willingness to learn new skills to your first experience.

You may or may not want to go to the trouble.

The bottom line is that you're reading this book because at least one of the thrilling adventures in it *turns you on.* It may not turn you on in a way that compels you to grab a phone book and begin a breathless search for the nearest hang gliding instructor, for example, but odds are good that it turns you on enough that you'd really like to know what it would be like to go flying—just once—in a hang glider.

This book will tell you.

You will fly, climb and run whitewater through the eyes of others just like you—others who have decided to take a state-of-the-art introductory ride or lesson in the thrill sport that turns them on. You will also find a listing of books, magazines and organizations that can tell you more about the sport, and a list of convenient places to observe it so you can see for yourself what really goes on.

You will learn to separate "thrill fact" from "thrill fiction." In the process, you will learn what measures you can take to assure safe-as-possible enjoyment of the thrill sport that calls your name. That way, if you do go for it, you'll know exactly how you can best look out for yourself.

You will learn about state-of-the-art instructional technique, all the common myths associated with your favorite thrill sport, ways for you personally to minimize risks and maximize rewards, and practical nuts and bolts pointers on how to select the safest and most exhilarating introductory experience from the maze of providers that service your area.

And, once you decide to take the leap or make the plunge, you will have at your fingertips a detailed listing of the best thrill sport resources in the state of California. The last section of each sport's chapter is a cream-of-the-crop guide to the instructors, guides, schools and outfitters who make a living turning your thrill sport dreams into reality, in the safest way possible.

You're about to find out how participation in thrill sports—at any level—can change your life for the better.

You can do it: in the sky, on whitewater or up against the face of a sheer rock wall. Or, you can do it with this book—from the absolute safety and comfort of your own living room couch.

Have fun and stay safe.

ABOUT DEATH—The Big P.S.:

OK, I admit it—it's true. You can get hurt or killed doing these things. The three biggest sources of injury and death in thrill sports are:

1) Beginners who teach themselves the basics or misplace their trust in an unqualified

friend or relative. The best way to create your own risk in a thrill sport is to get off on the wrong foot.

2) Exhilarated intermediates who are so obsessed with developing advanced skills that they forget or ignore well-established rules of safe progression within the sport. It's kind of like shooting yourself in the head.

3) Advanced participants who yearn to re-define the sport's outer limits and are willing to pay the ultimate price for exceeding those limits. That's their choice. You don't have to make it yours.

You can avoid the first major killer if you **start out with a pro.**

You can avoid the second major killer if you **consistently follow established rules of safe progression.**

You can avoid the third major killer in one of two ways:

1) **avoid advanced levels of participation all together;** or

2) **let others push the absolute edges while you constantly re-define your own.**

If you consistently and conscientiously avoid these three major pitfalls, safe participation in thrill sports becomes a simple matter of relentless risk management in the name of exceptional fun.

Isn't that what life is all about?

Who, Me?!

and other

Thrilling Issues

Tales of Growth and Perspective
Risk Without Danger?
Go With the Flow
Rides of Passage/Leaps of Faith

Chapter One

Who, Me?!

California's legendary thrill sports—the kind that get you up in thin air, down on white water, or pitted against terrain only a mountain goat could love—have two things in common:

• First, the core of their appeal is risk. They are thrilling because they are—as your mother says—*dangerous.*

• Second, whether you admit it or not, you personally have yearned to try at least one of these "crazy" sports at least once.

If you don't believe it, check out the following list:

Bungee jumping
Rock climbing
Whitewater rafting
Hot air ballooning
Parasailing
Skydiving
Hang gliding
Paragliding
Kayaking

Now check your pulse.

It's racing a little bit, right? And there's a smile on your face, right? That means there is a part of you that is *dying* to swoop through the air like an eagle, plunge down a stretch of whitewater like an otter, or scale new heights on the face of a rock wall like a mountain goat.

And what has stopped you? The shrill voices of loved ones yelping heartfelt concerns about your mental and physical health?

No matter how your particular stop signs read, rest assured they all boil down to one very personal and utterly rational question: Are the rewards of your favorite thrill sport worth the risks for you personally?

For many of us, the instinctive answer to that nerve-jangling question is NO WAY! But a little closer look at any one of the activities listed in this book invites a more open-minded response. At the introductory or "let's try this just once" level, risk management in each of these adventures is far more effective—and within your personal control—than you think.

Technological progress, improved teaching techniques and the creation of safer and more exciting introductory rides have taken the Russian roulette out of California's thrill sports. The simple truth is: All that stands between you and an exhilarating, highly rewarding adventure is a carefully calculated risk—the kind that even your mother would endorse.

At the introductory or "let's try this just once" level, risk management in each of these adventures is far more effective—and within your personal control—than you think.

So what's the big deal about thrill sports? Why take risks at all? Because acceptable risks are what life is all about. And there are few things on this planet that rival a thrilling adventure for making you feel alive.

Whether you enjoy them vicariously or in real life, each of California's thrill sports offers a unique and intensely personal adventure experience. First, you get to choose from three of nature's mediums: earth, water or air. Second, each sport offers multiple levels of involvement. If you don't want to take a hot air balloon ride, you can have enormous fun serving as ground crew for a friend who does. Finally, if kamikaze solo hang gliding turns you completely off, odds are that whitewater rafting with a group of friends (and an experienced guide!) will turn you on.

From a pure rewards perspective, *the thrill sport that turns you on* is the one that has the power to give you a very personal moment—a moment that will leave you breathless, give you a fresh new outlook on life, and perhaps allow you to grow in ways that you've never before imagined.

Remember, you don't actually have to go out and *do* these crazy things in order to get a big charge out of them. Believe it or not, when it comes to thrill sports, the knowledge that you *could do them if you really wanted to* is almost as rewarding as the doing itself.

So whether you prefer to grab your magic moment in the sky itself, or simply envision it from the comfort of your own couch, read on. Either way, this book will help you separate "thrill fact" from "thrill fiction."

Either way, the moment is yours for the seizing.

TALES OF GROWTH AND PERSPECTIVE

CALIFORNIA'S THRILL SPORTS ARE BOUNDLESSLY appealing. Men and women of all types and persuasions, of all ages, can and do find at least one thrilling adventure that does it for them.

Does what, for whom, you ask? The answers are as varied as thrill sports themselves, and as diverse as the adventurers who delight in them.

Take you, for example. Isn't there a definite gut-level appeal to the image of your own sweet self floating gently through a cloud-puffed sky in a hot air balloon, or bobbing along a stretch of whitewater in a raft full of grinning, shouting friends? You may even be a closet bungee jumper, an unusual type who secretly yearns for the kind of pure relief on the heels of sheer terror that you get only when you jump bungee.

Who knows what constitutes your private fantasy?

Everyone comes to thrill sports for a different reason. Your thrill may be your neighbor's chill and vice versa. In almost every case, something individual and unique—about you—will draw you naturally to your thrill sport. Invariably, that something is directly connected to your big payoff, the true and ultimate reward you will get from participating in (or vicariously enjoying) your favorite thrill sport.

In almost every case, something individual and unique—about you—will draw you naturally to your thrill sport.

Consider the following Tales of Growth and Perspective:

Growth

Marie Encke was a seven-year-old who never looked both ways before riding her bicycle on the street. She didn't think twice about walking behind strange horses either. Her failure to behave responsibly in potentially dangerous situations was driving her parents crazy.

Though they had been separated since Marie was just one year old, Mark Encke and Dana Kauffman were definitely together on this one. They wracked their brains in search of something that would put Marie in touch with the idea of taking care of herself.

When Mark suggested that Marie might benefit from a father/daughter whitewater rafting trip, Dana listened despite her misgivings. "I thought Marie might be a little too young to learn about safety by shooting through rapids with names like Meatgrinder, Troublemaker and Satan's Cesspool," recalls Dana.

But Mark was convinced that his daughter needed "something real" to confront and conquer.

"I didn't want to take her to Disney World or play Nintendo with her," recalls Mark. "Neither would teach her anything about responsibility. I felt like we needed an adventure where what we did or didn't do would make a difference."

"I didn't want to take her to Disney World or play Nintendo with her...I felt like we needed an adventure where what we did or didn't do would make a difference."

Mark called **Earth Trek** expeditions and tentatively scheduled a weekend trip on the South Fork of the American River. In the meantime, Dana checked things out.

"I talked to Earth Trek and they assured me that Marie, like everyone else, would wear a lifejacket and that she would be in the middle of the boat during rapids. Then I asked a rafting friend of mine for his opinion. He said that the Chili

Bar and Gorge runs—at their current level of flow—shouldn't be a problem for Marie.

"I was nervous about it, but since I knew I couldn't keep her in a box her whole life, I let her go."

"Marie was quiet and cautious during our first day on the river," recalls Mark. "All the talk about Troublemaker scared her so badly, she wanted out of the boat. Our guide said she could walk but that she'd have to watch out for snakes on the river bank. She decided that Troublemaker didn't look so bad after all."

"I ALMOST GOT THROWN OUT OF THE BOAT!!" recounts Marie. "But my dad grabbed me just before I went in. We got a picture of it!"

"Yeah, that kind of got her attention all right," says Mark. "The next day she couldn't wait to help our guide deliver the safety lecture to the new batch of rafters who joined us."

"I used some dolls to show them how to go down the river feet first so they wouldn't bonk their heads on a rock," says Marie. "And I handed out bailing buckets when we needed them after a rapid."

Mark and Dana agree that Marie's experience on the South Fork of the American River changed her for the better. "She usually looks both ways before taking her bike on a street," says Mark. "She's also pretty good around horses these days," agrees Dana.

Balance

Ask Brian Kasell, 39, of Venice, California, what he likes best about his new-found love, rock climbing, and he'll tell you straight up: "It's as much mental as it is physical. It's amazing how much you can conquer by bringing your best planning, concentration and mental focus to a climb."

"It's amazing how much you can conquer by bringing your best planning, concentration and mental focus to a climb."

Kasell sees the world through his right eye, the only good one he has. A flying baseball robbed him of vision in his left eye when he was 11 years old. Like anyone with monoscopic vision, Kasell has problems with depth perception. "The biggest problem is anything involving short distance and rapid movement," says Kasell. "I have a hard time catching a ball thrown from a few feet away."

Kasell also has problems with his sense of balance. "I've been a backpacker for over 20 years," he says. "I've always had more trouble than my friends when it comes to crossing streams or traversing narrow trails." It was all quite manageable for Kasell, however, until his life-long enthusiasm for hiking and camping in the mountains led him to rock climbing.

"My friends and I have been hiking off-trail (cross-country backpacking) for years. We've run into some situations where we could have used rock climbing equipment and skills." After a year of thinking about it, Kasell decided it was time to act. He called several places that teach rock climbing, picked the one he liked best, and signed up for lessons.

During his third day of instruction, Kasell came face-to-face with what he thought might be an insurmountable challenge. It involved both balance and rapid movement over a short distance.

"I was half-way up a vertical route called 'Greystoke' at Joshua Tree when it became apparent I was going to have to do a dynamic move. I was going to have to release both hand holds and quickly grab two holds higher up. Simultaneously, I'd have to throw my leg up in order to get to the next foot hold. It's the closest thing to flying in rock climbing. I knew if I didn't do it right, I'd come off the rock. Worse yet, I'd be stuck with some real doubts about my physical ability to pursue rock climbing. But I thought the whole sequence through, sucked it up, and went for it. No one was more surprised than I was when I made it on my first try."

"I thought the whole sequence through, sucked it up, and went for it."

Kasell's memorable move on the face of Greystoke dramatically reaffirmed one of his most cherished beliefs: sometimes, physical limitations are more perceived than real.

Perspective

Before he took up kayaking in 1984, San Franciscan Eric Fournier, 35, was drowning in a "total rock and roll lifestyle."

"I produced my first hit record at age 21," says Fournier. "Back when there was no such thing as AIDS, before anyone knew that cocaine is bad for you." Fournier embraced wine, women and drugs so completely that instead of producing more records, he started 'being' a record-producer.

"I was blowing it," recalls Fournier. "I was really dissatisfied with myself and who I had become. The lifestyle was so alluring, though, that I didn't think I'd ever be able to break away from it."

One night, while shooting pool and getting drunk with a friend, Fournier agreed to go sea kayaking with him the next day. "Doug Conner was an experienced kayaker," says Fournier. "I guess I was drunk enough that paddling around in a boat with him sounded like fun."

When a "fantastically hung-over" Fournier was wakened by Conner's call the next morning, he remembered that he was afraid of open water. It was a fear that didn't bode well for a would-be kayaker.

"Doug wouldn't let me off the hook, though, so the next thing I knew I was in a classroom full of people," says Fournier. "When it was my turn to introduce myself, the instructor asked me what had motivated me to take a sea kayaking lesson. '*Doug drugged me here!*' was my response. Truer words were never spoken."

Despite his hangover and fear of the water, Fournier thoroughly enjoyed his first kayaking lesson. "I concentrated on learning basic paddle strokes," says Fournier. "The experience was very empowering for me. It helped me overcome my fear and gave me the sense of control that was missing in other aspects of my life."

Kayaking also opened Fournier's eyes to nature. "I used to think of the outdoors as the space between a night club and a taxi cab," says Fournier. "I'm still basically an urban guy, but now I truly treasure the exposure to nature that kayaking gives me."

Fournier is out of the record business now and is much happier with his life. "I had become a real jerk," says Fournier. "The pleasure I got from [both river and sea kayaking] put me back in touch with my genuine self—the me that loved canoeing with my father when I was 16, the me that had been buried under a cloud of drugs and alcohol all those years."

Desire

Forget fear. Desire is the big issue for hang glider pilot Sally Tucker, 37, of Sylmar, California. Tucker has wanted to fly every since she can remember and hang gliding is the only form of flight available to her.

Tucker's mother and father think she is "absolutely crazy" for hang gliding. "I just tell them I learned from a great instructor, and they shouldn't worry," says Tucker. "The funny thing is, the biggest problem I had in hang gliding was finding someone who was willing to teach me."

For Tucker it is no less than the realization of a life-long dream, and the satisfaction of refusing to give in to a handicap that others consider insurmountable.

Tucker, like three of her four siblings, was born deaf. Because she is non-hearing, she'll never earn an airplane or helicopter pilot's license.

Instructor Rob McKenzie of **High Adventure Hang Gliding** in San Bernardino says that Tucker's handicap does not cause her any problems in the air. "Awareness of airspeed is critical to any student's ability to control a hang glider," says McKenzie. "While Sally can't judge air speed by sound like hearing students can, she's much better than they are at judging it by the feel of wind on her face and in the control pressures of her glider. Once we worked out a communication system for training, she was at no disadvantage whatsoever."

The payoff? For Tucker it is no less than the realization of a life-long dream, and the satisfaction of refusing to give in to a handicap that others considered insurmountable.

"I LUV HG" says the license plate on Tucker's van. "I'm going to fly until the day I die," says Tucker.

Feeling

When Jon Thompson, 25, of San Jose was 10 years old, a drunk driver ran him down. He has been confined to a wheelchair ever since. The loss of sensation in his legs, however, was replaced by a powerful feeling in his heart. "I like to live on the edge," says Thompson. "My main goal in life is to do things that even fully able-bodied people are afraid to do."

Thompson participates in traditional wheelchair sports like basketball, tennis, track and racquetball. But it's his passion for thrill sports that has enabled him to reach his goal time and time again. "I've gone tandem skydiving and tandem hang gliding," says Thompson. "And I've done whitewater rafting and sea kayaking. I've even rock climbed 250 feet on an 85 degree granite slab at Yosemite Valley."

So it came as no surprise to Thompson's friends and parents when he announced his intention to be the first paraplegic to patronize **Bungee Adventures** of Mountain View, California.

"My parents thought I'd lost my mind," says Thompson. Skeletal brittleness and muscular atrophy in his lower half were of particular concern. Would the shock of gradual deceleration at the end of a bungee cord—harmless to a non-disabled person—be too much for him? Undaunted, Thompson discussed the problem with the owners of Bungee Adventures. "We agreed that tying my legs together would prevent muscle injury and that attaching the bungee to my back instead of my front would protect my spine. I know I can bend safely frontward, but not rearward."

Thompson's 150-foot jump went perfectly. "I was screaming my head off when I jumped," recalls Thompson. "I mean the ground was *right there* instead of thousands of feet away like it is in skydiving! I loved every second of it."

The only problem, according to Thompson? "I don't know what to do next," he says. "It's kinda like I'm running out of edges to live on!"

Risk Without Danger?

You've just read about real people. People who used the thrill sport of their choice to help them overcome real or perceived limitations. But even if you have nothing in particular to overcome, or even if you have no intention of participating in any of these hairball activities, you've got to admit this much: fun is it's own reward and, when it comes to California's thrill sports, we're talking FUN!

There is such a thing as calculated risk—risk that is within your control.

But, yes, we're also talking risk.

Now that you know what's at stake reward-wise—personal growth and great fun—we're free to address the gnarly concept of risk and risk's fearsome sidekick: DANGER!

Is there really such a thing as risk without danger?

Not on your life.

But there is such a thing as calculated risk—risk that is within your control. In fact, personal control of calculated risk, in the name of extraordinary fun, is what thrill sports are all about.

The biggest factor in calculating risk, of course, is knowing enough to separate perceived risk from real risk.

Perceived risk is based on rumor, raw fear, misinformation, wild speculation and—all too often—"common sense." Real risk is based on knowledge, observable facts, self-awareness, personal responsibility and good sense.

These concepts, of course, conflict with popular opinion. Most people think that blind luck separates the living from the dead in thrill sports. Your mom, for example, is likely to rattle off the following questions the instant she hears that you've been within 100 yards of any apparatus that will spirit you off into thin air, or carry you down a set of rapids, or permit you to scale vertical rock walls:

- What if the wind stops?!
- What if an earthquake hits while you're climbing?!
- What if a big hunk of whitewater snatches you out of the boat?!
- Why would you want to jump out of a perfectly good airplane?!
- So what have I raised—a mountain goat?!
- Why did fate give me such a weird kid?!
- Don't you know you can get injured just *thinking* about this crazy stuff?!

What's a thrill-seeking person to do in the face of such impassioned reasoning?

Simple. Just remember two things: First, moms—even though they are usually right—can also be wrong. Second, moms are notoriously misinformed about the true nature of thrill sports. What's more, they have no desire whatsoever to hear anything positive about hang gliding or skydiving or any other such nonsense.

That means it's up to you to find out the true nature of the risk you will be taking when and if you sign up for a thrill sport. And it's up to you to share your new-found knowledge with your loved ones. You don't want to worry about them dying of a heart attack while you're out hang gliding, do you?

The fact is that catastrophes do happen to people who participate in thrill sports. But is that reason enough to avoid them like the plague? Does that mean that you just have to be *lucky* to survive thrill sports?

NO WAY!

That's like saying you should never drive on the freeway for fear of getting killed in a head-on collision, or you should never play outside for fear of getting struck by lightning. Or that the mere act of pointing a loaded gun at your head is going to kill you dead on the spot.

Listen. Pointing a loaded gun at your head can't possibly hurt or kill you—*unless you pull the trigger.*

And that's what's so great about thrill sports. Your finger—not fickle fate's, and not some bad driver's—is the one that's on the trigger. Believe it or not, YOU CONTROL THE LEVEL OF RISK when you participate in thrill sports. You control it by making your personal safety your number one priority every step of the way.

Your finger—not fickle fate's, and not some bad driver's—is the one that's on the trigger.

STEPS OF THE WAY: Personal Choices To Keep You Safe

1) *Choose your medium.* Earth? Water? Air? Pick the one that attracts you most—one that doesn't scare you to death. The first priority in thrill sport safety is: Avoid the initial heart-attack.

2) *Choose your initial level of involvement.* In relation to a specific thrill sport, do you want to: Read about it? Observe it? Help others do it? Try it out yourself? Remember that a little anxiety is good for you, while too much can compromise your safety. Remember that once you're comfortable at one level, you can always move on to

the next.

3) *Choose your provider.* Pick the resource that is best qualified to give you what you want in the safest, most enjoyable manner possible. Know industry standards, state-of-the-art instructional technique, and a little bit about the actual person who will guide you through your thrilling adventure.

4) *Accept responsibility for your own safety.* Trust only those you choose to trust and, above all, trust your own judgement. You are the only one who can truly know what constitutes an acceptable risk/reward ratio for you.

Risk in a Nutshell

There's a snappy quote that graces the walls of most sport aviation facilities in this country. It is a saying that applies equally well to all of California's thrill sports.

It goes like this: "Aviation itself is not inherently dangerous. But to an even greater extent than the sea, it is terribly unforgiving of carelessness, incapacity or neglect."

"Aviation is inherently dangerous," Meier says. "It's one of the most dangerous things you can do."

Mike Meier, in his paragliding training manual, dismisses this saying as "a comforting sentiment—cleverly written—one of those things that sounds so good that it *ought* to be true."

"Aviation *is* inherently dangerous," he says. "It's one of the most dangerous things you can do. And it does sometimes forgive, but not often enough, and not with any sense of fairness."

For the purposes of this book, then, we'll amend the aviation quote as follows:

"OK, OK, your mom is right. The thrill sport of your choice is inherently dangerous but, still, there are at least two good ways you can enjoy it safely:

•vicariously, from the safety and comfort of your own couch; or

•in real life, in accordance with Mike Meier's three requirements for a safe career in thrill sports."

Meier says only three things are required to be a safe thrill sport participant:

1) The *desire* to be safe.

2) The *understanding* of where safety comes from.

3) The *maturity* and *self-discipline* to act on your knowledge and desire.

Even if your thrill sport career is simply a memorable one-time experience, Meier's three rules apply. And, from the perspective of a first-time, one-time-only adventurer, rules two and three are the most important. If you want to minimize the risk of any thrill sport, you absolutely must understand it. And, once you understand it, you must bring every ounce of your maturity and self-discipline to bear—if you want to pursue it.

Go With The Flow

Everyone knows that California is the thrill sport epicenter of the world. But why is that? Because California has all the natural ingredients for thrill sports, that's why. And because California sunshine brightly illuminates bold new dimensions of time and space—the ones that will be magically revealed to you by the thrill sport of your dreams.

You want earth to climb around on? Boulder fields perhaps, or towering crags and slabs of granite? Joshua Tree National Monument in Southern California and Yosemite Valley in Northern California are both world-famous climbing sites.

Want some whitewater to plunge down in a raft or a kayak? Runnable stretches of river lace through foothills all along the Sierra Nevada Mountain Range. The South Fork of the American River alone channels over 100,000 boaters per year between its banks.

Ocean? California provides 1200 miles of coast and estuaries for sea kayakers to play around in, not to mention a bunch of off-shore islands. Most offer clean water, clean air and abundant sea life. The ocean also provides a venue for parasailing, the simplest of all air sports. Parasailing involves getting towed along behind a power boat in a round, ascending parachute. It is a popular ride for adventurers and vacationers in coastal communities like the Balboa Peninsula and the Catalina Island town of Avalon.

Then there are those sunny inland California skies. Recreational skydiving was pretty much born in the Southern California town of Lake Elsinore. And Southern California, with it's unique blend of mountain and desert terrain, is also the cradle and national hotbed of hang gliding. It promises to be the same for the relatively new sport of paragliding.

Northern California's Napa Valley wine country offers some of the best hot air ballooning in the world, as does Southern California's Temecula wine country, and the Del Mar coast.

Whether you're a doer or a dreamer, the first step in selecting your favorite thrill sport is picking the natural arena you'd most like to play in. Ask yourself: "Which medium electrifies me the most—earth, water or air?"

Blue sky, cool water and breathtaking land formations, however, are just the tip of the iceberg in California's thrill sports. We're also talking wild new dimensions of time, space and sensory involvement. Each of the sports covered in this book has its own unique ability to compress, elongate or elasticize time; and each gives you a whole new way to experience the world around you.

Because of their immense variety of medium, motion and sensory stimulation, California's thrill sports as a group are powerful catalysts for producing true "altered states."

Because of their immense variety of medium, motion and sensory stimulation, California's thrill sports as a group are powerful catalysts for producing true "altered states."

No drugs. No alcohol. Just natural altered states which can broaden your horizons, change your outlook on life and provide simultaneous focus and perspective.

In an attempt to give first-timers the vicarious experience of what those altered states are like, I have rated each thrill sport in this book according to the following variables:

- Speed
- Focus
- Your view of the world
- How does it compare to REAL life?
- How does it feel?

Speed

Generally speaking, speed translates to intensity. For example, in a hot air balloon you drift serenely in gentle breezes. On a skydive you plummet towards earth at a terminal velocity of 120 miles per hour. Similar differences can be found in water sports and earth sports.

Generally speaking, speed translates to intensity.

Within the context of your favorite medium (earth, water, air), what's your favorite speed? Plummeting with your hair on fire, or drifting with your mind in the clouds?

Focus

Now let's talk time in terms of tense: present, past and future.

In a sea kayak, for example, you have time to look all around and commune with nature as you slowly paddle through inland waterways. There is very little immediacy to the physical task of propelling yourself through an open expanse of calm water. You can daydream and mentally experience mysterious blends of past, present and future.

As a whitewater kayaker, on the other hand, you are locked in the present. Time, quick and precious, is as here-and-now as the river itself. The whole world seems to plunge downstream with you. You must spend all of your time either evaluating obstacles immediately ahead or physically reacting to avoid hitting them.

How do you prefer to spend your time? Riveted to a hot, mind-sharpening encounter with the present? Or transformed by a cool, soulful stroll through your own personal perceptions of past, present and future?

Your view of the world

Thrill sports boldly take you where you've never gone before.

Some thrill sports will make you swear you've discovered the fourth dimension or, better yet, visited another planet.

Some suspend you in wide-open space, and permit you to move up, down and all around. Others force you into a narrow corridor with only one way out. Still others will make you swear you've discovered the fourth dimension or, better yet, visited another planet.

Sea kayaking, for example, plops you in the middle of a huge expanse of water, while river kayaking (literally) channels you downstream between two narrow banks.

Parasailing, for another example, has a "wide-open" feel to it, even though it is basically an "up and down" activity. In parasailing, you start from inside a speeding boat. You are attached to a round, ascending parachute that is already inflated and attached to the boat via a line on a winch. The operators basically reel you up to an altitude of about 300 feet, then reel you back down 10 minutes later. You don't have to do anything to control the parasail, so you'll have plenty of time to enjoy both the view and the sensations of being suspended in mid-air.

Bungee jumping, on the other hand, is tremendously "channeled" in an up-and-down direction. As you prepare to leap, you will be aware only of the space between you and the ground. You don't have to do much, but you do have to decide to JUMP! That decision commands all of your attention. Once you've jumped, every last ounce of your being and awareness will be riding a straight line between your launch point and the surface of the earth.

Which is more appealing to you: 360-degree awareness of the wide-open world around you, or "straight-line" fever? OK, OK: Which is less scary?

How does it compare to REAL life?

Some thrill sports, like kayaking, modify your sense of space in subtle ways: Gently bobbing over ocean swells or plunging down a rapid—with your fanny just a hull's thickness away from direct contact with the water—is a unique spatial experience.

Many first-time hang gliding passengers report that the unique time/space sensations of high altitude hang gliding actually cause tingling in their spines.

Other thrill sports, like hang gliding, alter your perception of space so dramatically that you think you're in another world. Hang gliders go up, down and all around. Untethered, they climb, glide, swoop and dive in an eerie, engineless silence. Many first-time hang gliding passengers report that the unique time/space sensations of high altitude hang gliding actually cause tingling in their spines.

Do you want to feel like you've visited another planet and discovered the elusive fourth dimension of space? Or do you like the world just the way it is, thank you, only with a little more color, a little more texture?

How does it feel?

All thrill sports involve you physically in some way, shape or form. The variety of kinetic experience is almost endless. Thrill sports allow you to play with gravity, to experience its power in unique and memorable ways.

At one extreme is bungee jumping. Anyone who has done it knows that bungee jumping is a multiple-climax unnatural act—one that will leave you wild-eyed and panting. The instant you jump from a bridge, crane or hot air balloon your brain shrieks out to your heart: "We're gonna dieeeeeeee!!" A split-second later, as the stretching bungee arrests your fall, your heart gasps back to your brain: "We're gonna liiiiiiive!!" Another split second later, as you go weightless at the top of your first rebound, your stomach flips 180 degrees in anticipation of yet another plunge towards earth. The whole cycle is repeated 3 to 4 times—in diminishing intensity—until you finally swing to rest some 50 feet to 100 feet in the air.

Anyone who has done it knows that bungee jumping is a multiple-climax unnatural act—one that will leave you wild-eyed and panting.

Compare the gut-wrenching reversals of bungee jumping to the gentle, gravity-defying sensations your body experiences on a hot air balloon ride. Compare it to the rhythmic rotation of your shoulders, and the steady huff of your own breath as you and your friends paddle a whitewater raft through the calm water between rapids—ears tuned for the first grumbling sound of the next stretch of whitewater.

Each of these adventures is physically rewarding in a unique way, and each offers a similar level of physical risk. All the variables of time, space and sensory stimulation contribute to the quality of the experience. The question is: What turns *you* on?

RIDES OF PASSAGE/ LEAPS OF FAITH

Freeze-frame the image of you diving into thin air, clawing your way up a rocky crag, or floating along towards a growling stretch of whitewater.

NOW THAT YOUR HEAD IS FILLED WITH CRISP images of earth, water or air; and now that your imagination craves contact with bold new dimensions of time and space; admit this much: you can actually see yourself cruising along in at least one of the strange contraptions that thrill sports enthusiasts use to immerse themselves in their favorite natural medium. It's kind of fun just thinking about it, isn't it?

Freeze-frame the image of you diving into thin air, clawing your way up a rocky crag, or floating along towards a growling stretch of whitewater.

First we need to talk about thrill sports in relation to their biggest consideration this side of deadly risk: Degree of difficulty, both practical and psychological, is the second most important factor to consider in selecting a thrill sport.

There are major differences between "easy" thrill sports and "hard" ones. And you should know about them. There's certainly no point in signing up for an adventure that calls on you to make more of a sacrifice of time, effort and personal resources than you're willing to make.

When it comes to thrill sports, it's all a matter of perspective. One person's easy is another person's hard. Even so, there are two natural groupings of thrill sports: "rides of passage" are relatively easy for most people while "leaps of faith" are relatively hard.

See if these "easy/hard" groupings make sense to you. Remember that when it comes to thrill sports, the words "hard" and "easy" have psychological as well as practical implications. **Rides of passage** would include hot air ballooning, parasailing, bungee jumping, first-day rock climbing and whitewater rafting. **Leaps of faith** would include hang gliding, paragliding, skydiving and kayaking.

The difference between rides and leaps becomes clear if you think about how you would go about meeting your responsibility to assure your own safety.

Rides of passage include hot air ballooning, parasailing, bungee jumping, first-day rock climbing and whitewater rafting.

•A **ride of passage** is a carefully researched decision to place your life in the hands of others. Your biggest responsibility is to select the right provider. Once you've done that, you just show up for your ride.

•A **leap of faith**, on the other hand, is a declaration of your willingness to assume direct responsibility for your own well-being. Not only must you pick the right provider, but you must also be willing to concentrate, stay focused, maintain self-awareness, and be willing to learn new skills throughout the entire process of your adventure.

Leaps of faith include hang gliding, paragliding, skydiving and kayaking.

Generally speaking, the variables that distinguish rides from leaps are:

Rides:

1) Minimal commitment of time, effort and money
2) Minimal skill/learning requirement
3) Risk more perceived than real
4) Risk controlled by provider; participant merely along for the ride
5) Participant's primary safety responsi-

bility is to find a provider that offers a safe ride.

Leaps:

1) Significant commitment of time, effort and money
2) Significant skill/learning requirements
3) Risk both perceived and real—but surprisingly manageable
4) Risk controlled by participant and provider together, as a team
5) Participant must bring self-awareness, focus, and a high degree of personal responsibility for his or her own safety to the adventure.

Okay. Now you are armed with all the thrill sport theory you need. You know how to choose your thrill sport based on what your favorite medium is, and what kind of thrilling experience you want to have. You understand the meaning of risk and danger, and know that you can take control of them. You know to ask a lot of questions before choosing your thrill sport provider. You understand that some thrill sports require a bigger commitment of effort and energy than others. You are prepared to take responsibility for your own safety. Now you are ready.

So many thrill sports, so little time!

Have fun.

BUNGEE JUMPING

Crescent City
Yreka
Mt. Shasta
Alturas
Eureka
Redding
Red Bluff
Chico
Ukiah
Yuba City
Santa Rosa
Placerville
Sacramento
South Lake Tahoe
San Francisco
Oakland
Stockton
Sonora
Lee Vining
Yosemite
San Jose
Santa Cruz
Merced
Monterey
Salinas
Bishop
Fresno
Visilia
Lone Pine
Kettleman City
Death Valley Jct.
San Luis Obispo
Bakersfield
Santa Maria
Wheeler Ridge
Mojave
Baker
Barstow
Santa Barbara
Ventura
Palmdale
Needles
Los Angeles
San Bernardino
Santa Ana
Long Beach
Palm Springs
Oceanside
Escondido
Blythe
San Diego
El Centro
Yuma
101
5
97
139
89
299
395
44
36
99
20
80
29
50
108
120
580
680
1
152
41
136
190
65
46
127
14
40
247
10
62
95
215
15
86
8
1
2
3
4
5
6
7
8
9
10
11
12
13
14
15
16
17
18
19
20
21

CHAPTER TWO

BUNGEE JUMPING

THE MAXIM "WHAT YOU SEE IS WHAT YOU GET" applies to bungee jumping more than any other thrill sport. But what you see scares your pants off, while what you get is relatively harmless.

Done correctly, bungee jumping is no more life threatening than a roller coaster ride. But don't try to tell that to your heart, mind, body and soul. The instant you launch into your first bungee jump, every fiber of your being will scream bloody murder.

I found that out while researching this book. I also stumbled upon a new love: reverse bungee jumping, otherwise known as "slingshotting."

Whether you do it from a bridge, a hot air balloon or a construction crane, bungee jumping is absolutely the *hairiest* "ride of passage" on planet earth. Even for a jaded ten-year thrill sport veteran such as myself.

FIRST PERSON: The Author Jumps

I knew going in that bungee jumping would be nothing less than sheer terror and pure relief compressed into just a few split seconds. The instant I leapt from a cage suspended 200 feet in the air by a construction crane, I was absolutely certain I was going to die. The short plummet towards hard earth—less than 200 feet below—was the most incredible rush I'd ever felt this side of a skydiving free-fall.

I knew going in that bungee jumping would be nothing less than sheer terror and pure relief compressed into just a few split seconds.

The best part of the ride, however, came just a few heartbeats after the jump itself. That's when the four bungee cords attached to the harness around my hips and chest *strrrrrretched* to twice their original length. And that's when I felt myself shooting back up towards heaven.

Talk about salvation.

A brief instant of weightlessness at the top of my first rebound started the whole cycle over again. Three or four "boings" later, I swung at the end of the bungee cords, mouth agape and eyes wide open, waiting to be lowered gently back to earth.

On the way down I shrieked: "THAT WAS GREAT! I WANNA GO AGAIN!" I must have registered a solid nine on the excitement scale because the nice folks at **Bungee Adventures** of Mountain View agreed to let me.

My second jump—with the bungee attached to my ankles rather than my waist—was pure art: a perfect arching swan dive, followed by a high-pitched rebound and the weird sensation of being lowered, head first, back to mother earth.

"My second jump was pure art—a perfect arching swan dive followed by a high-pitched rebound and the weird sensation of being lowered, head first, back to mother earth."

I hadn't had that much blood in my head in years.

"No-brainers don't get any better than this!" I said to myself. At the time, I didn't realize that there was more to bungee jumping than "normal" bungee jumping.

I found that out the next day when I showed up at the Dixon Fairgrounds to check out another Bay Area bungee jumping outfit called **Total Rebound**. I had pretty much resigned myself to the grimmest duty in journalism: watch everyone else have fun, then talk with them afterwards about how great it was—for *them.*

I had already sopped up a fair amount of

excitement from three or four post-jump interviews when **Total Rebound** owner, John Wilkinson, sidled up to me, looked me in the eye and said: "So, Erik—how'd you like to give 'slingshotting' a try?"

"Uhhh, John," I replied, "what *exactly* is 'slingshotting' anyway?" I thought the term 'slingshotting' sounded a little lame, frankly, but I definitely wanted to hear more about it.

"It's reverse bungee jumping, Erik," smiled John. "We attach the bungee to your back, then five of us hold you down while the jump cage rises and stretches the bungee out. About the time you think you can't take the pressure anymore, we let you go. You just get snatched right off the ground—boinged right up into the air by a recoiling bungee."

"How do I know that this, this—this slingshotting—won't splatter me up against the bottom of the cage like some big hairy bug?" I asked wisely. As a thrill sport expert I felt compelled to ask at least one intelligent question before yelling "HECK, YES!" at the top of my lungs.

John assured me that he and his cohorts had carefully worked out the all-important "distance to death vs. bungee stretch capacity" calculations, so I agreed to give slingshotting a try.

When my turn came, John and crew piled on top of me while I lay face down on the grass. About 15 seconds of increasing pressure on my chest told me that the bungee was ready to work its magic. The next thing I knew I was *zooming* away from the ground, with a big handful of grass in each hand.

"What a gas!" I thought to myself before the weightlessness at the top of the recoil demanded my full attention. The same "we're gonna die!—no we're not!" sensations of regular bungee

If YOU decide to try slingshotting, be sure to read the precautions on page 49. It is NOT necessarily the safest way to bungee jump.

jumping followed, but when I was lowered back to the ground I knew I had just experienced something different—something totally unique in the wild and wacky world of thrill sports.

"This slingshotting stuff opens up thrill sports to a whole different breed of cat," I said. "*You don't have to decide to jump!* You just lie on the ground—trapped under a pile of grunting humans—and *wait for the bungee to set you FREE!*"

FIRST RIDE
(Cost: $40-$125 per jump, depending on height and structure)

You get up one morning. You go out and leap off a bridge, balloon or crane. Three or four big rubber bands attached to your chest or ankles magically transform certain death into a celebration of life. You plummet, scream, spring skywards and go weightless. Several times. You go to bed that night—and have the *wildest* dreams.

Bungee Jumping from Bridges

Unless you count the "vine-jumping" rites of South Pacific Islanders, the first bungee jumps were off a bridge in England. And all the big bungee jumping operations in New Zealand operate from bridges.

Bridges are great.

They offer both aesthetic and psychological advantages. Most are surrounded by breathtaking scenery, and most have cool water rather than hard earth directly underneath them.

The problem in this country is that almost all bridge jumping is either illegal or profoundly discouraged by state and local authorities. If you're jumping off a bridge in the United States, odds are overwhelming that you're breaking the law.

The bottom line? Bungee jumping outfits that use bridges are, by definition, covert operations. They must employ both wit and guile (and well-positioned sentries with radios) to get their jumps in before the heat arrives to shut things down.

The problem, in this country, is that almost all bridge jumping is either illegal or profoundly discouraged by state and local authorities.

If this "cat-burglar" sort of approach appeals to you, go for it. Just don't expect bridge jumping outfits to have a stable base of operations, or a gift shop, or—uhhh—you know—insurance.

One other warning about bootleg bridge jumping. Avoid "head-dips" altogether. Head dips—where the bungee stretches just enough so that you just barely splash into the water head first—require precise calculations. Your body weight, bungee stretch characteristics, height of bridge, wetness of the bungee and even air temperature all must be taken into account. Otherwise you can hit the water harder than is good for you. Bungee jumping operators who have one eye out for the cops are less likely to get your personal "head-dip" calculation done properly. It only takes one screw-up to leave you with a broken neck.

Bungee Jumping from Hot Air Balloons

When **Bungee Adventures**, the first domestic bungee jumping operation in the United States, was chased away from the Wards Ferry Bridge, it began jumping customers from a hot air balloon. Hot air balloons, like bridges, are aesthetically appealing. But balloons are also Federal Aviation Administration regulated aircraft.

At this writing, the FAA has made no official stand on the subject of bungee jumping from hot air balloons. Some FAA representatives are for it. Others are against it. In the absence of an official FAA position on the subject, bungee jumping from a tethered (attached to the ground) hot air balloon is neither legal nor illegal. Stay tuned.

The biggest drawback to hot air balloons as jump platforms is that they can fly only within a few hours of dawn—when the winds are calm enough to assure safety. The simple truth is that bungee jumping enterprises do much better financially when they use a launch pad that can be used all day long.

Bungee Jumping from Construction Cranes and Towers

In light of all this, the domestic bungee jumping launch pad of choice is a construction crane or a fixed structure such as a tower. Yes, cranes are noisy and ugly. And yes, both cranes and towers definitely lack the aesthetic appeal of a bridge or a balloon. But they also offer a number of advantages.

First, liability insurance and necessary permits are easier to come by for bungee jumping businesses that have a fixed base of operations. That means you won't have to slink around like a criminal when you go bungee jumping.

The simple truth is that bungee jumping enterprises do much better financially when they use a launch pad that can be used all day long.

Second, you can jump from a crane or tower all day long. That means you don't have to get up before dawn and hope the winds stay calm long enough for you to have your turn from a balloon.

Reverse Bungee Jumping (also known as "Slingshotting")

Reverse bungee jumping is controversial. Insurance companies are skeptical about it and so are some operators. At this time, the North American Bungee Jumping Association (see resource listing at the end of this chapter) does not endorse it.

The nut of the problem is precise control over the amount of stretch given the cord before the rider is released. Too much stretch, obviously, can splatter the "jumper" up against the launch platform.

If you decide you want to try slingshotting, here are some guidelines:

- Cranes are the only way to go for slingshotting. They're the only launch platform that gives operators precise control over stretching the bungee, while you stay pinned on the ground. The crane operator stops stretching just when the "anchor group" holding you down starts to come off the ground. At that point, their combined weight roughly equals the load placed on the bungee link.

- Always insist on knowing the combined body weight of the people holding you down. Obviously, if the anchor group weighs too much, they won't come off the ground until the bungee is stretched tight enough to endanger your life. Talk it over with your operator. If he can't explain his intentions to you precisely—in terms of load capacity/stretch characteristics of the bungee link, and the combined weight of your anchor group—forget about slingshotting until you find someone who can.

Always insist on knowing the combined body weight of the people holding you down.

Mechanics

Guidelines for reverse bungee jumping:
1) Cranes are the only way to go.
2) Make sure the operator has calculated the load capacity/stretch of the bungee link, and the combined weight of your anchor group.

The quality and safety of your bungee jump, no matter what platform you're on, depends on proper bungee attachment at both ends of the line. The end attached to the launch platform must be only one thing: SECURE!

The end attached to your body has to be both secure *and* compatible with the all-important goal of keeping you in one piece. These are the possible points of attachment:

Mid-body, front: The bungee is attached to you via a secure "chest/waist" harness. This is the most common point of attachment in the world of bungee jumping. As any skydiver or rock climber will tell you, your body is designed to withstand forces (like gravity) that tend to compress it rather than elongate it. The chest/waist harness keeps you right-side up and transfers most of the "G-force" of deceleration to your hips. When the bungee starts to stretch, everything north of your hips—including your spine—is slightly compressed towards the hips. That's good.

Three possible points of attachment to the bungee harness: mid-body in the front, mid-body in the rear and at the ankles

Mid-body, rear: Attaching a bungee to the rear of a chest/waist harness isn't much different from attaching it to the front—from a load-distribution point of view. The advantage of back attachment is that you get a better ground rush because you're facing down while the bungee stretches. The argument against back attachment is that you can't afford to lose consciousness, which can actually happen (rarely) if you get scared enough to faint. If you do faint, your head will slump forward, which could conceivably block off your airway so you can't breathe. That's bad.

Ankle jumps: Many people think ankle jumps are more fun. You dive, like an Acapulco cliff diver, into an electrifying face-first encounter with a wonderful thing called "ground rush." There's good news and bad news about ankle jumps. The bad news is that your body isn't designed to take forces (like gravity) that try to elongate it. When a bungee attached to your ankles starts to stretch, the force of deceleration is transferred to all parts south. It pulls, rather than presses, on your legs and spine. That's bad.

The good news is that ankle jumps seem to be manageable *if* you follow a couple of simple rules: First, insist on at least 100 feet of bungee for an ankle jump (and sufficient ground clearance, of course!). The longer bungee will make the deceleration softer than it would be on 50-foot cords. Second, use your legs as shock absorbers. Keep them slightly bent at the knee. That will give the big muscles in your legs some control over the amount of shock that gets to your spine. Third, do a number of chest/waist jumps first. That way you'll be more likely to remember the rules we just discussed.

ANKLE JUMP GUIDELINES:
1) Insist on at least 100 feet of bungee, with sufficient ground clearance.
2) Use your legs as shock absorbers, keeping them slightly bent at the knee.
3) Try the chest/waist jump first so you get the feel of it.

MYTHS

"Crazy New Zealanders—real outdoorsy types —invented bungee jumping about five years ago."

Nope. **The truth is:** Bungee jumping was invented over ten years ago by a group of bored, tuxedoed, champagne-sipping rich kids from England. They called themselves "The Dangerous Sports Club," and they are generally credited with performing the first true bungee jump off Clifton Bridge in Bristol, England.

Just a few years ago, however, a bunch of thrill

seekers in New Zealand started leaping off bridges on a regular basis. They are generally credited with launching commercial bungee jumping on its current inexorable march toward the heart of mainstream America.

At this writing, bungee jumping outfits are springing up everywhere. The epicenter of domestic bungee jumping is, of course, California. **Bungee Adventures** of Mountain View, California, was the first commercial operation in the states. They were the first to use balloons, the first to use a crane, and among the first to secure liability insurance. They and a handful of others are the pacesetters for bungee jumping, American style.

"If the bungee cord breaks on my jump, I'm a dead duck, right?"

Well, yeah. But not many people are crazy enough to bungee jump with just one bungee cord attached. **The truth is:** Most domestic commercial jumping operations use THREE or FOUR cords per jumper—enough to withstand at least five times the load of your plummeting body weight. Operators who use a single New Zealand-style all-rubber cord claim that 1,500 separate strands of rubber and double carabineer attachments at both ends of the cord ensure redundancy throughout their "bungee chain".

Most domestic commercial jumping operations use three or four cords per jumper–enough to withstand a load equaling at least five times your plummeting body weight.

Bungee jumping operators guard against cord failure in two other ways: They sheath the rubber core of their cords with nylon to protect them from the damaging effect of the sun. And they inspect and replace their cords on a regular basis, or at any obvious sign of cord imperfection such as nicks, soft spots, frays or abrasions.

If you happen to run into an operator that

doesn't shield his cords from the sun, keep running.

"If the bungee cords are too strong, they'll break me in half, and if they're too weak, they'll splatter me against the ground!"

Well, yeah. But a bungee jump operator knows that. He also knows that breaking you in half with bungee cords that don't stretch enough, or splattering you against the ground with bungee cords that stretch too much will kill his business in a heartbeat.

That's why bungee jump operators use different combinations of cords for different body weights. That's why they only buy bungee cords that have predictable and consistent stretching characteristics. **The truth is:** Bungee jumping operators make *very careful calculations* involving your body weight, bungee stretch characteristics, and height of jump platform before they'll allow you to jump.

"So if the cords are strong, nothing can go wrong, right?"

Wrong. The cords must be securely attached to the jumping platform and to the jumping person. If something breaks at either end, it doesn't matter how strong the cords are.

The truth is: All carabineers, harnesses, knots and rigging have to work and work right. Strength isn't the only issue. The harness, for instance, should not transfer the shock of the stretching cords to one rigidly fixed spot on your body. Most harnesses feature a sliding attachment point which puts the load at the most appropriate spot between the jumper's

All carabineers, harnesses, knots and rigging have to work and work right. Strength isn't the only issue.

navel and chest. The "sweet-spot" for any given jump depends on the angle of your body in relation to the ground when the bungee starts to stretch.

"Speaking of angle in relation to the ground! If the cords happen to twang between my legs, can I still have children?"

No matter what angle your body is at when the cords take hold, gravity will automatically pivot you around so that the force of deceleration gets taken between your chest and waist.

Sure—if you want to. **The truth is:** No matter what angle your body is at when the cords take hold, gravity will automatically pivot you around so that the force of deceleration gets taken between your chest and waist. If you want to have children—or even if you don't—stay well away from anyone who tries to *attach* the bungee between your legs.

"I heard that ankle jumps—even if they don't tear me apart—might pop my eyes out of my head!"

The truth is: At least one doctor has claimed that ankle jumps, by forcing too much blood into your head, can cause retinal damage to your eyes. Most operators regard this claim as unfounded—as long as the bungee is "soft" enough.

More specifically, current National Bungee Jumping Association guidelines specify a maximum 3.5 "G-loading" for ankle jumps, as opposed to a maximum of 4.5 "Gs" for chest/waist harness jumps. This assures a softer bungee.

"Since rubber can't possibly be 100% predictable, blind luck must determine whether I'll get a 'hard' or 'soft' bungee to jump with!"

The truth is: Each different size and kind of

bungee cords has predictable shock absorption characteristics within a certain range. Operators know what those ranges are. Operators pick their cord combinations in accordance with a simple rule. A cord combination is too "hard" if your plummeting body weight does not cause it to stretch to at least double its normal length. More is okay, given enough ground clearance, high-stretch bungee cords, or an adequately modified bungee replacement schedule. The further a bungee cord stretches, you see, the faster it wears out.

"The coolest form of bungee jumping is 'stunt' or 'hot dog' bungee jumping!"

If you've seen people on TV or in promotional videos jumping to within a few feet of the ground and snatching beer cans from the hands of their friends, you've seen "stunt jumping." Stunt jumping *really* requires careful stretch/load calculations. And—because rubber is rubber—those calculations cannot be 100% precise.

Avoid stunt jumping altogether.

Avoid stunt jumping altogether. From a safety perspective, it's not much different from playing Russian roulette. At best, there is one bullet in a stunt jumper's six-gun. If you don't know what you're doing, you're looking at five.

TRUE CHILLS
(And how to avoid them)

The bungee jumping term for a fatal accident is "zeroing out" or "splatting." Take your pick.

So far, not one bungee jumping customer—and only one careless instructor—has "zeroed out" in the state of California. Stunt jumpers, however, have been killed.

A good example of a stunt jumping fatality is the "instructor" in Reno who jumped from the top of a billboard with the idea of attracting attention to himself and his business. He died because he hooked himself to a bungee cord that was just a few feet too long. Was his death due to the random dangers of bungee jumping? Or was it a tragic case of unbelievably poor planning on his part?

The one commercial bungee jumping fatality involved an instructor who was jumping from a hot air balloon. After supervising the jumps of his customers, he rushed to make the final jump of the day himself—before high winds forced him to pack up and go home. In his haste, he failed to hook his carabineer through the loop at the end of his bungee cords. Instead, he jammed the ends of the cords through the oval formed by the carabineer.

Miraculously, friction held everything together through the first rebound. But cords and carabineer came apart in the weightlessness at the top of his first rebound. Did he fall to his death because of unsuitable/unsafe equipment? Or was he done in by his own carelessness?

Although mass scale bungee jumping is a new phenomenon in this country, a single national organization has already emerged. The North American Bungee Association (NABA) has recently published professional bungee jumping guidelines covering equipment selection, testing, maintenance, operating procedures and personnel requirements.

From a consumer's perspective, the key to the NABA's guidelines can be summed up in two words: "parallel redundancy." Parallel redundancy basically means "for Heaven's sake, use at least TWO of everything that could possibly break or screw up!!"

NABA guidelines represent only one arm of bungee jumping's new "quality control" system. The other is the long arm of the law. As of January 1992, the state of California defines bungee jumping as an "amusement ride." As such, it is subject to regulation by the California State Department of Industrial Relations, Division of Occupational Safety and Health, Elevator Unit, Amusement Ride and Ski Lift Section. (Are you out of breath yet?) Director James Meyer says that all California amusement ride operators—including all bungee jumping operators who want to describe themselves as legal, licensed and insured—must show him three things:

From a consumer's perspective, the key to the NABA's guidelines can be summed up in two words: "parallel redundancy."

•Stress analysis tests of all equipment they use (bungee cords, harnesses, carabineers, etc.). Tests must be conducted by an engineer.

•Proper licenses, certifications and lease papers for their balloons, cranes, structures, sites, etc.

•Proof of liability insurance in the amount of $500,000 to $2,000,000, depending on the requirements of all involved.

Bungee operators who meet these requirements are issued a permanent operating permit that is subject to annual review. Those who try, in good faith, to meet them are eligible for a temporary operating permit. Those who refuse to cooperate are cited and ordered to shut down.

Despite NABA's guidelines and California's state regulation, however, there are a number of renegade bungee jumping businesses—ones who operate without insurance, permits or a secure site, or any intention of getting these things. That means it's still up to you to distinguish legal and insured bungee jumping operators from quasi-legal and clearly illegal ones.

For starters, if you have any doubts about the permit status of any bungee jumping business in the state, you can call the Elevator Unit of the California State Department of Industrial Relations at (916) 920-6361. Meyer and his staff will be happy to tell you one of four things:

•the business has a current, permanent operating permit;

•the business has a current, temporary operating permit;

•the business has not co-operated with permit procedures and is in clear violation of the law;

•the business is unknown to the state.

If you have any doubts about the permit status of any bungee jumping business in the state, you can call the Elevator Unit of the California State Department of Industrial Relations at (916) 920-6361.

The following questions will help you determine if your prospective bungee jumping outfit—whether it has a California state permit or not—is operating in accordance with current NABA guidelines.

Equipment Considerations

What follows is the proper terminology for the primary equipment of bungee jumping:

Bungee cord: Each individual length of bungee.
Bungee link: The combination of two, three or four cords that will give you a safe jump.
Bungee chain: All the equipment that connects the jumper to the jump structure: harness, carabineers, bungee link and structure-anchor.

Armed with this terminology, you can ask

your bungee operator these pertinent questions:

What kind of bungee cords do you use?

The operative word here is cord**S**. Redundancy in all parts of the system is crucial to bungee safety. Most U.S. operators form the "bungee link" with a series of 5/8-inch or 3/4-inch diameter cords that have a cotton interbraid, a rubber core and a nylon sheath. A New Zealand-style all-rubber cord (made up of about 1,500 individual rubber strands) is OK as long as it is attached by double carabineers to both jumper and jump platform.

How much load can each cord withstand?

Load capacity depends on the cord. Generally speaking, 5/8-inch cords are good for 1,000 pounds, and 3/4-inch cords are good for 1,400 pounds.

Are the individual cords protected from the sun?

The nylon sheath on braided cords protects the rubber core from damage as a result of direct exposure to the sun. UV protection is essential.

Is the bungee link used in my jump strong enough to withstand five times the load I'm going to put on it when I jump?

If the previous three questions convince you that the operator knows his bungee cords, this question and the next two will go a long way toward proving that he knows his bungee links. The cord combination for your jump should be at least five times the load placed on it by your plummeting body weight. If you weigh 150 pounds and your operator uses a series of 5/8-inch diameter cords, he should use three cords for your jump.

MODERN BUNGEE JUMPING— TRUE FACTS

•Bungee jumping, done right, is no more dangerous than a roller-coaster ride.

•Bungee jumping is the hairiest "no-brainer" thrill sport on planet earth.

•The maxim "You can run, but you can't hide," definitely applies to your first bungee jump—even if you're an experienced thrill seeker.

•In California, bungee jumping is officially considered an amusement ride. The only legal, insured bungee businesses in this state have an operating permit issued by the Amusement Ride Section of the California State Department of Industrial Relations.

Are the individual cords in the bungee link sheathed together so that I won't get tangled in them on rebound?

The reason most operators sheath their cords together is to keep them from separating—like strings of spaghetti squash—during rebound. If you're rebounding up into a tangle of four splayed cords, you're more likely to get tangled.

What's your target stretch factor for each jump?

Most operators want the bungee link to double its length (at least) at the bottom of your fall. Less than that tends to make the deceleration too hard. More is okay, given enough ground clearance and a bungee cord that is designed for longer stretching.

How do you know when your bungee cords or bungee links need replacement?

Regular visual and physical inspection of the cords will reveal wear. If one cord in a link is suddenly a few inches or feet longer than the others, or part of the cord looks either lumpy or thin, it needs to be replaced. Sections that feel lumpy, soft or kinked also indicate wear. Under ideal conditions, cords are good for between 200 and 1,500 jumps, depending on manufacturer recommendations. Good operators have regular cord inspection intervals and keep good written records of their inspections.

Do you have a "bumper" on the bungee link nearest the jumper?

A soft, cylindrical pillow of foam rubber on the jumper end of the bungee link prevents the "bungee burns" and fat lips that *will* happen from time to time when a raw bungee link whacks you in the face or neck.

Can you tell me something about the harnesses, carabineers and anchors you use to attach the bungee link to the jumper and the jumping structure?

The important concept here is parallel redundancy. You should have two harnesses (chest/waist), two carabineers attaching the bungee link to the harnesses, and two more carabineers attaching the other end of the bungee link to two anchor points on the jumping structure. All should have a strength/load ratio of better than 5-1.

Questions to Ask Regarding Operations

How long have you been in business?

No one has been in business more than four years.

Can you legally use your jump site?

The key here is that insurance is not available to operators who use unsecured sites. Bridge sites and untethered balloons are, by definition, illegal.

Do you have liability insurance?

Only the operators that have secure sites can answer yes. Cranes or towers on private property, tethered balloons, and legal bridges (although none exist in California at this time) are the only jump structures that can possibly be approved by insurance companies. And, as you've read, only insured operators qualify for amusement ride permits in the state of California.

What are the jump options in terms of height and attachment point?

Ask this question in conjunction with your

•Bungee cords are just one component of the critical "bungee chain."

•2-4 bungee cords plus a sheath make up the bungee link of a bungee chain. Other links are: Your harness, the carabineers that attach your harness to the bungee link, the carabineers that attach the other end of the bungee link to the jumping structure, and the anchor points on the jumping structure.

•The three most important things to look for in a bungee jumping operation are: proper strength and stretch characteristics on the specific "bungee link" you'll be jumping with, double attachments and fasteners (system redundancy) throughout the bungee chain, and a load safety factor of 5 to 1.

questions about the load/stretch characteristics (and length) of the bungee link you will jump with. You don't want to jump a 50-foot bungee link from a structure that is 75 feet off the ground. If you do you'll "zero out" with 25 feet of stretch still left in the bungee.

Questions to Ask About Actual Jump Procedures

Do you have several bungee links on hand to accommodate jumpers of different weights?

Operators should have enough separate bungee links on hand to cover the body weights of all jumpers. Most have at least three links to accommodate weights of 100 to 200 pounds.

Do you treat each one of these cords as if they were the umbilical cord of your unborn baby?

Observe for a while. Shy away from operators who allow their bungee links to be stomped on, pinched by a descending crane basket, or buried in mud or dirt.

How many operators are on hand and what does each one do?

There should be enough staff people to deliver a safety talk, supervise harnessing, collect your money, operate the jumping apparatus, coach you through launch, communicate between launch and landing, and manage the switching of bungee links to accommodate different size jumpers.

TRUE THRILLS

Here's how bungee jumping stacks up in relation to the reward variables I've outlined for thrill sports:

Speed

How fast can you recite this poem?:
"DIE!?"
"Die-Yi-Yiiiiiiiiiiiiiiiiiiiii!!!"
"Live-Liv-Livvvvvvv???"
"Die-Yi-Yiiiiiiiiiiiiii!!"
"Liv-Liv-Livvv!?"
"Die-Yi-Yiiiiiiii!"
"Live-Liv-Liv!"
"Dieeee?"
"LIVE!!"
That's exactly how fast bungee jumping is.

Focus

You're completely in the here-and-now. Period.

Your view of the world

Before you jump? Wide open! You take one last look at the world as you know it. When you jump? Straight-line fever followed by a series of random looping arcs between launch and the ground below.

How does it compare to REAL life?

Tough call in the air. Depends on your overall mental health and the depth of your religious beliefs. Odds are good that your first bungee jump will feel like quick, back and forth visits between heaven and hell. Once you're down on the ground, don't be surprised if you can actually see a post-jump "aura" emanating from yourself and all who went before.

Odds are good that your first bungee jump will feel like quick, back and forth visits between heaven and hell.

How does it feel?

Alimentary. Stomach more than anything else. Right in the pit: The jump grabs it; the first yank of bungee squeezes it; the weightlessness at the top of the first rebound flips it over. Churn three to four times in diminishing intensity. You end up—gape-mouthed and puckered—dangling at the end of a yo-yo string.

RESOURCES FOR DOERS AND DREAMERS

Admit it. Part of you is whispering, "*This bungee jumping sounds like great fun!*" The other part, however, is probably yelling "WHAT?! ARE YOU NUTS?!" Here are a few resources for those of you who would like to look into this bungee jumping madness a little further before actually signing up.

National Organizations

North American Bungee Association: 1500 East Kearns, Suite E 300, Park City, Utah 84060. (801) 645-9862. President: Thomas Woodard. Recently released NABA Jumping Guidelines are available to members only for a fee of $50.

Books, Magazines, Videos

There isn't much. Here's what there is:

Bungee Cords: Publication of the North American Bungee Association: see listing above. Editor: Gregg Glassock.

Videos: A few bungee jumping operators have promotional videos for sale. (See resource guide for details.)

Observation Points

For a good time—heh, heh—call any of the bungee jumping operators listed in the resource guide below. Most of them welcome observers with open arms. The only ones who don't are the ones who face logistical problems at illegal jump sites. With them you might have better luck if you volunteer to "look out for the cops."

RESOURCES FOR DOERS

The following operators all use systems which feature parallel redundancy throughout the bungee chain.

Crane, Balloon and Tower Operators

Bungee Adventures: 2218 Old Middlefield Way #G, Mountain View, California 94043. (415) 903-3546. World record holders (2,000-foot jump from a hot air balloon) John and Peter Kockleman have been in business since 1988. Theirs is the first commercial operation in the United States. Chest/waist harness jumps and ankle jumps from a balloon or a 250-foot crane. Promotional video available. Insurance and state permit in effect. Call for directions to the jump site.

See #1 on map page 42.

Total Rebound: 398 11th Street, Suite 302, San Francisco, California 94103. (415) 864-0704. Owner John Wilkinson operates, with state approval, at the Solano County Fairgrounds, adjacent to Marine World. Insurance and state permit in effect. Chest/waist harness jumps from a balloon and a 320-foot crane. "Slingshots" from crane only. Uses unique high-

stretch bungee cords.
See #2 on map page 42.

California Bungee: 16785 Beach Boulevard, Huntington Beach, California 92647. (800) 272-JUMP. Owner Ricco Nel has been in business nearly as long as the Kocklemans. He operates out of Perris Valley Airport. Jumps are from a 144-foot crane and a 300-foot balloon. Chest/waist harness and ankle jumps. Observers welcome. From 215 South, take the 4th Street exit west in the town of Perris. Go straight on Redlands past 4th Street. Go left on Ellis after 0.9 miles and it's 0.4 miles on the right. A separate business called "Quantum Leap" is a traveling bungee operation for state fairs and other occasions.
See #3 on map page 42.

Cowa Bungee: 11684 Ventura Boulevard, Studio City, California 91604. (808) 760-3957. Owners Dave Barlia and Steve Klassen use a 150-foot crane and offer balloon jumps from 300 feet. They operate out of the Lancaster area. Chest/waist harness jumps only. Call for directions to the jump site.
See #4 on map page 42.

Boing Bungee: 716 East Valley Parkway #200, Escondido, California 92025. (619) 432-8817. Brothers Rick and Russ Armstrong head the family business. Mom and sister do all the bookings. They offer balloon and crane operations and have been in business since 1991. Rick and Russ are lifelong balloonists from Albuquerque. Chest/waist harness jumps. Call for directions.
See #5 on map page 42.

Balloon Bungee/Sunset Balloon Flights, Inc.: 2201 San Dieguito Drive Suite 1, Del Mar, California 92014. (619) 481-9122. Frank Reed is one of the few commercial balloon operators in the state who has totally embraced bungee jumping. Most others feel that bungee madness violates the purity of the balloon experience.

See #6 on map page 42.

Pacific Bungee: P.O. Box 91757, Santa Barbara, California 93190. (805) 569-5303. Owners Michael Komp and Patrick Carey. They operate along foothills of Santa Barbara. Chest/waist and ankle jumps. Weekend mornings, by appointment only.

See #7 on map page 42.

Jumping Joe Bungee: Murietta Hot Springs, (800) 944-JUMP. Alan Trull and Rick Weibel, owners. Balloon jumps from 160 feet. Chest/waist harness. Weekends only with reservations.

See #8 on map page 42.

Topa Topa Outdoor Adventures: Owner John Christian. 1498 Old Telegraph Road, Fillmore, California 93015. (805) 524-4569. Jumps from a balloon normally; crane for special occasions. Chest/waist and ankle jumps. Weekend mornings, by reservation.

See #9 on map page 42.

Fantasy Balloon Flights/Bungee Jumping Division: 83701 Avenue 54, Thermal, California 92274. (800) GO ABOVE. Owners Cindy and Steve Wilkinson have been in the balloon business for 10 years. Bungee operations new in 1991. Chest/waist harness jumps only.

See #10 on map page 42.

Bungee Masters: P.O. Box 1804, Mill Valley, California 94942. (800) GO BUNGEE. Owner Jack Kramer has the second oldest balloon operation in the state. Jumps from 100, 200 and 300 feet. Also does 100 and 200 foot crane jumps in Rio Vista. Chest/waist harness and ankle jumps.

See #11 on map page 42.

Vertical Addictions: 3175 South Hoover, Suite 232, Los Angeles, California 90007. (800) 321-JUMP. Ryan Magnussen is new to Southern California but has several years experience (over 20,000 jumps) jumping from bridges in Northern California and balloons in Boulder, Colorado. Currently offers chest/waist harness and ankle jumps from a balloon in the Palmdale area. Magnussen is hot on the trail of a fixed crane site in the LA area.

See #12 on map page 42.

Bungee Fever, Inc.: 2702 California Avenue, Long Beach, California 90806. (800) TRY-BUNGEE. Owner Derek Whittaker offers ankle jumps over water from a construction crane. Last year Bungee Fever operated out of Lake Elsinore. Look for them in a new location this year.

See #13 on map page 42.

Bungee Quest: 993 Butte Drive, Santa Rosa, California 95403. (707) 545-JUMP. Owner Randy Mitchell offers ankle and chest/waist jumps from a crane and balloon at Sonoma/Marin Fairgrounds in Petaluma. Insurance and state permit in effect. Serves Sonoma, Marin, Mendocino counties.

See # 14 on map page 42.

Air Boingo: 1405 Washington Street, Colton, California 92324. (714) 824-JUMP. Owner Bill Draney has the only fixed tower operation in the state. Insurance and state permit in effect. Offers chest/waist jumps from a 75-foot Sport Tower. Open weekends and weekday evenings.

See #15 on map page 42.

Rapid Descents Bungee Jumping: 14011 Ridgehill Road, El Cajon, California 92021. (619) 561-6179. Manager Rick-O Bartoldus offers "New Zealand"-style jumps from a 140-foot crane. Predominantly ankle jumps. Some chest/waist harness jumps. Insurance and state permit in effect. Crane is located at Marshall Scotty's Amusement Park in El Cajon. Call for directions.

See # 16 on map page 42.

Bridge Operators

Bridge operators tend to flit from one bridge to the next like fireflies. "Call for details" is standard operating procedure for bridge jumpers.

Adventure Sports Unlimited: Sacramento. Owner Jonathan Bowlin: (916) 481-5967. Call for details. Excellent bridge operator according to industry pros.

See #17 on map page 42.

Bungee Experience: P.O. Box 1874, Los Gatos, California 95031. Owner Glen Bruno. (408) 395-7075. Knows where to go. Good sneaker. Call for details.

See #18 on map page 42.

Primal Instincts: Olympic Valley, Tahoe area. (916) 581-5867. Partners Jim Fritsch and Roger Stoneburner offer bridge jumps in Northern California. Call for details.

See #19 on map page 42.

Vertigo Bungee: Lake Tahoe. Owner Mike Stine. (916) 583-7220. Very experienced. Call for details.

See #20 on map page 42.

Odyssey Productions: P.O. Box 3127, Chico, California 95927. (916) 342-6624. Co-owners Jim Isherwood, Scott Tapley and Bill John. Call for details.

See #21 on map page 42.

Rock Climbing

Crescent City
Yreka
Newell
Mt. Shasta
Alturas
Eureka
Redding
Red Bluff
Susanville
Chico
Fort Bragg
Ukiah
Yuba City
Santa Rosa
Placerville
South lake Tahoe
Sacramento
San Francisco
Oakland
Stockton
Sonora
Lee Vining
Yosemite
San Jose
Merced
Santa Cruz
Bishop
Monterey
Salinas
Fresno
Lone Pine
Visilia
Kettleman City
Death Valley Jct.
San Luis Obispo
Bakersfield
Santa Maria
Wheeler Ridge
Mojave
Baker
Barstow
Palmdale
Needles
Santa Barbara
Ventura
Los Angeles
San Bernardino
Santa Ana
Palm Springs
Long Beach
Oceanside
Escondido
Blythe
San Diego
El Centro
Yuma

CHAPTER THREE

ROCK CLIMBING

ROCK CLIMBING IS BOOMING IN POPULARITY, both indoors and out. It is the most "upwardly mobile" segment of a vast group of movement/survival skills known as mountaineering.

You could argue that mountaineering is the world's original thrill sport. Long before we invented sophisticated contraptions to carry us through sky or whitewater, we wandered higher and higher into the mountains, although usually for some more practical purpose than getting a few thrills.

Naturally, the sheer faces of rock and ice we encounter in the high country give rise to questions like:

• "Can I climb that thing without killing myself, or not?"
• And: "*Why* do I really want to climb that thing in the first place?"

Just as naturally, the answers echo back:

• "Sure I can climb it—if I use the right equipment and techniques."
• And: "I want to climb it—obviously—for the FUN of it."

"Free" rock climbing is one of two branches of technical climbing—the kind of climbing that exposes you to fatal falls, unless you know

Mountaineering is the world's original thrill sport. Long before we invented sophisticated contraptions to carry us through sky or whitewater, we wandered higher and higher into the mountains.

how to deploy and use protection. Protection consists of solid, properly mounted anchors, plus rope, carabineers and climbing harnesses. A climber's protection system quickly stops any accidental fall.

Don't confuse "free" climbing with "aid" climbing, the other branch of technical climbing. "Aid" climbers are experienced mountaineers with very technical talents and tastes. They use their protection (bolts set in the rock, ropes, etc.) to help them move upwards.

Free climbers, on the other hand, navigate vertical rock walls using only natural "holds" in the rock plus high-friction shoes. They wouldn't think of using ropes and anchors for propulsion. Free climbers use protection simply to save their lives if they "come off" the rock.

As far as we beginners are concerned, free climbing must be divided into two segments: "top-roping," and "lead climbing."

Protection consists of solid, well-mounted anchors, plus rope, carabineers and climbing harnesses. A climber's protection system quickly stops any accidental fall.

Top-roping is the easiest form of technical free climbing and it is the only kind suitable for beginners. As a top-roper under the supervision of a rock climbing guide or instructor, you are always attached to a rope that has been securely mounted at the top of the climb. When you make a mistake as a top-roper, you don't really fall. You just "come off the wall." A manned, solidly anchored "belay" rope keeps you from falling more than a few feet.

As a lead climber, on the other hand, you must be experienced and talented enough to select and mount rope-anchor points on the way up a climb. If you don't do your job correctly, the entire climbing party is in grave danger.

If you suspect that your safety as a top-roper is entirely in the hands of your lead climber, you are a beginning rock climber with an excellent head on your shoulders.

For the purposes of this book, rock climbing is narrowly defined as beginning, professionally supervised, technical, top-rope free climbing. It too can be divided into two main groups.

Your safety as a top-roper is entirely in the hands of your lead climber.

Traditional free climbing is done outdoors, on natural rock crags or walls such as the ones found at Joshua Tree National Monument in Southern California and Yosemite National Park in Northern California. The goal of traditional rock climbing is to plan the best route to the top and then climb it without making mistakes.

Sport climbing takes place either indoors or outdoors. Sport climbers typically make shorter climbs that are more physically challenging. That's why sport climbing is also called *gymnastic* climbing. Pre-set protection allows you to be more physically aggressive, more technically sophisticated in your movements. As a sport climber you don't mind coming off the wall several times while rehearsing and refining your movements. Your ultimate goal is the same as a traditional climber's—a complete ascent of the route you're working on.

As a beginning, professionally supervised, top-rope free climber, either indoors or outdoors, you are in for an exhilarating mental and physical challenge and very little real danger.

In fact, rock climbing—as defined above—is the ultimate ride of passage. A basic rock climbing lesson is merely the first step in a dance with the mountains that will take you as high and as far as you care to go.

Amelia Rudolph is a professional dancer and choreographer who started rock climbing three years ago. Her first experience was at a crag in Tuolumne Meadows. She was under the supervision of a long-time rock climber/friend who had all the essential qualifications: rock climbing skills, rock climbing equipment and five years experience guiding in the Sierras.

She tells her story:

VERTICAL DANCE: Amelia Rudolph and The Project Banda Loop Dance Troupe

"I learned that dance principles like balance and centering apply directly to rock climbing—with one key difference: In rock climbing, I had to balance and center my weight on vertical as well as horizontal planes."

"I had been intrigued by rock climbing for some time when a friend of mine invited me to go climbing with him at Tuolumne Meadows. The first thing we did when we got there was hike up the backside of the small dome we'd be climbing. When we got to the top, he picked a spot for the anchor of our top-rope. Then he showed me how to set it. Knowing first hand that our protection was secure really helped me relax.

"Back at the bottom of the climb, we warmed up by 'bouldering.' We did climbing moves just a few feet off the ground and spotted for each other. I learned how to use my 'sticky' shoes. I also learned that dance principles like balance and centering apply directly to rock climbing—with one key difference: In rock climbing, I had to balance and center my weight on vertical as well as horizontal planes.

"We did some traverse climbing and I was impressed right away by the subtle shifts in weight between my hands and feet as I moved across the rock. It felt similar to the movement I was learning in T'ai Chi class.

"Next, George showed me how to put on a harness and how to make the right knots for attaching our top rope to the harness. Then we went over 'belay' techniques. [A "belayer" is like a bottom anchor—a human manager for the end of the rope that isn't attached to the climber. A belayer applies his or her body weight, through the rope, to stop the climber when a fall occurs.]

"Once I got comfortable with the equipment, and learned the right way to communicate while on belay, George let me climb. We had a great time. It was the start of a relationship that's lasted to this day.

"I liked climbing so much that I kept on doing it. When **CityRock Gym** opened in Emeryville in November of 1990, I realized that I had a great opportunity to combine dance with rock climbing. But first I had to turn some rock climbers into dancers or turn some dancers into rock climbers. I did a little of both.

"Turning a veteran rock climber like Hans Florine into a dancer was easy. Just like a great dancer, he was so balanced in his movement that he made very difficult moves look fluid and easy. I just talked to him while he climbed: I'd tell him to do more of the natural climbing moves that were attractive as dance, and less of the moves that weren't.

"Turning some of my Project Banda Loop Dancers into climbers was a different story. I watched while a **CityRock** instructor named Lawrence LaBianca gave five of them a first-day rock climbing lesson. It was tough for him because dancers who are faced with a new challenge are a very peppy group. They were all over the place, pressing Lawrence to get them 'climbing the walls' as quickly as possible.

"Lawrence did manage, despite the pressure, to get them through a pretty normal first lesson. Their indoor lesson wasn't much different from my first lesson with George at Tuolumne. The main difference was that the anchors were already set at the top of the gym's wall, and the ropes were already in place. They bouldered, learned about knots and harnesses, and learned how to trust and communicate with each other from both ends of belay. Easy routes up the wall were followed by harder routes. I got a kick out of watching other dancers use dance techniques on a vertical rock wall.

"At the end of the lesson we had five dancer/climbers all buzzed up and ready for more. Everyone loved it, except maybe for Lawrence. He told me later that he went home that night and cried his eyes out."

Postscript: Amelia Rudolph and The Project Banda Loop Dancers launched into a whirlwind of soulful climbing and hard choreography. It eventually became a series of vertical dance performances by the entire troupe. They called it "Off the Ground—Tales of Gravity and Perspective." The troupe played to packed houses at CityRock Gym in May, June and November of 1991.

A week after the final June performance, "Off the Ground's" lead climber/dancer, Hans Florine, won a national climbing competition held at CityRock. He credits his win, in part, to improvement in his grace and fluidity as a result of wall-dancing with The Project Banda Loop Dancers.

FIRST LESSON (Cost: $25-$90, depending on length; weekend courses: $125-$200)

Introductory rock climbing lessons are available both indoors and out. Generally speaking, indoor lessons are shorter (1 to 3 hours) and more focused on climbing/movement skills. Anchors and ropes are already securely in place before an indoor lesson even begins.

Outdoor lessons are longer (4 to 6 hours) and more focused on protection. Anchor placements must be selected and anchors set before the climbing part of the lesson can begin.

Rock climbers have widely varying opinions about the pros and cons of indoor and outdoor climbing. At introductory levels, however, the experiences are similar—with one important qualification.

Don't expect that indoor training will automatically qualify you for outdoor climbing. The two most obvious deficits that indoor beginners bring to their first outdoor experience are: no experience picking hand and foot holds by reading natural rock, and very little knowledge or ability to place or set anchors for their top-ropes.

Conversely, outdoor beginners shouldn't be too surprised if their indoor counterparts can climb circles around them. Because of the phenomenal convenience of indoor walls, beginners get to practice more sophisticated climbing techniques—as much as they want—very early in their climbing careers.

Don't expect that indoor training will automatically qualify you for outdoor climbing. The two most obvious deficits that indoor beginners bring to their first outdoor experience are: no experience picking hand and foot holds by reading natural rock, and very little knowledge or ability to place or set anchors for their top-ropes.

Basic Introductory Lesson Sequence

All or most of the following steps will be taken —in approximately the same sequence—during any introductory rock climbing class:

1) *Introductory talk.* Your guide will map out the sequence of your lesson. You'll be introduced and fitted to the equipment. You'll also learn terminology for technique, equipment and communication between climbers. Finally, transportation, logistics and environmental issues will be laid out for you.

2) *Place anchors, set anchors, install top-ropes above routes to be climbed.* If an instructor sets an anchor, he or she will either show it to you or explain to you where and how it is set. If it is already set, the instructor will point it out to you and explain how it is set.

3) *Warm-up and stretching.* At the introductory level, rock climbing is only moderately physically demanding. It does, however, place unusual stresses on your muscles, ligaments and tendons. The simple act of warming up and stretching goes a long way towards eliminating muscle pulls and strains and general stiffness on the following day.

4) *Bouldering or slab traversing.* You'll practice free climbing moves just a few feet off the ground, and you'll learn how to spot for others who are doing the same thing. This process familiarizes you with the unique qualities of climbing shoes, and tunes you into the idea of looking after your fellow climbers. It also gives you some experience with basic climbing technique including balancing, aligning hips over feet, foot and hand placement, and conserving energy by using your arms and legs most efficiently.

The simple act of warming up and stretching goes a long way towards eliminating muscle pulls and strains and general stiffness on the following day.

5) *Harness and knots.* You learn how to buckle harness, double back on buckled harness, and tie into the top-rope for climbing.

6) *Belay techniques.* Starting on flat ground or less than vertical slab, you'll learn basic belay techniques including belayer anchoring techniques, communication between climber and belayer, giving and taking slack, need for belayer

to keep brake hand on rope at all times, and braking techniques for belay device being used.

7) *Climbing easy routes on less than vertical slabs.* You will start on easy routes on non-vertical rock so that you can focus on basic climbing and belaying skills. Easy routes usually mean more, bigger or better-spaced hand holds or usable rock features. This translates into less of a requirement for strength, coordination or balance in the early going.

8) *Climbing harder routes on increasingly vertical rock faces.* Once you and your climbing partners become skilled and comfortable with looking out for one another, you will be allowed to climb more challenging routes. Harder routes require increasing measures of strength, balance and coordination because the holds and features on the rock are smaller, fewer or less conveniently spaced.

9) *End of the lesson review.* Helps you focus on what you liked or didn't like about the lesson, puts you in touch with your personal strengths and weaknesses as a climber, helps you set future climbing goals.

MYTHS

Myths about rock climbing, like myths about most other high-risk sports, usually spring from one of three sources:

• Accidents or fatalities involving careless, ignorant or poorly trained beginners. Self-taught beginners and those who place their trust in an unqualified teacher create their own risk.

• Accidents or fatalities involving eager beavers who ignore established, safe routes of progression during their intermediate stages of skill development.

• Accidents or fatalities involving leading-edge climbers who either did something foolish, or tackled a challenge so difficult that it could not be met using state-of-the-art equipment and technique.

Place yourself under the supervision of a professional instructor. There is no better way to assure that you'll be climbing with good protection and people who know how to make it work.

Risk does indeed exist in rock climbing, but it's a lot more controllable than the myths surrounding the sport would lead you to believe. Let's start with the big one:

"If I make a mistake while rock-climbing, I'll plummet and die."

Make all the mistakes listed below—in the exact sequence listed below—and you may very well die:

1) Go rock climbing alone, or without harness, rope, carabineers and anchors.
2) Climb higher than you care to fall on Class IV and Class V climbs.
3) Fall.
4) Hit the ground hard enough to bust your noggin.
5) Die.

Or, you can do steps 2 through 5 with poorly set protection, or a poorly trained belayer who doesn't take proper care of the rope while you climb.

Avoid the whole mess simply by placing yourself under the supervision of a professional instructor. There is no better way to assure that you'll be climbing with good protection and people who know how to make it work.

The truth is: If you make a mistake while you are protected—which you will be in any basic rock climbing course—you don't really fall. You simply come off the rock. Your belayer, who is watching you like a hawk, simply accepts your weight through the rope you're both attached to and you stay right where you are. If you decide to try again, you get back on the rock and go from the same spot you came off. If you want down, your belayer lowers you down, and you try again on the next climb.

If you make a mistake while you are protected—which you will be in any basic rock climbing course—you don't really fall. You simply come off the rock.

"I heard you have to learn how to use grappling hooks and drive big spikes into granite if you want to climb vertical rock walls."

You're thinking of that scene in *The Dirty Dozen* where Charles Bronson has trouble getting a grappling hook onto that chateau full of helpless German officers, aren't you? Or maybe you're thinking of aid climbers who bolt whole campsites onto vertical rock during multi-day big wall ascents.

The truth is: Free climbing is more like vertical gymnastics or vertical dance than anything else. It really has nothing to do with technical expertise in the use of hammers and spikes. Other than the simple rope/harness/anchor system which protects you from an accidental fall, the only mechanics involved in free climbing are the human mechanics of leverage, balance and precise application of muscular force.

Free climbing is a whole body/soul experience, not a whole hardware store experience.

"If I don't have the upper body strength of a Cyborg Terminator, I won't be any good at climbing rock."

You definitely develop upper body strength—especially in the forearms—through rock climbing, but you don't have to be particularly strong to start with. At the early stages, technique, balance, flexibility and concentration are more important than upper body strength.

The truth is: If raw upper body strength were the be-all, end-all for free climbers, all the best rock climbers would be bodybuilder men. But non-bodybuilder women do very well in rock-climbing. In fact, many think that a woman named Lynn Hill is the best free climber in America today.

"If I'm scared of heights, I can't possibly try rock climbing."

Everyone is afraid of heights. We are programmed to be afraid of heights—especially if we have no control over the circumstances or machinery that takes us there and brings us back.

The truth is: Rock climbing is a great way to overcome a fear of heights. Once you experience how well the protection system works, you realize that you're in control. You can come down any time you want and you don't have to go up any further than you want.

Also, you're much less likely to dwell on your fear of heights while rock climbing. You'll be so thoroughly focused on making your next move that fear will seem almost irrelevant.

TRUE CHILLS
(And how to avoid them)

If you fail to take the proper precautions, rock climbing—at any level—is extremely dangerous.

Listen. Any time you're higher off the ground than you'd care to fall, you're at risk. Your protection, and the people who make it work, have to function properly every single time you come off the rock. If your protection doesn't work properly, you could be the victim of a fatal accident.

Rock climbers have a word for a fatal accident. They call it *"cratering."*

If you hear one rock climber say to another "Did you hear that [so and so] 'cratered' yesterday?" that's major bad news. But if you stick around long enough to find out the circumstances of [so and so's] demise, odds are overwhelming that you'll learn that [so and so] did something stupid or careless that led directly to his or her death.

Any time you're higher off the ground than you'd care to fall, you're at risk. Your protection, and the people who make it work, have to function properly every single time you come off the rock.

The good news is that once you, as a beginner, place yourself in the hands of a qualified basic instructor, you're pretty much assured that all proper precautions will be taken during your lesson. Under those circumstances, rock climbing is probably no more dangerous than driving a car.

Overuse Injuries

Tendonitis in the fingers, elbows and shoulders is the most common rock climbing injury. You are not likely to suffer from tendonitis on an introductory level, especially if you warmed and stretched your body prior to climbing.

Top echelon rock climbers guard against tendonitis and other over-use injuries by observing the following rules:

- Never climb more than two days in a row. Take it easy on the second day.
- Pay attention to all aches and pains: know when to back off.

- Use proper technique (which minimizes stress on fingers, arms, shoulders).
- Always warm up and stretch before climbing. Cool and stretch afterwards.

Levels of Difficulty

Although we're talking about Class V free climbing on extremely steep terrain, you should be aware of the other levels of climbing as well. Some experience at lower levels may whet your appetite for the big stuff—the stuff that can kill you if you don't consistently follow the simple safety procedures.

Class V Climbing: Extremely steep terrain. Protection is absolutely necessary because, without it, a fall will almost certainly kill you.

Class I Climbing: The equivalent of hiking up a fairly steep hill.

Class II Climbing: Climbing that requires higher steps over rougher terrain.

Class III Climbing: Often called "scrambling," this kind of climbing requires that you use your hands for both balance and upward propulsion.

Class IV Climbing: This is the level where you want to start thinking about protection. The climbing is still easy in comparison to Class V, but a fall could result in serious injury.

Class V Climbing: Extremely steep terrain. Protection is absolutely necessary because, without it, a fall will almost certainly kill you.

Bouldering

Peter Mayfield of **CityRock Gym** describes bouldering as "a chapter of poetry in the novel of mountaineering."

The term bouldering refers to free climbing moves of any difficulty level that are done so close to the ground that no protection is necessary. Because the movement is so free and unencumbered, many climbers describe bouldering as "pure dance."

One caution about bouldering: While it is difficult to kill yourself if you fall while climbing around just a few feet off the ground, it may be easier to hurt yourself. Properly supervised beginning top-ropers almost never fall more than a foot or two before their weight is supported by belay. On the other hand, a six- to 12-foot fall while bouldering can easily result in a twisted ankle or a wrecked knee.

One caution about bouldering: While it is difficult to kill yourself if you fall while climbing around just a few feet off the ground, it may be easier to hurt yourself.

Equipment Considerations

The equipment you need for introductory free-climbing will be provided by the school or guide that gives you your first lesson.

All you really need at the beginning level is a well-fitting pair of basic "sticky" climbing shoes, a harness, some carabineers, and rope of the right strength and length. If you're learning outdoors on natural rock, you may want to wear a helmet. Your guide will also have an assortment of anchoring devices that will be used to anchor a rope at the top of your climbing route.

While all the equipment is fairly simple, it has to be absolutely reliable and in a good state of repair. You can't afford to have a rope, carabineer, harness or anchor break on you. It's that simple.

Fortunately, most climbing equipment—ropes, carabineers, etc.—is tested to standards of the U.I.A.A. (Union International des Associations d'Alpinisme), and once you select a qualified school or instructor, you can count on them to use safe, well-maintained equipment.

It's always a good idea, however, to ask a few questions about the equipment you will be us-

MODERN TOP-ROPE ROCK CLIMBING—TRUE FACTS

• *Professionally supervised introductory rock climbing gives you a great physical and mental challenge without exposing you to significant risk.*

• *Professionally supervised "top-rope free climbing" — indoors or out — is the only kind of Class V (technical) climbing that is suitable for beginners.*

• *Safety in top-rope free climbing is assured only by the proper use of "protection."*

• *Protection in top-rope free climbing consists of a secure anchor for the top-rope, rope, carabineers, and a climbing harness.*

ing during your lesson. And it doesn't hurt to visually inspect it as well—*before* you attach yourself to it and trust it to protect you from a fall.

Here are some questions you can ask if you feel uncomfortable about the equipment. Most guides actually enjoy explaining to you how strong their equipment is.

What is the strength rating of the carabineers I'll be using?

Aluminum, non-locking "ovals" are rated up to 3,500 pounds. Aluminum, locking "D's" are rated up to 5,500 pounds. Steel, locking "D's" are rated up to 11,000 pounds.

How much load can the harness I'll be wearing withstand?

The tensile strength of one-inch tubular harness webbing is up to 4,000 pounds. The tensile strength of two-inch tubular harness webbing is up to 6,000 pounds. **Note:** Harness buckles and fasteners are usually the weakest part of a harness system. The important concept is that they should have a known strength value, either through testing by the U.S. Military or the U.I.A.A.

Do you have a helmet available if I decide I want to wear one?

The only acceptable answer is "yes."

How often or under what circumstances do you replace your top-ropes?

Ropes should be replaced when there is any visible sign of damage, such as nicks, cuts, fraying or permanent kinks. They should also be replaced if they are stretched repeatedly by falls, or after two years of regular use with conscientiously minimized exposure to the sun. Ultraviolet (UV) rays from the sun weaken rope. Consequently, climbing ropes should never be left lying in the sun when not in use.

All good climbers constantly have their eyes peeled for signs of wear and tear on their equipment. You should do the following:

•Visually inspect the rope: Noticeable fraying is a bad sign.

•Visually inspect the harness: Is it in good shape? Do all buckles and adjustments work properly?

•Try on your rental shoes. They should be snug, but not painful.

•If you're going to wear a helmet, try it on. If it doesn't fit right, it will distract you throughout your lesson.

School/Guide Considerations

Your biggest responsibility as a beginning rock climber is to make sure that the person who is showing you the ropes is worthy of your trust.

Whether they call themselves guides, instructors, friends or acquaintances, the people who teach you basic rock climbing skills truly have your life in their hands. With so much at stake in such a rapidly growing sport, you'd think there would be a universally accepted industry standard for guide/school qualifications.

There isn't.

A fairly new organization called the American Mountain Guides Association (AMGA), however, has made significant progress in establishing standards. The AMGA has created and implemented an accreditation program for climbing schools as well as a certification pro-

• A free climber is attached to one end of a protection loop and a "belayer" is attached to the other. The belayer uses the rope to "catch" the weight of a free-climber when the climber "comes off the rock," either accidentally or on purpose — so he or she can be lowered back down to the ground.

• Balance, flexibility and leverage are more valuable to a free climber than pure strength. Done well, rock-climbing is like vertical gymnastics, or vertical dance.

gram for climbing guides. Although only a handful of California schools and instructors have been accredited/certified by the AMGA, several others have joined the association.

All AMGA members are required to meet the following requirements:

•Must be current and actively involved in providing guide services.

•Must submit climbing resume with application.

•Must operate with licenses and permits where necessary.

•Must maintain liability insurance coverage.

•Must be able to provide brochure or written response to inquiries about service.

Beware of "rogue" guides or instructors, especially the ones who have no insurance, no permits to use climbing areas, and only minimal climbing experience.

The recommendation here is that you look for all five qualifications in any guide service or climbing school, whether or not it is formally affiliated with the AMGA. The AMGA acknowledges that many fine guides and schools in California have not yet gone through the certification/accreditation process. As long as the guide or school meets all or most of the AMGA's membership criteria, odds are good that it is worthy of your trust.

Beware of "rogue" guides or instructors, especially the ones who have no insurance, no permits to use climbing areas, and only minimal climbing experience. Also beware of friends, acquaintances, or relatives who offer to teach you rock-climbing. While there are definitely some good rogues and relatives out there, you really have no way of knowing who they are—or where to find them.

BUT, if you insist on climbing with a non-certified guide, pay close heed to the advice of Tom Anderson, a long-time guide who helped develop the climbing program for a Costa Mesa adventure sports outfitter called **A-16**. (See resource guide at the end of this chapter.)

Says Anderson: "A good guide is a good climber and a *great* teacher. A good guide should be experienced, knowledgeable, safe and responsible. Some climbing programs and guide services are 'certifiable' [by the AMGA], some are not."

TRUE THRILLS

Here's how beginning top-rope rock climbing looks in relation to the reward variables I've outlined for thrill sports:

Speed

There is very little physical speed involved in rock climbing. Your mind, however, definitely races *way* ahead of your body. At the bottom of a climb, the first thing you do—instinctively—is scan the rock as far as you can see. You mentally place yourself at every point along the route, and try to picture what you'll do when you get there. The instant you start your climb, your brain speeds up even more. Every hold, every step, brings new information to process, new options to choose from.

Your physical movement may be slow, deliberate and precisely planned during a climb, but the rest of you pretty much **smokes** *all the way to the top.*

Your physical movement may be slow, deliberate and precisely planned during a climb, but the rest of you pretty much *smokes* all the way to the top.

Focus

Rock climbing is as here-and-now as it gets on this planet. All your senses, every muscle fiber in your body is focused on your next move, and the next, and the next—all the way up.

Your view of the world

As a beginning top-roper, your goal is to climb a fairly straight route, bottom to top. But, again, it's just your body that must crawl along a fairly narrow corridor. Your mind lays claim to all the area within immediate reach of your arms and legs, plus a wide pie-shaped expanse of rock above. It may not look like much space to someone watching from the ground, but it will seem like the whole world to you.

How does it compare to REAL life?

The huge disparity between physical speed and mental speed gives rock climbing a definite other-worldy feeling—especially when you combine the time warp with the unique physical sensations of defeating gravity on a totally vertical plane.

How does it feel?

Huffing, prying and leveraging your way up a vertical rock wall is a great way to thumb your nose at gravity.

If you subscribe to the theory that gravity is your mortal enemy, that it will ultimately drag your lifeless form back into the ground, you'll love rock climbing. Huffing, prying and leveraging your way up a vertical rock wall is a great way to thumb your nose at gravity. Rock climbing is also a solid whole-body workout.

RESOURCES FOR DOERS AND DREAMERS

Organizations

American Mountain Guides Association (AMGA): P.O. Box 2128, Estes Park, Colorado 80517. (303) 586-0571. Accreditation program for schools. Certification program for guides. Membership services for schools and guides.

American Sport Climbers Federation: Ralph Erenzo (212) 865-4373. This organization coordinates sport climbing competitions in the U.S.

The Access Fund: P.O. Box 67A25, Los Angeles, California 90067. The coordinator is Sam Davidson, 126 North 2nd Street, Salinas, California 93906. (408) 443-9507. The goal of this fundraising group is to keep climbing areas across the U.S. open and available to climbers.

Books, Magazines, Videos

Learning to Rock Climb, Michael Laughman, Sierra Club Books, 1981. ($12.95) Good book for beginners because it shows hip belay and basic rappel technique that climbers used before the advent of belay and rappel "devices." Terminology and technique is current enough to be useful for beginners. Equipment shown in photos and illustrations is somewhat dated.

How to Rock Climb, John Long, Chockstone Press, 1989. ($9.95) Excellent book for beginners. Illustrations, static photos of moves, and action photos of climbs make it a fun book to read. Climb difficulty rating system clearly spelled out. Current information on gear, techniques and movement skills.

Face Climbing, John Long. Chockstone Press. 1991. Chapter on slab climbing will be of particular interest to beginners. Rest of book deals with more advanced skills and techniques.

The Basic Essentials of Rock Climbing, Mike Strassman, ICS Books, 1989. This book really needs to be re-titled. "*Basic Bouldering*" or "*Basic Climbing Movement*" would be a far more appropriate title given the information contained in the book. Safety information is totally inadequate for anything above Class III climbing. Very little information on protection. Good basic movement information. Illustrations are excellent but totally misleading in terms of protection.

The Basic Essentials of Mountaineering, John Moynier, ICS Books, 1991. A great little book for those who want a peek at what's involved in mountaineering. Not intended to be a self-guiding tool.

Basic Rockcraft, Royal Robbins, La Siesta Press, 1989. Great coverage of all aspects of basic climbing, especially protection. Strong on knots, harnesses, belay techniques. Well-illustrated with photos of climbers wearing outdated shoes.

Southern California Bouldering, Craig Fry, Chockstone Press, 1990. Complete maps and descriptions of Southern California bouldering sites.

Climbing Magazine, P.O. Box 339, Carbondale, Colorado 81623. (303) 963-0372. Since 1970, the premier magazine in the sport. Wide coverage of all aspects of climbing.

Rock and Ice Magazine, P.O. Box 222295, Carmel, California 93922. (408) 625-6222. General interest coverage of rock, ice and sport climbing.

Sport Climbing Connection, P.O. Box 3203, Boulder, Colorado. (303) 442-5242. New publication devoted entirely to sport climbing.

"Basic Rock Climbing" (video): With John Long. Vertical Adventures Productions, (818) 883-4921.

"Moving Over Stone" (video): Narrated by Doug Robinson. Ridge of Light Productions, P.O. Box 2906, Mammoth Lakes, California 93546.

"Training to Rock Climb" (video): Hosted by Christian Griffith. The Vertical Club, Inc. (206) 283-8056. Gym workouts involving stretching, bouldering, endurance and strength training.

Observation Points

The following locations offer excellent, convenient viewing of rock climbers in action. Check the resource guide at the end of this chapter for phone numbers and other information.

Donner Summit: Call Alpine Skills International (ASI) for details.
See #1 on map page 72.

Yosemite National Park: El Capitan distance viewing, and training site viewing. Call Yosemite Mountaineering School for details.
See #2 on map page 72.

Joshua Tree National Monument: (numerous sites throughout park). Call Vertical Adventures or Wilderness Connection.
See #3 on map page 72.

Idyllwild: (Tahquitz and Suicide Rock). Call Vertical Adventures.
See #4 on map page 72.

Mickey's Beach: (Red Rock Beach). North of San Francisco, one mile south of Stinson "clothing optional" Beach. Cliff on south end of beach.
See #5 on map page 72.

Castle Craggs: (base of Mount Shasta). Distance viewing. Some hiking necessary. Call Shasta Mountain Guides.
See #6 on map page 72.

Tuolumne Meadows: Call Yosemite Mountaineering for details.
See #7 on map page 72.

Lake Perris: Call A-16, Costa Mesa.
See #8 on map page 72.

Mission Gorge: San Diego. Call Aquarius Adventures.
See #9 on map page 72.

Stonewall Peak: Julian. Call Aquarius Adventures.
See #10 on map page 72.

Lovers Leap: South Lake Tahoe. Off Highway 50. Call High and Wild Mountain Guides.
See #11 on map page 72.

Stony Point: Chatsworth. Call First Ascent.
See #12 on map page 72.

Mt. Tamalpais: Bay Area. Call Marin Discoveries. See #13 on map page 72.

Buttermilk: bouldering area, Owens Valley. Call John Fischer.

See #14 on map page 72.

Owens Gorge: sport climbing area. North of Bishop off 395. Call John Fischer.

See #14 on map page 72.

Indoor Climbing Gyms: These are the most convenient ways for city dwellers to get some exposure to rock-climbing. See resource guide for details.

RESOURCES FOR DOERS

Rock Climbing Schools and Guide Services with Membership in the American Mountain Guides Association: (AMGA)

The AMGA is a relatively new organization that is gaining recognition within the climbing community. It is the only active organization that offers an accreditation program for climbing schools, a certification program for climbing guides, and a general membership program for guides. The California schools/guides listed below are all affiliated with the AMGA.

Yosemite Mountaineering School: Yosemite National Park, California 95389. (209) 372-1244. Bruce Brossman, Director. One of the best rock climbing resources in the world. Certainly the highest profile climbing school in the state. These are the people who gave us the famous "Go Climb a Rock" T-shirts. All levels of rock climbing instruction plus a guide service for the more experienced. Call or write for brochure.

See #2 on map page 72.

Able Mountaineering: P.O. Box 18, Coloma, California 95613. (916) 626-6208. Guides: William G. Anderson and John G. Cleary (AMGA certified rock guide.) Rock climbing, ice climbing and mountaineering in the Sierras.

See #16 on map page 72.

Alpine Guide Service, Inc.: 10033 Angel Court, Spring Valley, California 92077. (619) 426-9108. Dick Cole, director/guide. Rock climbing, mountaineering, ski-mountaineering and backpacking all over California.

See #9 on map page 72.

Alpine Skills International: (AGMA accredited school), P.O. Box 8, Norden, California 95724. (619) 426-9108. Guides: Bela and Mimi Valdasz, co-directors. Rock climbing, ice climbing, mountaineering, trekking, expeditions, mountain medicine and rescue, winter skills courses, avalanche programs, ski-mountaineering, snowboard mountaineering. California and international.

See #1 on map page 72.

Aquarius Adventures: 302 N. Granados Avenue, Solano Beach, California 92075. (800) 328-5776. Guide: Bart Berry, director. Rock climbing, ropes courses, outdoor-based management training. Teaches "Basic Rock Climbing Weekend" at Joshua Tree, Idyllwild, Lake Perris, Mission Gorge (San Diego) and Stonewall Peak (Julian). Holds a sport climbing course at UC Riverside on 36 foot by 100 foot outdoor wall. Private guided instruction also available.

See #15 on map page 72.

High & Wild Mountain Guides: P.O. Box

11905, Tahoe Paradise, California 95708. (916) 577-2370. Guide/owner, Jay Smith, has been climbing for over 20 years. Rock climbing, ice climbing, mountaineering, trekking, expeditions, ski-mountaineering. Basic instruction is generally at Lovers Leap, which is just off Highway 50 near South Lake Tahoe. Climbing at Phantom Spires and Sugarloaf are also available.

See #11 on map page 72.

John Fischer: P.O. Box 694, Bishop, California 93514. (619) 873-5037. Or call Wilson's East Side Sports in Bishop (619) 873-7520. Independent guide John Fischer is on the AMGA board of directors, and has been climbing 30 years, guiding for 22. Rock climbing, ice climbing, mountaineering, trekking, expeditions, mountain medicine and rescue courses, ski-mountaineering. Basic lessons in Buttermilk area, which is one of the best bouldering areas in the world.

See #14 on map page 72.

Shasta Mountain Guides: 1938 Hill Road, Mount Shasta, California 96067. (916) 926-3117. Owner/guide Michael Zanger has been climbing for 31 years and guiding for 20. Rock climbing, ice climbing, mountaineering, trekking, expeditions, winter skills courses, ski-mountaineering, photography workshops. Basic instruction usually takes place at Castle Crags State Park near the base of Mount Shasta.

See #6 on map page 72.

Sky's The Limit: (AGMA accredited school), HCR 33, Box 1, Calico Basin, Nevada 89124. (702) 363-4533. Guide: Randall Grandstaff, director. Rock climbing, ice climbing, mountaineering, trekking, expeditions, winter skills courses, ski-mountaineering. Although his school is in Nevada, Randall Grandstaff draws most of his customers from California. He also teaches and guides mostly in California.

Other Rock Climbing Guides/Schools Who Meet AMGA Membership Standards

Adventure 16 (A-16): Large retail outfitter chain. Basic instruction at Lake Perris, Joshua Tree, Idyllwild area, and other Southland locations. In-house wilderness outing coordinators at three locations:

A-16/Costa Mesa: 1959 Harbor Boulevard, Costa Mesa, California 92627. (714) 650-3301. Has Orange County's best indoor climbing wall.
See #17 on map page 72.

A-16/San Diego: 4620 Alvarado Canyon Road, San Diego, California 92120. (619) 283-2374.
See #9 on map page 72.

A-16/West L.A.: 11161 West Pico Boulevard, West Los Angeles, California 90064. (213) 473-4574.
See #12 on map page 72.

Vertical Adventures: P.O. Box 7548, Newport Beach, California 92658. (213) 540-6517. Owner/guide Bob Gaines has been in business since 1981. Trains at various locations in Joshua Tree, and—during summer months—at outdoor crags in the Idyllwild area.
See #17 on map page 72.

Marin Discoveries: 11 First Street, Corte Madera, California 94925. (415) 927-0410. Guide Annie Callaway instructs rock climbing for this non-profit organization. Basic courses on Mount Tamalpais. Intermediate classes in Napa.

See #13 on map page 72.

The Wilderness Institute: 28118 Agoura Road, Agoura Hills, California 91301. (818) 991-7327. President/guide Brad Childs heads up this non-profit organization. Rock climbing coordinator is Joe Anders. Basic courses at Stony Point in Chatsworth. Intermediate and special classes for beginning women taught by Brenda Waugh. Special classes for teens taught by Randy Childs. Special "Learn to Rappel" class.

See #12 on map page 72.

First Ascent: 9855 Topanga Canyon Boulevard, Unit 111, Chatsworth, California 91311. (818) 347-4011. Owner/guide Greg Shaw has been climbing 15 years. Basic lessons at Joshua Tree, Idyllwild and Stony Point in Chatsworth. Hourly private guiding available at Stony Point which is right in Chatsworth. Unusually low (3-1) student to instructor ratio.

See #12 on map page 72.

Indoor Rock Climbing Gyms

CityRock Gym, Emeryville: 1250 45th Street, Suite 400, Emeryville, California 94608. (510) 654-2510. Peter Mayfield opened the premier rock climbing gym in the country in November of 1990. Climbing for all levels, beginning to advanced. In addition to providing all levels of instruction, CityRock serves as an indoor mecca for Bay Area climbers. National competitions have been held at CityRock. Innovative programming includes "Vertical Dance" performances by Amelia Rudolph and the Project Banda Loop Dance Troupe.

See #18 on map page 72.

Class 5 Fitness: 25-B Dodie Street, San Rafael, California 94901. (415) 485-6931. Bennett White and Yale Smith's indoor cross training center includes 7,000 square feet of climbing surface and a 50-foot overhang. Introductory courses include "Beginning Belay/Equipment" and "Beginning Movement."

See #18 on map page 72.

Club One, San Francisco: 360 Pine Street, 6th Floor, San Francisco, California 94104. (415) 398-1111. Indoor rock climbing program in a high quality health club. Program managed by Peter Mayfield of CityRock Gym.

See #18 on map page 72.

Retailers with Referral Arrangements to Lcoal Guides/Schools

Alpenglow Sports: 415 N. Lake Boulevard, Tahoe City, California 96145. (916) 583-6917. Full service climbing outfitter. Refers lessons to Alpine Skills International.

Marin Outdoors: Retailer of outdoor equipment and apparel. Will point you in the right direction for lessons. Four stores:

San Rafael: (415) 453-3400
Petaluma: (707) 763-9393

Fairfield: (707) 426-1222
Santa Rosa: (707) 544-4400

Recreational Equipment International (R.E.I. Co-Ops): The following R.E.I. stores have referral arrangements with local climbing guides/schools. Call for details.

Berkeley: (415) 527-4140
Carson: (213) 538-2429
Santa Ana: (714) 543-4142
San Diego: (619) 295-7700

Western Mountaineering/Marmot Mountain Works: Sister stores that retail outdoor equipment and apparel. Will point you in the right direction for lessons. Western Mountaineering is in San Jose at (408)984-7611. Marmot Mountain Works is in Kentfield at (415) 454-8543.

Wilson's East Side Sports: Bishop (619) 873-7520. Very knowledgeable about local climbing scene. Refers lessons to John Fischer.

Adventure 16 (A-16): Large retail outfitter chain. The three A-16 stores that don't have an in-house wilderness outings coordinator refer to the ones that do:

A-16/San Fernando Valley: 5425 Reseda Boulevard, Tarzana, California 91356. (818) 345-4266.

A-16/Solana Beach: 143 South Cedros, Solana Beach, California 92075. (619) 755-7662.

A-16/Horton Plaza: Log Cabin on The Sports Deck, San Diego, California 92101. (619) 234-1751.

University-Affiliated Climbing Schools

Outdoors Unlimited Co-Op UC San Francisco: P.O. Box 0234-A, San Francisco, California 94143. (415) 476-2078. Steve Leonoudakis, Director. Call or write for catalog which details classes, programs and trips.

CAL Adventures UC Berkeley: Department of Recreation and Sports, 2301 Bancroft Avenue, Berkeley, California 94720. (510) 642-4001. Rick Spitler, coordinator. Call or write for catalog which details classes, programs and trips.

UCSB Outdoor Recreation Program: Trailer 303-B, Robertson Gym, U.C. Santa Barbara, Santa Barbara, California 93106. (805) 893-3737. Wayne Horodowich, director of outdoor recreation. Climbing program is 20 years old.

Outdoor Adventures UC Davis: MU-Recreation, University of California, Davis, California 95616. (916) 752-1995. Dennis Johnson, director. Rock climbing director: Chris Rosamond. 24- by 100-foot climbing wall in Recreation Hall. All beginning classes start indoors. Outdoor climbing runs April to November at the Cosumnes River Gorge. Beginning rock climbing course is one day plus an evening.

Adventure Outings: California State University Chico, BMU 750, Chico, California 95929. (916) 898-4011. Rowland McNutt, coordinator. Rock climbing: introductory classes on a 60- by 60-foot indoor wall at the Chico State Gym. One day instructional outings to Bidwell Park, Bald Rock and Feather River Canyon/Grizzley Dome. Video tape of your climbs aids in instruction.

WHITEWATER RAFTING

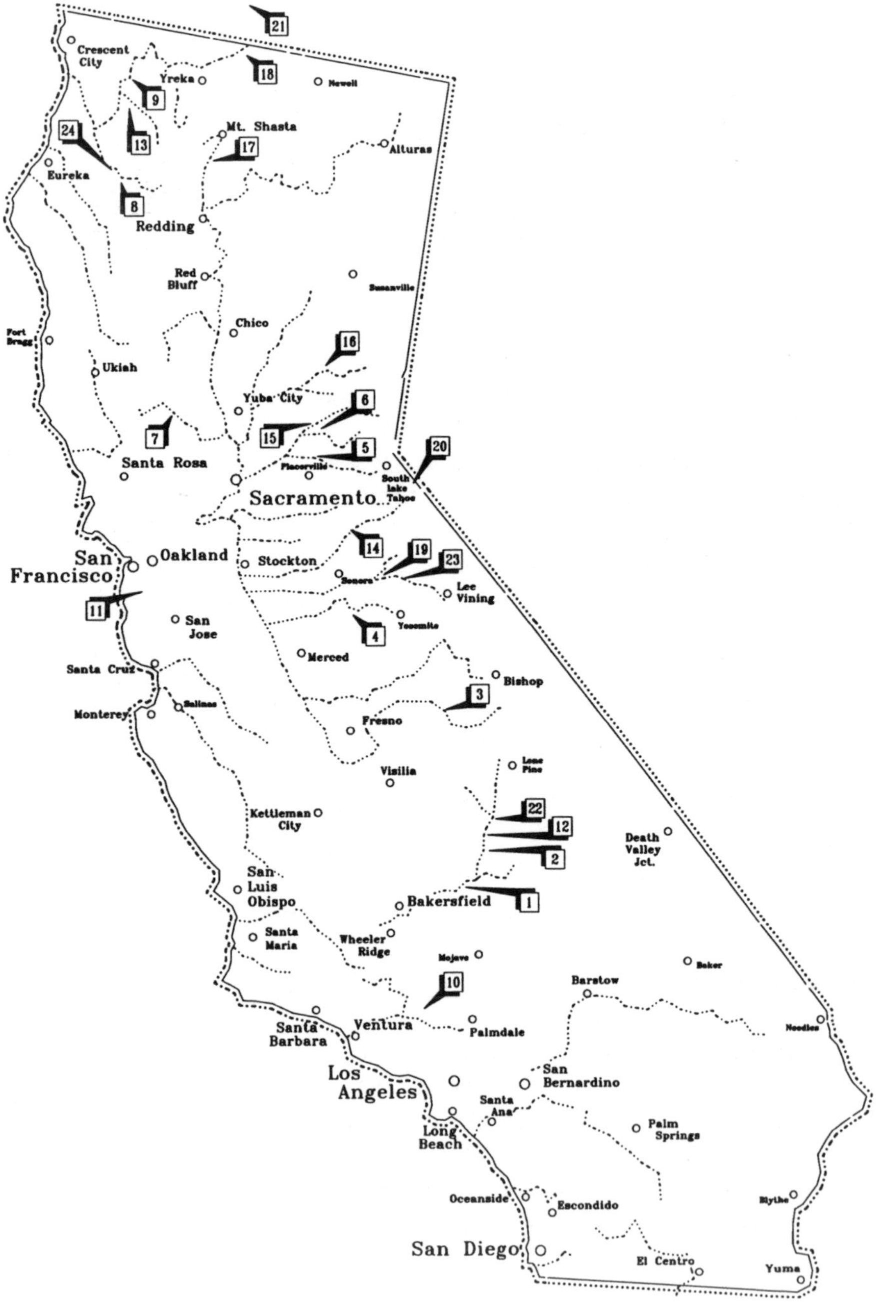

Crescent City
Yreka
Newell
Mt. Shasta
Alturas
Eureka
Redding
Red Bluff
Susanville
Chico
Fort Bragg
Ukiah
Yuba City
Santa Rosa
Placerville
South lake Tahoe
Sacramento
San Francisco
Oakland
Stockton
Sonora
Lee Vining
San Jose
Yosemite
Merced
Santa Cruz
Bishop
Monterey
Salinas
Fresno
Visalia
Lone Pine
Kettleman City
Death Valley Jct.
San Luis Obispo
Bakersfield
Santa Maria
Wheeler Ridge
Mojave
Baker
Barstow
Santa Barbara
Ventura
Palmdale
Needles
Los Angeles
San Bernardino
Santa Ana
Long Beach
Palm Springs
Oceanside
Escondido
Blythe
San Diego
El Centro
Yuma
21
18
9
13
24
17
8
16
6
7
15
5
20
14
19
23
11
4
3
22
12
2
1
10

Chapter Four

Whitewater Rafting

Whitewater rafting is the only sport covered in this book that brings honest to goodness group intensity to thrilling adventure. While hot air ballooning is also done in groups of two to ten, the group *does nothing* except sit back and enjoy the ride. And, although rock climbers definitely depend on one another during a climb, they aren't required to come up with an immediate, coordinated group response—on shrill command—in order to avoid some huge obstacle that appears suddenly, almost magically, from a tumultuous flow of "in yer face" whitewater.

Whitewater rafting is the only sport covered in this book that brings honest to goodness group intensity to thrilling adventure.

Jib Ellison, author of *The Basic Essentials of Rafting* (see resource guide), has shrieked "PADDLE FORWARD!!" to thousands of first-time whitewater rafters. As a long-time river guide, his main mission in life is introducing others to "an exciting sport that brings you face to face with the forces of nature."

The opening passage of Jib's book describes an average scene on an average paddle boat trip —complete with shrieking guide, scrambling rookie paddlers, accidental "swims," and wild cheering at the end of the ride. Here's how it happens from the guide's point of view:

SHOOTING A RAPID: Jib Ellison Tells It Like It Is

"The sound is unmistakable. Like a lion's roar, the rapid warns that it lies in wait—just downstream. The spring sun filters through the tall pine trees, their smell mixed with the bite of thin mountain air. Although your heart is racing, you feel strangely calm. Time seems to move slowly. Butterflies flutter about in your stomach. You yawn, although sleep is the farthest thing from your mind.

"This is the proverbial calm before the storm.

Your entire being is focused on the obstacles ahead. Rocks and waves and white foaming water are everywhere.

"The noise is deafening now. You have to scream loudly in order for your team of paddlers to hear you. Although you're almost on top of the churning rapid, you still cannot see downstream below the horizon line. You stand. Your entire being is focused on the obstacles ahead. Rocks and waves and white foaming water are everywhere. Suddenly, you see the route through the rapid and you call out a command. The crew responds by paddling forward as the boat slides into the rapid.

"A wave hits the bow and slaps the raft sideways. You call a turn, trying to regain control and get the raft back on course. Some of the crew hear you, others don't. You scream out the command again, this time with more urgency. A house-sized boulder lies downstream. It looked far away just a few seconds ago. Now it looms big. The boat hits it sideways and [gets] pushed up onto the rock. You call 'ROCK SIDE!!' and this time everyone knows what to do. Your crew scrambles to the high side of the raft. Their quick reaction keeps the raft from flipping.

"The raft peels off the rock and goes over a small ledge into a hole. The impact sends two of the crew into the river. Bobbing like corks in their life-jackets, they come up right next to the boat. You reach over and pull them quickly back into the raft.

"The rapid is not over yet. No time to think about what went wrong; only time to decide where to go from here. Looking downstream you [pick] a new route and call another command. 'RIGHT TURN!,' you scream. The [crew's] response is quick. It turns the boat into the next wave. Suddenly you're in control again. Another rock lies ahead but this time you avoid it easily.

"Next thing you know you're at the bottom [of the rapid]—in a calm pool—wet and totally exhilarated. Everyone lets out a cheer!

"You have experienced life to the fullest."

FIRST RIDE
(Cost: widely varied, depending on duration, location of trip)

If you have a close personal friend or a trusted acquaintance who happens to be an experienced river guide—and that specific person offers to take you on a whitewater rafting trip—go for it. Otherwise, your best bet is to place yourself in the hands of a reputable commercial whitewater outfitter.

Outfitters provide all necessary equipment and personnel, including rafts, paddles, life-jackets, experienced guides, transportation to and from the river, and exceptionally good food. Most important of all: They know the flow on the rivers they use—and you don't.

Most important of all: Outfitters know the flow on the rivers they use—and you don't.

Nothing is more critical to safe, fun whitewater rafting than knowing how much water is flowing down the river, month to month, day to day, hour to hour, instant to instant. The same stretch of the same river can provide a totally enjoyable beginner's ride at one volume of flow, and turn into either a crashing bore or total death at another.

Flow comes from one of three main sources: water run-off from rains, run-off from melting snow-packs high in the mountains above the river, or specifically timed releases of water stored behind upstream dams. That's why flow changes from year to year, season to season, day to day, even instant to instant.

The amount and kind of whitewater you will encounter on a rafting trip are determined by flow, overall steepness of the river bed, shape of the river bed (at all points along the stretch that's being run), and the nature of the obstacles in the river bed at all points along the run. River people have developed a rating system which helps them—and you—determine if a river is likely to give you a safe, fun ride that is appropriate for your level of experience.

Here's the internationally accepted whitewater rating system:

Class I Whitewater: Moving water with small waves. Few or no obstructions.

Class II Whitewater: Easy rapids with waves. Wide, clear channels that are obvious without scouting from shore prior to running rapid. Some maneuvering required.

Class III Whitewater: Rapids with high, irregular waves that are capable of capsizing a boat. Narrow channels that may require complex maneuvering and/or scouting from the shore.

Class IV Whitewater: Long, difficult rapids with constricted passages that often require precise maneuvering through very turbulent water. Scouting from shore often necessary. Conditions may make rescue difficult.

If Class I whitewater looks a little too tame to you, but Class V and VI has "crazies only" written all over it, you are a beginning rafter with an excellent head on your shoulders.

Class V Whitewater: Extremely difficult, long and very violent rapids with highly congested routes that nearly always must be scouted from shore. Rescue conditions are difficult and there is significant hazard to life in the event of a mishap.

Class VI Whitewater: Many consider "Class VI" whitewater unrunnable. Even the proverbial experts admit that they are at significant risk when they tackle this stuff.

If Class I whitewater looks a little too tame to you, but Class V and VI has "crazies only" written all over it, you are a beginning rafter with an excellent head on your shoulders.

But don't worry. A vast majority of the rafting trips designed for first-timers take place on whitewater that is rated between tough Class II and easy Class IV. You'd be hard-pressed to call easy Class II a thrilling adventure, and anything wilder than easy Class IV is not suitable for those without whitewater experience.

An example of a tough Class II run would be the Kern River between The Powerhouse and Kernville, at a flow of 400 to 1,000 cubic feet per second (cfs). This popular Southern California run is usually called the Powerhouse Run of the Upper Kern.

The most popular run in the state, by far, is a Class III stretch along the South Fork of the American River between Chili Bar and the

Salmon Falls Bridge. Normal dam releases of 800 to 1,700 cfs are perfect for beginners. The controlled flow also translates to an exceptionally long (March to October) season.

Finally, an example of an easy Class IV run would be the Kern River from below Lake Isabella to Democrat Hot Springs, at a flow of 2,500 cfs or lower. This run is known as the Lower Kern.

Duration Considerations

California whitewater rafting trips vary widely in length: length of the stretch of river being run, and length of time it takes to make the run. Here are the main divisions:

Lickety Splits: (Cost: about $20) Extremely short runs of one or two miles. These trips can be completed in less than two hours, or less than half a day. An example is The Powerhouse run on the Lower Kern in the southern Sierras, which usually takes about an hour and a half.

Day Trips: (Cost: $70-$100) Runs of three to 12 miles that can be completed during daylight hours. Popular examples are runs called The Gorge and Chili Bar on the South Fork of the American River.

Non-Wilderness Overnighters: (Cost: $130-$200) Tens of thousands of Northern and Southern Californians make weekend pilgrimages to the South Fork of the American River every year. Most do The Gorge one day and Chili Bar the next, with a night of camping thrown in between. You don't have to take any gear on the river. Your outfitter's shuttle driver will meet you in a full-service, vehicle-access campground at the end of your first day of rafting.

Wilderness Overnighters: (Cost: $200-$280) Wilderness overnighters are special. You get two days of whitewater rafting separated by one night of wilderness camping. Because there is no vehicle access to the banks of a river that runs through a wilderness area, you must bring all your equipment (food, stoves, tents, sleeping bags, water, etc.) down the river with you.

Wilderness overnighters give you much more than a thrilling whitewater adventure. They also put you directly in touch with the most cherished value of river people everywhere: complete and utter devotion to environmental preservation.

Wilderness overnighters give you much more than a thrilling whitewater adventure. They also put you directly in touch with the most cherished value of river people everywhere: complete and utter devotion to environmental preservation.

The most popular of the few remaining wilderness river runs in California is on the Tuolumne between Lumsden Campground and Wards Ferry.

Multi-Day Trips: (Cost: $250-$1,000) Californians must leave the state for multi-day trips for one good reason: With few exceptions, longer runs aren't available in California. That's because the Sierra Nevada Mountains are relatively steep. The runnable stretches of rivers fed by Sierra snowmelt are short and sweet because they are naturally designed to get rid of large amounts of water quickly.

Multi-day trips usually involve several successive days on longer wilderness rivers such as the Rogue in Southern Oregon, the Salmon in Idaho, and the granddaddy of them all—the Colorado River, through the majestic Grand Canyon, in neighboring Arizona.

Boat Considerations

Whitewater rafts come in two configurations: paddle boats and oar boats. Paddle boats are more fun if you're the type that wants in on the action. Unless you and your group specifically request an oar boat, your outfitter will provide paddle boats on lickety splits, day runs and non-wilderness overnighters.

Oar boats—which are controlled by one expert oarsman—are essential on wilderness overnighters and multi-day trips for two reasons: they're better suited to carry large amounts of gear, and they provide needed respite from the demands of paddling. Some multi-day trip outfitters, like those on the Grand Canyon, use oar boats almost exclusively. Others will take a few paddle boats along and rotate people in and out of them for the sake of variety.

MYTHS

"If we fall out of the boat in the middle of a rapid, we'll drown, right?"

Whitewater rafting drownings are almost unheard of—except among those misguided souls who get drunk and/or decline to don a life jacket.

Any time you're in the water—even the proverbial one inch of water—you can drown. But if you're wearing a life jacket, and you're sober, odds are overwhelming that you'll bob to the surface near the boat and get snatched back in before you can bat an eye. In the worst case, it's not that difficult—in mild to moderate whitewater—to swim over to the nearest riverbank where you can wait to be picked up.

The truth is: Whitewater rafting drownings are almost unheard of—except among those misguided souls who get drunk and/or decline to don a life jacket.

"It's OK if I get a little chilly on this trip, isn't it? I really don't want to bring any extra clothing or wear a life jacket."

No responsible outfitter will allow you to set foot in one of their rafts if you aren't wearing your life jacket. But, for the sake of argument, let's say you went for an accidental swim without a life jacket and lived to tell about it. Now you're wet. Unless you have proper clothing, you'll soon be cold. If you get too cold and stay that way for any length of time, you could possibly die.

Hypothermia—or loss of heat at your body's core—is the biggest single cause of whitewater fatalities. The best protection from hypothermia is a wetsuit, a paddle jacket and neoprene booties. Life jackets also protect you from hypothermia.

The truth is: Hypothermia—or loss of heat at your body's core—is the biggest single cause of whitewater fatalities. The best protection from hypothermia is a wetsuit, a paddle jacket and neoprene booties. Life jackets also protect you from hypothermia.

Always wear a life jacket on the river.

"It doesn't matter if I don't paddle, does it? The raft can only go downstream anyway, right?"

If your river guide suspects you of bringing that attitude into the raft, he or she will look you in the eye and say: "We're not on a track, you know. This isn't the Amazon River Boat ride at Disneyland." Expect a few hard looks from your fellow passengers as well. After all, they *need* you as much as you need them.

The truth is: Your paddlestrokes, like everyone else's, make a difference. Even a single paddlestroke at the right time can spell the difference between a triumphant plunge past a looming boulder and an "exciting group swim" at the bottom of a rapid.

MODERN WHITEWATER RAFTING: TRUE FACTS

- *Whitewater rafting is a true group experience. You depend on others and others depend on you to come through when it's time to paddle, hard and smart, in the middle of a rapid.*

- *Your first whitewater rafting trip should take place on mild to moderate whitewater (Tough Class II through Easy Class IV).*

- *Whitewater drownings are virtually unheard of* — **if** *you are wearing a life-jacket.*

- *Almost all commercial whitewater rafting in the state of California takes place between mid-spring and early fall.*

It's this simple: A big part of the thrill of whitewater rafting is knowing—in your heart and bones—that you personally contributed to a mighty group effort that miraculously became much more than the sum of its parts.

"What's the big hurry? We can go whitewater rafting any time, can't we?"

Whitewater rafting is the most seasonal thrill sport there is. It is usually done between mid-spring and early-fall in the best of circumstances.

The truth is: Most California whitewater depends on water run-off from melting snow-packs in the Sierra Nevada Mountains. Direct run-off feeds some rivers. Others are fed by releases from the reservoirs behind upstream dams. Run-off, of course, is what feeds the reservoirs. Run-off is always seasonal, and it can be scarce—especially in drought years when the snow-packs are small.

Even in drought years, however, excellent whitewater trips are still available. The whitewater season is much shorter, though, so you have to know when and where to go. And you have to be flexible enough to go with the flow. Stay in touch with your local outfitters. They know all about run-off and the timing of water releases from upstream dams. Consider them your precious whitewater resource.

"If the boat gets swamped with water, it'll sink like a stone and we'll all have to walk home, right?"

Actually, even a conventional raft filled to the brim with water won't sink like a stone. It won't be very maneuverable, however, and you may not be able to stop it from careening down the next rapid like a big old hunk of driftwood. **The truth is:** conventional rafts are equipped with "pickle buckets," or bailing buckets, which are manned by designated "swampers." Swampers scoop the river out of the raft and dump it either back in the river, or on the head of some uppity boat-mate.

A swamper's job is kind of fun, actually.

Pickle buckets and swampers, however, seem to be walking the path of the buffalo (towards extinction!), due to the increasing use of "self-bailing" rafts.

The truth is: Self-bailing rafts are becoming more and more popular. Self-bailers have been around, in their current form, since 1983 when Jim Cassady and an outfit called Whitewater Manufacturing produced the first inflated-floor self-bailer. Because the floor floats above the river, any water that gets into the boat simply drains out of the dozens of grommet holes around the edge of the floor. The holes are also used to lash the floor to the rest of the boat.

"If the boat hits a sharp rock, it'll blow up like a cheap balloon and we'll all get our money back, right?"

The truth is: Whitewater rafts have hides as tough as rhinoceros skin. Also, there are specific kinds of rafts for specific kinds of whitewater. The bottom line is that boats never blow up. They all have several compartments of air on each side and both ends of the boat. They can, however, get punctured and spring leaks from time to time. When that happens you and your boat-mates get to joke around with the guide while he patches the doggone boat.

TRUE CHILLS
(And how to avoid them)

Keep the following facts in mind: The danger of hypothermia increases at high water levels, during spring snowmelt, when the river is cold, at high elevations, and in the rainy season when the days are short and air temperatures are low.

The most common term for a fatal accident in whitewater rafting is "hypothermia."

If you get too cold, you die. It's that simple. The good news is that you don't have to get too cold. As one river expert puts it, "hypothermia is the killer of the unprepared."

At the introductory level you don't have to worry about hypothermia—especially if you've placed yourself in the hands of a competent whitewater outfitter. Your outfitter will give you the following list of suggestions on how to avoid hypothermia on your river trip:

Hypothermia Busters

1) Always wear your life-jacket. It helps protect you from heat loss at your core.

2) Don't wear cotton clothes. Wet cotton makes you colder.

3) Wear wool clothes or, better yet, clothes made with synthetic materials like Polypropelyne that are specifically designed to protect against heat loss when wet.

4) Wear a wetsuit when appropriate. Ask your guide if he thinks a wetsuit is needed.

5) Wear shoes or, if it's colder, neoprene booties. You can lose a lot of heat from your feet.

Keep the following facts in mind: The danger of hypothermia increases at high water levels, during spring snowmelt, when the river is cold, at high elevations, and in the rainy season when the days are short and air temperatures are low.

A good rule of thumb is: When air and water temperatures *combined* add up to less than 120 degrees Fahrenheit, the chances of hypothermia are greatly increased.

Equipment Considerations

Always select a qualified professional whitewater outfitter to give you your first rafting experience.

That's because there are no regulations regarding the design, manufacture, distribution and sale of whitewater rafting equipment. You, as a consumer, have no reliable means to distinguish dangerous rafting equipment from safe rafting equipment—unless you place yourself under the guidance of a licensed professional outfitter.

You, as a consumer, have no reliable means to distinguish dangerous rafting equipment from safe rafting equipment—unless you place yourself under the guidance of a licensed professional outfitter.

All river outfitters must be licensed to use the stretches of river that they use for commercial boat rides. The licensing agent is whoever has jurisdiction over the stretch of river in question. For example, the licensing agency for the Kern River in Southern California is the U.S. Forest Service.

The U.S. Forest Service has developed outfitter licensing requirements that are quite specific to the Kern River. Standards for type of rafts, construction of rafts, necessary safety equipment, etc. must be met by any outfitter who wants to operate on the Kern.

If you want a list of licensed Kern River outfitters, call the Cannell Ranger District of the U.S. Forest Service in Kernville, and they'll send it to you.

The licensing agent for the popular South Fork of the American River, on the other hand, is the El Dorado County Department of Planning in Placerville. They have their own set of outfitter licensing standards that are specifically tailored to assure safe, fun commercial rafting on the American River.

And so on. There are almost as many licensing agencies as there are rivers.

A listing of the licensing agents for all California rivers can be found in the book *California Whitewater* by Jim Cassady and Fryar Calhoun. (See the resource guide at the end of this chapter.)

Provider Considerations

For the same reasons described above, you're better off selecting a qualified professional outfitter to give you your first rafting experience. If you go rafting under the supervision of a beer buddy—in a flimsy department store raft—and you don't wear a life jacket, you are creating your own risk.

Licensing agents for California's rivers also have standards governing the training and experience of river guides—the people who will be the captain of your raft during your whitewater trip.

You're almost always better off sticking with a licensed outfitter. There are a few outfitters, however, who give great, safe, fun rides—but for one reason or another don't have an official license.

If you run into one, call the appropriate licensing agency and ask specifically about that operator. They'll either assure you that the outfitter is O.K. or they'll warn you off.

Beyond that, it's always a good idea to talk to your guide first—either on the phone or in person. With competence and experience pretty much assured through licensing, what you really want to know about your guide is: "Do I like this person? Is this someone I can have a little fun with out on the river—while he or she is screaming at me to PADDLE RIGHT!?"

Other Safety Considerations

Pay careful attention to your outfitter. Especially when he or she tells you to:

1) Wear shoes.
2) Protect yourself from sunburn.
3) Stay away from poison ivy and poison oak.
4) Secure your glasses—and anything else you don't want to lose—with a safety strap.

TRUE THRILLS

Here's how introductory whitewater rafting stacks up in relation to the reward variables I've outlined for thrill sports. The coolest part about whitewater rafting is that—due to seasonal and daily variations in flow volume—no two rides are exactly the same.

Speed

Whitewater boating is an infinitely variable speed sandwich. Each time you get on the river, you know only one thing for sure: You're in for several bursts of rapid action—each sandwiched between a couple of bobbing or cruising floats.

Whitewater boating is an infinitely variable speed sandwich.

Focus

Again, infinitely variable, depending on the river and the flow. Rest assured you'll tend to focus on the here and now when a boulder jumps out at you from the middle of Big Daddy rapid. At the bottom of that same rapid, don't be surprised if everyone on board starts yakking about "next time." Finally, the lazy float down to Little Mama is a good time to relax and enjoy the scenery.

Your view of the world

It's hard to describe a whitewater rafting trip as anything but the ultimate definition of a narrow view of the world, but there is plenty of variety within your river channel. The river widens and narrows and gets steeper or flatter. Narrow and steep means more focus on the here-and-now because there's a lot more action. Wide and flat opens things up, but tames the action.

How does is compare to REAL life?

Stretches between rapids simply brighten and freshen the world as you already know it. Rapids, on the other hand, are worlds unto themselves. Each is like a miniature planet. Rafting trips offer quick—"Here we come! There we go!"—glimpses of unique churning worlds that will never look quite the same again, no matter how many times you run past them.

Forget spatial considerations. What really makes a white-water rafting trip feel "other worldly" is the sound. It's a roar you will never forget.

But forget spatial considerations. What really makes a whitewater rafting trip feel "other-worldly" is the sound. It's a roar you will never forget.

How does it feel?

From your body's point of view, whitewater rafting is a veritable flow—sometimes quick, sometimes slow—of sensory associations and sudden changes in heart rate and breathing. Everything is triggered by sound.

You can't always see rapids, but you can always hear them. When you hear them coming, your heart beats faster. When you hear them going, you breathe deep and easy.

After a few miles, visual associations kick in. You learn that narrowing, steepening banks signal the sound and beat of upcoming rapids;

and widening, shallowing banks eventually lead to multiple sighs of relief.

A waiting pool at the bottom of a rapid triggers gut-level sensations: either the thrill of victory or the agony of defeat. It all depends on how you arrive—within the boat or without it. Either way, you and your new comrades feel like a gang of human otters as you head downstream *listening* for the first grumblings of the next big wet surprise.

RESOURCES FOR DOERS AND DREAMERS

If you're intrigued by whitewater rafting and want to find out more about it before actually doing it, consider any of the following resources.

Organizations

American Rivers, Inc.: 801 Pennsylvania Avenue Southeast, Suite 203, Washington, D.C. 20003. (202) 547-6900. This is a national river conservation organization.

Friends of the River (F.O.R.): Fort Mason Center, Building C, San Francisco, California 94123. (415) 771-0440. This is a state river conservation organization. Its regular publication, *Headwaters*, also includes articles with a recreational focus.

F.O.R. has an excellent booking service for all of California's rivers. They also have an inexpensive whitewater guide school.

America Outdoors: 531 Gay Street, Suite 600, Knoxville, Tennessee 87902. Will provide a list of established whitewater schools and outfitters in your area.

Project RAFT: 2855 Telegraph Avenue, Suite 309, Berkeley, California 94705. (415) 704-8222. A non-profit organization that utilizes wilderness as a forum for empowering people to positive action in their lives, communities and world.

Books, Magazines, Videos

California Whitewater, Jim Cassady and Fryar Calhoun. ($19.95) Revised 1990, North Fork Press, Berkeley, California. This is the definitive text on California whitewater. Detailed maps, critical flow and gradient information, plus rapid by rapid descriptions of every runnable stretch of whitewater in the state.

The Basic Essentials of Rafting, Jib Ellison. ($4.95) 1991, ICS Books, Inc. This great little book is ideal for anyone thinking of taking up whitewater rafting. All the basics, presented in a friendly, inspirational style.

Whitewater Rafting in Western North America: A Guide to Rivers and Professional Outfitters, Lloyd D. Armstead. 1990, Globe Pequot Press. Excellent, detailed descriptions of virtually all boatable whitewater runs in the Western United States.

The Complete Guide To Whitewater Rafting Tours, Rena Margulis. 1986, Aquatic Adventure Publications. This book, though somewhat dated, is chock full of every little detail about most of California's outfitters.

The Whitewater River Book, Ron Watters. 1984, Pacific Search Press. A well-illustrated guide to whitewater techniques, equipment, camping and safety. Rafts and kayaks.

Headwaters: The Newsletter of Friends of the River, Fort Mason Center, Building C, San Francisco, California 94123.

Paddler Magazine: P.O. Box 697, Fallbrook, California 92028.

Currents: Newsletter of the National Organization of River Sports, P.O. Box 6847, Colorado Springs, Colorado 80904.

"Whitewater Bloopers I and II" (video). Gayle Wilson Video Productions. Ashland, Oregon. Hilarious bloopers from California's "Slammin' Salmon."

"California Whitewater" (video). Camera One, P.O. Box 75556, Seattle, Washington 98125. Excellent video tour of a sampling of California's best whitewater.

"The Great White Hunter: In Search of The Unrunnable." (video). Rivers and Mountains. (800) 234-5522. Excellent and entertaining footage of exploratory Class V runs. Non-representative equipment bias towards catarafts—a fringe kind of river-running craft.

Whitewater Tales of Terror, William Nealy, Menasha Ridge Press. Hilarious cartoon exposure to river culture. Mostly kayak stuff, but some classic rafting scenes in this great little book.

Kayak: An Animated Manual of Intermediate and Advanced Whitewater Technique, William

DROUGHT-BUSTERS

Drought doesn't kill whitewater rafting. It does, however, shorten the season. Here are some tips to help you get your whitewater in spite of drought conditions:

- *Stay in touch with your local outfitters and river flow hotlines (listed in the resource guide). That way you'll know when and where to strike.*

- *Pre-arrange with your boss or spouse to take some spontaneous time off on weekdays. Water releases from upstream dams are more likely during the week in drought years.*

- *Open your mind to travel: Because drought particularly affects the Kern and the Kings Rivers, Southern Californians will probably want to think Northern*

Nealy, Menasha Ridge Press. Forget the word "kayak" in the title. This highly entertaining cartoon-illustrated book carries valuable information about whitewater hydraulics that any river person should know.

Observation Points

There are three good ways to get in on the excitement of a whitewater rafting trip without actually taking the trip yourself:

1) Go to any "put-in" site—where rafters enter the river—and check out the buzz of excitement and anticipation among the paddlers and passengers.

2) Go to a place where you can watch rafters shoot rapids. You'll hear howls of anticipation before the rapid and hoots of victory afterwards.

3) Go to any "take-out" site—where rafters exit the river—and check out the tired but excited chatter that goes on while the rafts and gear are packed up and carried to the shuttle vehicle.

Here are some of the most popular and easily accessible whitewater observation locations in the state. You can drive right to them.

Sandy Flat put-in: (Lower Kern) May-September. See #1 on map page 106.

Chili Bar put-in: (South Fork American) April-September. See #5 on map page 106.

Ewings rapid: (Upper Kern): Class II-III, April-mid-July. See # 2 on map page 106.

Limestone rapid: (Upper Kern): Class IV, April-mid-July. See #12 on map page 106.

Banzai rapid: (Kings): Class III+, May-July. See #3 on map page 106.

Troublemaker rapid: (South Fork American): Class III+, April-September. See #5 on map page 106.

Ned's Gulch rapid: (Merced) Class IV, April-early July. See #4 on map page 106.

Freight Train rapid: (Salmon) Class V, April-early July. See #13 on map page 106.

Democrat Picnic area take-out: (Lower Kern), May-September. See #1 on map page 106.

Kernville Park take-out: (Upper Kern), April-mid-July. See #2 on map page 106.

See the resource guide at the end of this chapter for the phone numbers of outfitters that provide trips on the river you want to visit. They'll be happy to give you directions to Troublemaker, Banzai, Freight Train and all the rest. Or consult the book *California Whitewater* by Jim Cassady and Fryar Calhoun.

The "River Menu" that follows in the resource guide was prepared by Jim Cassady himself—with beginners specifically in mind.

RESOURCES FOR DOERS

California offers rafters and other boaters the widest range of whitewater in the country. There are three main areas of whitewater: rivers of the southern Sierra Nevada, rivers of the central and northern Sierra Nevada, and the rivers of the coast ranges in the northwest part of the state.

California. Northern Californians may want to consider the Klamath and Trinity Rivers near the Oregon border.

- *Take advantage of bargains on out-of-state trips: When California's whitewater season is shortened by drought, many California outfitters extend their season with bargain basement packages for trips to rivers in New Mexico, Utah, Oregon, Idaho and Colorado.*

- *Take advantage of some classic runs that are only available during drought conditions, when water levels plunge in dams. The old "Camp Nine" run of the Stanislaus River and the "Poe Run" of the Feather River then become accessible.*

Only the rivers that support commercial rafting operations are listed, along with their average season, degree of difficulty (Class II to Class V), duration of trip available, and recommended flows in cubic feet per second (cfs).

Commercial runs for for beginners

Lower Kern: June-August, Class IV (some V). Two days. 1,000-3,000 cfs. See #1 on map page 106.

Upper Kern: April-July, Class II, III, IV. Half day, full day. 600-3,000 cfs. See #2 on map page 106.

Kings: May-August, Class III. One or two days. 1,000-6,000 cfs. See #3 on map page 106.

Merced: May-June, Class IV. Two days. 800-3,000 cfs. See #4 on map page 106.

South Fork American: May-September. Class III. One or two days. 800-4,000 cfs. See #5 on map page 106.

Middle Fork American: June-August. Class II, Class IV with portage. One or two days. 800-2,000 cfs. See #6 on map page 106.

Cache Creek: June-August. Easy Class III. One day. 400-1,000 cfs. See #7 on map page 106.

Upper Trinity: June-August. Class III. One day. 500-2,500 cfs. See #8 on map page 106.

Lower Klamath: June-September. Class III. One, two, or three days. 1,000-8,000 cfs. See #9 on map page 106.

Magic Mountain/"Roaring Rapids:" April-October. Class II. Three minutes.** See #10 on map page 106.

Great America/"Rip Roaring Rapids:" April-October. Class II. Four minutes.** See #11 on map page 106.

(**Yes, it's hard to believe, but those amusement park rapids really do qualify as Class II runs. Jim Cassady and Fryar Calhoun, authors of *California Whitewater*, were impressed enough with the 3-4 minute "runs" that they rated them and listed them in their book.)

Commercial runs for aggressive beginners

North Fork Stanislaus: May-August. Class IV+. One half or one day. 400-2,000 cfs. See #14 on map page 106.

North Fork American: April-June. Class IV+. One day. 600-4,000 cfs. See #15 on map page 106.

North Fork Yuba: May-June. Class IV, some V. One or two days. 800-4,000 cfs. See #16 on map page 106.

Upper Sacramento: May-June. Class IV. One day. 600-3,000 cfs. See #17 on map page 106.

(California) Salmon: May-June. Class IV, some V. One or two days. 600-3,000 cfs. See #13 on map page 106.

Upper Klamath: June-September. Class IV+.

One or two days. 1,200-3,000 cfs.
See #18 on map page 106.

Wilderness camping runs

Tuolumne: May-September. Class IV+. Two or three days. 800-4,000 cfs. See #19 on map page 106.

East Fork Carson: May-June. Class II. Two days. 500-3,000 cfs. See #20 on map page 106.

Rogue (Oregon): May-June. Class III. Three to five days. 1,000-5,000 cfs. See #21 on map page 106.

Advanced commercial runs: experience definitely required

Class V Portion of Upper Kern: May-June. Class V. One day. 1,000-3,000 cfs. See #12 on map page 106.

Forks of Kern: May-July. Class V. Two or three days. 600-4,000 cfs. See #22 on map page 106.

Upper Tuolumne: June-September. Class V. One day. 800-2,000 cfs. See #23 on map page 106.

Giant Gap Run: North Fork American, May-June. Class V. Two days. 500-2,000 cfs. See #15 on map page 106.

Burnt Ranch Gorge Run: Trinity, June-August. Class V. One or two days. 500-2,000 cfs. See #24 on map page 106.

For Updated Information on River Flow and Where to Go

The River Flow Hotline: (916) 322-3327. The recorded message is updated three times a week.

Pacific River Supply, El Sobrante: (510) 223-3675. Owners Jim Cassady and Mike Martell will be happy to tell you where to go. PRS also prints a free Flow Update Information Sheet that can be mailed or faxed.

California whitewater outfitters who operate on Southern Sierra Nevada rivers

Chuck Richards Whitewater: Box W. W. Whitewater, Lake Isabella, California 93240. (619) 379-4685. In business since 1975, owner Chuck Richards was one of the first to offer commercial rafting on the Kern River.

Kern River Tours: P.O. Box 3444, Lake Isabella, California 93240. (619) 379-4619. Owner Rick Roberts has run trips on the Kern River since 1975.

Outdoor Adventures: P.O. Box 1149, Point Reyes, California 94956. (800) 323-4234. Since 1972, owner Bob Volpert has run trips on the Kern in the south, and on the Tuolumne in the north. He also runs trips on the Rogue (Oregon) and the middle and main forks of the Salmon (Idaho).

Sierra South: 11300 Kernville Road, Kernville, California 93238. (619) 376-3745. In business since 1985. Brother-sister team Tom Moore and Marriane Moore-DeChant operate out of a full-service retail store. Raft rides for beginners include Lickety Splits, (one hour trips on the Powerhouse Run) plus half and full day trips on various stretches of the Upper Kern.

Whitewater Voyages: P.O. Box 906, El Sobrante, California 94803. (800) 488-RAFT. Owner Bill McGinnis has been in business since 1975. McGinnis has authored a couple of books on whitewater rafting and guiding. Trips on the American (South, Middle, and North forks), Cache Creek, California Salmon, Carson (East Fork), Kern, Klamath (upper, lower), Merced, Rogue (Oregon), Stanislaus (North Fork), Trinity, Tuolumne, and Yuba (North Fork).

Spirit Whitewater: 1001 Rose Avenue, Penngrove, California 94951. (707) 795-7305. In business since 1975, owner John Munger specializes in trips on the Kings River.

Zephyr River Expeditions: P.O. Box 510, Columbia, California 95310. (209) 532-6249. In business since 1973, owner Bob Ferguson runs trips on the Kings, American (South Fork), Carson (East Fork), Merced, and Tuolumne rivers.

Kings River Expeditions: 211 North Van Ness, Fresno, California 93701. (209) 223-4881. Owner Jeb Butchert has run Kings River trips since 1972.

California outfitters who operate on rivers throughout California

Note: The "Camp Nine" run on the Stanislaus River is only runnable during drought years when water levels in the downstream reservoir are low. Many of the outfitters listed below offer "The Stan," but only when it's available.

Adventure Connection: P.O. Box 475, Coloma, California 95613. (916) 626-7385. Owner Nate Rangel has run trips on the American (South, Middle, and North forks) since 1982.

All Outdoors Adventure Trips: 2151 San Miguel Drive, Walnut Creek, California 94596. (415) 932-8993. In business since 1974, owner George Armstrong runs trips on the American (South, Middle, and North forks), California Salmon, Klamath (upper and lower), Merced, Stanislaus, and Tuolumne Rivers.

ARTA (American River Touring Association): Star Route 73, Groveland, California 95321. (800) 323-ARTA. ARTA has been around since 1963. Manager Steve Welch has been on board for the last 12 years. Trips on rivers throughout the West: the American (South, Middle, and North forks), California Salmon, Green (Utah), Illinois (Oregon), Klamath (upper, lower), Merced, Rogue (Oregon), Idaho Salmon (Middle Fork, main), Selway (Idaho), Tuolomne, and Yampa (Utah).

Environmental Travelling Companions (ETC): Fort Mason, Building C, San Francisco, California 94123. (415) 474-7662. This group serves the general population, but their true mission—and it makes them unique—is to provide whitewater rafting adventures to special populations, including physically handicapped individuals and groups. They also do whitewater kayaking for general populations.

Beyond Limits Adventures: P.O. Box 215, Riverbank, California 95367. (800) 234-RAFT. Although they offer beginning-level trips, partners Mike Doyle and West Walker's specialty is hairy whitewater. Since 1986 Doyle has been serving up Class V whitewater to customers who call themselves "Team Extreme." In keeping with their leading-edge mind-set, Beyond Limits was the first outfitter to offer river body-boarding. Rivers run include: American (South, Middle, and North forks), Carson (East Fork), California Salmon, Klamath (upper, lower), Scott, Stanislaus, Trinity and Yuba (North Fork).

Earthtrek Santa Ana: 23342 Madero, Suite B, Mission Viejo, California 92691. (800) 229-TREK. Jerry Ashburn runs one of the few whitewater services in Southern California. Earthtrek's specialty is one and two day trips on the South, Middle, and North forks of the American River. Two day weekend trips include round-trip charter bus service, five meals, overnight camping, and 21 miles of river between Chili Bar and Folsom Lake.

Echo: The Wilderness Company: 6529 Telegraph Avenue, Oakland, California 94609. (415) 652-1600. Owners Dick Linford and Joe Daly have been in business since 1971. Rivers include: American (South, North forks), California Salmon, Rogue (Oregon), Idaho Salmon (Middle Fork, main), and Tuolumne.

Libra Whitewater Expeditions: P.O. Box 4280, Sunland, California 91041 (818) 352-3205. In business since 1980, Jon Osgood runs trips on the South, Middle and North forks of the American River.

Mariah Wilderness Expedition: P.O. Box 248, Point Richmond, California 94807. (415) 233-2303. Owners Donna Hunter and Nancy Byrnes have run trips on the American (South, Middle, and North forks) and the Merced since 1982.

O.A.R.S.: P.O. Box 67, Angels Camp, California 95222. (209) 736-4677. Owner George Wendt has been running rafting trips all over the West since 1969. Rivers include: American (South, North forks), California Salmon, Carson (East Fork), Colorado (Grand Canyon), Dolores (Colorado), Klamath (lower), Merced, Rogue (Oregon), San Juan (Utah), and Tuolumne.

South Bay River Rafters: P.O. Box 243, Hermosa Beach, California 90254. (213) 545-8542. In business since 1977. Owner Pat Fischer runs trips on the South Fork of the American River.

Tributary Whitewater Tours: 20480 Woodbury Drive, Grass Valley, California 95949. (916) 346-6812. In business since 1978, owner Dan Buckley runs trips on the American (South, Middle, and North forks), California Salmon, Carson (East Fork), Trinity, and Yuba (North Fork.)

W.E.T. (Whitewater Expeditions and Tours): P.O. Box 160024, Sacramento, California 95816. (916) 451-3241. Owner Steve Liles has been in business since 1979. Trips on the South, Middle, and North forks of the American River.

Whitewater Connection: P.O. Box 270, Coloma, California 95613. (916) 622-6446. Owner Jim Plimpton has been in business since 1980. Trips on the South, Middle and North forks of the American River, California Salmon and on the upper Klamath River. Small store on premises.

Whitewater Voyages: P.O. Box 20400, El Sobrante, California 94820. (800) 488-RAFT. Owner Bill McGinnis has been in business since 1975. Trips on the American (South, Middle, and North forks), Cache Creek, California Salmon, Carson (East Fork), Kern, Klamath (upper, lower), Merced, Rogue (Oregon), Giant Gap, Stanislaus (North Fork), Trinity, Tuolumne, and Yuba (North Fork).

Zephyr River Expeditions: P.O. Box 510, Columbia, California 95310. (209) 532-6249. In business since 1973, owner Bob Ferguson runs trips on the Kings, American (South Fork), Carson (East Fork), Merced and Tuolumne.

Whitewater Excitement: P.O. Box 5992, Auburn, California 95603. (800) 327-2386. Since 1979, owner Norm Schoenhoff has run trips on the American River (South, Middle and North forks), and on the Merced.

Outdoor Adventures: P.O. Box 1149, Point Reyes, California 94956. (800) 323-4234. Since 1972, owner Bob Volpert runs trips on the Kern in the south, and on the Tuolumne in the north. He also runs trips on the Rogue (Oregon) and the middle and main forks of the Salmon (Idaho.)

Turtle River Rafting Company: 507 McCloud

Avenue, Mount Shasta, California 96067. (916) 926-3223. Owner: Rick Demarest. In business since 1976. Trips on the South Fork of the American, California Salmon, Klamath (upper, lower), Owyhee (Oregon), Sacramento (upper), and Trinity.

Sunshine River Adventures: 18341 Kennedy Road, Knight's Ferry, California 95361. (209) 848-4800. Owner Jim Faust has been in business since 1984. He runs trips on the Mokelumne and the lower Stanislaus.

Sierra Mac River Trips: P.O. Box 366, Sonora, California 95370. (209) 532-1237. One of the older outfitters in the state, Marty McDonnell has offered trips on the upper and main Tuolumne since 1965. He also runs Giant Gap on the North Fork of the American.

River Runners-California: 23801 Killion Street, Woodland Hills, California 91367. (818) 340-1151. Since 1973. Trips on the South Fork of the American River.

River Mountain Action: 5916 W. 77th Place, Los Angeles, California 90045. (818) 348-3727. In business since 1979, owner Roger Mugford runs trips on the South Fork of the American River.

Wilderness Adventures: P.O. Box 938, Redding, California 96099. (916) 243-3091. In business since 1979, owner Dean Munroe rafts the California Salmon, Klamath (upper, lower), Sacramento (upper) and Trinity rivers.

Electric Rafting Company: P.O. Box 3456,

Eureka, California 95501. (707) 445-3456. Trips on the California Salmon, lower Klamath, and Trinity River. Owner Bill Wing has been in business since 1979.

California River Trips: P.O. Box 460 Lotus, California 95651. (916) 626-8006. Owner: Bill Center. In business since 1978. Trips on all forks of the American River.

American River Recreation: 11257 South Bridge Street, Rancho Cordova, California 95670. (800) 288-0675. Owner: Don Hill. In business since 1974. Trips on all forks of the American River.

James Henry River/Wilderness Journeys: P.O. Box 807, Bolinas, California 94924. (415) 868-1836. Owner James Katz has recently re-entered the California river market after concentrating on out-of-state and international rivers for many years. Specialty is "environmental awareness" and "natural history" interpretive programs for youth groups and UC Adult Extension Schools.

Action Adventures Wet 'N Wild: P.O. Box 13846, Sacramento, California 95853. (916) 641-6676. Owner Loren Smith has been in business since 1958. He is one of the very first whitewater rafting operators to set up shop in the state. Rivers: American (South, Middle, and North forks), Carson (East Fork) and Tuolumne.

Ahwahnee Whitewater: 22511 Parrott's Ferry Road, Columbia, California 95310. (209) 533-1401. In 1990, current owner Jim Gato bought Outdoors Unlimited, a rafting company that was established in 1969. Trips on the Merced and the Tuolumne.

University programs that run rafting trips

Adventure Outings: California State University, Chico, BMU 750, Chico, California 95929. (916) 898-4011. Rowland McNutt, coordinator. Beginner river rafting trips to Trinity River. Lower Klamath, South Fork American.

CAL Adventures: U.C. Berkeley, 2301 Bancroft Avenue, Berkeley, California 94720. (510) 642-4001. Rick Spitler, coordinator. Bobby Dery, whitewater director. Various trips.

Outdoor Adventures: U.C. Davis, MU-Recreation, University of California, Davis, California 95616. (916) 752-1995. Dennis Johnson, director. Various trips.

Outdoors Unlimited Co-Op: U.C. San Francisco, P.O. Box 0234-A, San Francisco, California 94143. (415) 476-2078. Steve Leonoudakis, director. Various trips.

Hot Air Ballooning

Crescent City
Yreka
Newell
Mt. Shasta
Alturas
Eureka
Redding
Red Bluff
Susanville
Chico
Fort Bragg
Ukiah
Yuba City
Santa Rosa
Placerville
Sacramento
South lake Tahoe
San Francisco
Oakland
Stockton
Sonora
Lee Vining
Yosemite
San Jose
Merced
Santa Cruz
Bishop
Salinas
Monterey
Fresno
Lone Pine
Visalia
Kettleman City
Death Valley Jct.
San Luis Obispo
Bakersfield
Santa Maria
Wheeler Ridge
Mojave
Baker
Barstow
Palmdale
Santa Barbara
Ventura
Needles
Los Angeles
San Bernardino
Santa Ana
Palm Springs
Long Beach
Oceanside
Escondido
Blythe
San Diego
El Centro
Yuma

Chapter Five

Hot Air Ballooning

Hot air balloon pilots are a special breed. They pride themselves as much on their ability to help others appreciate the magic of ballooning as they do on their piloting skills. Pilot Kris Heffleger of **High Adventures** in Mission Hills, California, has authored a description of a day of hot air ballooning, which we repeat here:

ADVENTURE ALOFT: Kris Heffleger Shares the Experience

"It's dawn on a cool morning in the green rolling hills of Southern California. As the rising sun begins to scatter shafts of golden light, an energetic, laughing group of adventurers prepares for a morning of hot air ballooning. Pilots, crew and passengers alike buzz in eager anticipation of what many have described as a magic carpet ride. First-time flyers in particular look forward to a rare experience. By the end of the morning, each will have logged an hour aloft in a hot air balloon.

"The fabric (bag) portion of the balloon is attached to the gondola and spread out. While two passengers hold open the mouth of the balloon, a gasoline powered fan fills it with cold air. The pilot briefs other members of the crew on their roles in getting the balloon to an upright, flying position. Then he ignites the balloon's powerful gas burner.

"In less than 30 seconds the gentle giant is up and ready to go.

"A special emotion wells in all who witness a balloon inflation. It's as though they were privy to the manipulations of a magician as the spectacular rainbow-colored Goliath comes to life.

"Passengers for the first flight clamber aboard the wicker gondola. The pilot briefs them on what to expect in their upcoming flight. Shortly after he unleashes a blast of heat from the burner, the balloon slowly floats into the sky. The earth, and—it seems—even gravity itself are left behind.

A special emotion wells in all who witness a balloon inflation. It's as though they were privy to the manipulations of a magician as the spectacular rainbow-colored Goliath comes to life.

"There is no true feeling of motion when aloft. The balloon rises and descends more gradually than an elevator. And no breezes can be felt because in a balloon *you are the wind*, travelling at its same speed. Except for the occasional roar of the burner, it is so quiet that you can hear a dog barking 1,500 feet below.

"There is no set destination in a hot air balloon. That's because a balloon pilot's control is limited to changing altitudes, finding different directions in the breezes, and maneuvering for landing in an open field.

"It has been said that ballooning is the form of travel where the destination is irrelevant, and the trip is everything. After an hour of spectacular 360-degree views from varying heights, the craft is brought gently to rest near a rural road.

"The balloon is tethered to the ground. Passengers exchange places with the chase-crew who followed the flight of the balloon in a recovery vehicle. The job of the chase crew is both fun and challenging. By maintaining visual or radio contact with the pilot of the balloon, they must anticipate where the balloon will land and be there—preferably in time to witness touchdown.

"Crewing can be more difficult than it seems because the balloon is at the whim of mother nature. A balloon pays no attention whatsoever to the path that an earth-bound vehicle must take. Often, the landing is only the halfway point of the morning's adventure.

A balloon pays no attention whatsoever to the path that an earth-bound vehicle must take. Often, the landing is only the halfway point of the morning's adventure.

"At the final landing of the day, the balloon is deflated by opening a valve at the top. In minutes it is gathered up and packed into a large bag. Then it's time for the traditional champagne toast and brunch. Passengers, pilot and crew exchange tales of the morning's adventures as they toast the day.

"A morning of hot air ballooning will truly give you a memory that will last a lifetime."

FIRST RIDE (Cost: $135-$200 for a one-hour ride)

Hot air balloon rides are like snowflakes: No two are alike. Even flights in the same balloon over the same terrain will be different from one day to the next. Wind and weather conditions differ, even in calm sunrise and sunset conditions when nearly all balloon flights take place.

You can, however, pick the general type of experience you will get by asking yourself the following questions:

Am I looking primarily for a gripping aviation experience or a mellow scenic ride?

Altitude gains of more than 3,000 feet and extreme distances are more likely with specific companies in specific locations. Scenic rides are far more common. They allow you to gaze upon beautiful scenery from moderate altitude or follow the contours of the countryside at a very low altitude.

Am I looking for a private ride? A romantic experience with that special someone? A ride with a hand-picked group of friends, family or co-workers? Or, a group ride with strangers?

All are available and different companies specialize in different kinds of experience. Two person "sweetheart" rides usually cost more per head than six- to ten-person "cattle" rides.

Do I want personal contact with my balloon's pilot during the flight?

Some companies encourage comraderie between passengers and crew. Others put the pilot in a separate part of the balloon's basket which allows the passengers to socialize more privately among themselves.

How long a flight do I want?

There are no guarantees, of course, because the wind is in charge. Consider a half hour the bare minimum, and expect to be mildly disappointed if that's all you bargained for. A full hour is better and is far more likely with a company that does only one or two rides per balloon per day. Companies that do three or four "hops" in each balloon sometimes have to cut one short in order to get the last one in before increased winds force re-scheduling. Ask: "How long is the flight?" and "How many hops?"

Am I a morning person or an evening person?

Since a great majority of all balloon flights in California take place within three hours of dawn, ballooning is pretty much a sport for morning people. Generally speaking, you have to be at the launch site by dawn in order to take off at sunrise. Sunset flights along the coast of Del Mar near San Diego are the exception rather than the rule.

Do I want to go with a large company—one that offers sales, service, gift shop, and a catered champagne brunch? Or, would I rather go with a smaller operator, like a medium-sized mom and pop shop; or one that gives rides weekends only, as much for fun as for profit?

Generally speaking, the larger companies have big balloons that carry six to 10 passengers per flight while smaller companies tend to fly smaller balloons with two to four passengers per flight.

The point is this: Before you sign up for anything ask enough questions to assure yourself that the ride you'll be getting in real life matches the one you have in your head.

No matter what, make sure your pilot has a Commercial Balloon Pilot's Certificate issued by the F.A.A. Anyone who sells hot air balloon rides is required by federal law to have one.

MYTHS

Hot air ballooning is such a gentle activity, and its safety record is so nearly perfect, that most people hesitate to call it a thrill sport. Still, it is a form of flight—and like any other form of flight—it is plagued by a host of myths involving fear, safety and control. And here they are:

"*A hot air balloon ride can be really scary!*"

A hot air balloon ride definitely gets your attention. But most people don't find it scary at

Some say the experience approaches the scary side of exhilarating but, by and large, first-time balloonists uniformly describe the ride as awe-inspiring, even heavenly.

all. Some say the experience approaches the scary side of exhilarating but, by and large, first-time balloonists uniformly describe the ride as awe-inspiring, even heavenly.

Scary, of course, is in the mind of the beholder, but **the truth is** that the feeling of fright and the act of hot-air ballooning seem to be strangely incompatible—especially at the "Balloon 101" stage—which is the stage that all balloon ride operators stick to when dealing with first-timers.

"No one can control a hot air balloon—not even a balloon pilot!"

Wrong. No one can control the wind. And the wind does indeed control the speed and direction of a hot air balloon. But does that mean you can't control the path the balloon takes in relation to the ground? No way!

You control a balloon by correctly judging wind conditions and by controlling its altitude. Want to avoid a 15-mile-per-hour landing? Don't fly in 15-mile-per-hour winds! Want to go higher (or fly longer to avoid an obstacle on the ground)? Use your heater to heat the air inside the balloon, and it will rise faster the hotter it gets. Want to go lower? Don't heat the air inside the balloon, and it will descend faster the cooler it gets. Throw in the fact that the wind blows at different speeds and directions at different altitudes, and you can see that skilled balloon pilots do indeed have quite a bit of control over where and how a hot air balloon flies and—most importantly—lands.

"Only champagne-sipping wimps take hot air balloon rides!"

Don't say that too loudly at a balloon race or rally. You will be politely objected to—in no uncertain terms. The world of hot air ballooning is a world of rugged elegance and—more to the point—tradition. A post-flight champagne toast or brunch is part of that tradition. It's just one of those things. Most people, whether they drink champagne or cider or nothing at all, think it's a nice thing at that.

The truth is: People of all types and persuasions, from every age group and every walk of life find something magical in a hot air balloon ride. And it has nothing to do with the drink they're offered when the day is done.

"Hot air balloon rides are way more dangerous than airplane rides!"

Facts prove otherwise. In the past 20 years there have been no more than a handful of fatal accidents involving first-time balloon passengers.

TRUE CHILLS (And how to avoid them)

Pilots who misjudge weather conditions create extra risk. So do pilots who fly worn, non-airworthy balloons. Doing both at the same time is double jeopardy.

Although fatal balloon accidents are extremely rare, they do happen. Pilots who misjudge weather conditions create extra risk. So do pilots who fly worn, non-airworthy balloons. Doing both at the same time is double jeopardy. For example, two balloonists died in Albuquerque a few years ago when they flew a balloon destined for the scrap heap in extreme weather conditions over Sandia Peak, an area known for turbulent air. Post-crash inspection of the balloon revealed that it was more than just worn. The vent at the top was held together completely by velcro—even the seams that were supposed to be sewn. The two pilots may have survived the strong weather in a better balloon. They may have been able to get away with flying their bogus balloon in mellower conditions. But they couldn't do both.

Weather-related balloon accidents are entirely avoidable for pilots who routinely check weather conditions, then follow the adage: "When in doubt, sit it out." In August of 1990 there were a number of balloon crashes on the same day in the Napa Valley. Balloonists who failed to call the weather service that day were surprised by the high winds and turbulent air. The ones who called recognized unusual conditions and stayed on the ground. Fortunately, there were no fatalities.

The maxim "what goes up, must come down" applies to anything that flies, including hot air balloons.

The maxim "what goes up, must come down" applies to anything that flies, including hot air balloons. Unfortunately the maxim does not include the absolute assurance that what goes up must come down in one piece—or that it must come down at a speed compatible with the preservation of human life. That means you cannot totally eliminate equipment-related problems as a source of true risk. Next to weather, balloon equipment is the biggest consideration in the "fly-no fly" question.

Equipment Considerations

In any form of flying, there is always the possibility of structural failure, mid-air collision and crash landing. That's as true in a hot air balloon as it is in a commercial jetliner—but it doesn't seem to be any truer than that. Balloon people contend that structural failures are rare and usually attributable to poor maintenance.

At the very worst, you can trust the airworthiness of balloons every bit as much as you can trust the airworthiness of airplanes. That's because balloons, like airplanes, must be certificated by the FAA. Certification assures that minimum airworthiness standards were met when the balloon was built.

At the very worst, you can trust the airworthiness of balloons every bit as much as you can trust the airworthiness of airplanes. That's because balloons, like airplanes, must be certificated by the FAA.

Also, FAA regulations mandate a thorough annual inspection for each and every certificated hot air balloon. FAA certificated repair stations perform the annual inspections, and a record of those inspections must be kept by the owner of the balloon.

Here are some questions you can ask about balloon equipment:

Who made this balloon?

The primary manufacturers of hot air balloons are: Aerostar International, The Balloon Works and Cameron USA. Smaller manufacturers include Thunder & Colt and Head Balloons. A few pilots design and/or manufacture their own balloons. Home-builts are subject to FAA regulations as well, but they cannot legally carry passengers as "balloons for hire."

Is the balloon I'll be flying in certificated and "in-annual?"

Certificated means it has a standard airworthiness certificate. "In-annual" means that it has been inspected, as required by law, within the last 12 months.

Can I see the balloon I'm going to ride in before I ride in it?

You may have to come observe for a day to accomplish this particular mission. You can't expect balloon operators to grant you a condi-

Bright, crisp, beautiful balloons are good. Faded, frayed or ugly ones warrant—at the very least—a few pointed questions.

tional flight booking subject to your "expert" inspection. Bright, crisp, beautiful balloons are good. Faded, frayed or ugly ones warrant—at the very least—a few pointed questions.

Pilot Considerations

The primary source of true risk in hot air ballooning is—you guessed it—balloon pilots.

The FAA participates in protecting the public from incompetence or inexperience on the part of all pilots. Three separate balloon pilot certificates are issued by the FAA:

Student Balloon Pilot: Don't sign up for a ride with one of these.

Private Balloon Pilot: Don't sign up for a ride with one of these—unless you personally know and trust that person.

Commercial Balloon Pilot: This is the top balloon pilot rating. Commercial pilots can teach as well as sell rides. A commercial pilot's certificate is, without question, the balloon industry's standard for those who sell hot air balloon rides to the general public.

As you have already learned, balloon safety depends almost entirely on the competence, experience, and—most importantly—*skill* of your balloon pilot. Skill in manipulating altitude by heating trapped air is just the tip of the iceberg for a balloon pilot. Judgement of wind conditions, selection of flying sites that are suitably free of obstacles, and ability to avoid obstacles during approach and landing is what separates a good pilot from a bad pilot in hot air ballooning.

Consequently, you should interview your pilot either over the phone or—better yet—in person. The one concrete question you should ask is: "How many 'commercial pilot' hours have you logged?" Look for an absolute minimum of 100 hours as pilot in command. Most companies want their pilots to have a least 300 hours. While experience certainly doesn't guarantee skill, it does show that the pilot has demonstrated his ability to survive with the skill he has.

You also want to get to know if you and your pilot can hit it off on a personal level. This person will be escorting you through a magical experience. It'll be even better if he or she is someone you can relate to—someone whose company you're likely to enjoy.

The one concrete question you should ask is: "How many commercial pilot hours have you logged?" Look for an absolute minimum of 100 hours as pilot in command.

If you want a referral to a good local balloon pilot or company that matches up well with what you're looking for in a balloon ride, look in the phone book under "U.S. Government, Department of Transportation." Find the sub-listing "Flight Standards District Office." Call that number and ask for the number of the local Balloon Pilot Examiner. If there isn't one of those around, ask for the number of the nearest Balloon Accident Prevention Counselor. That will put you in touch with the people who know the most about the balloon pilots in your area. They may be able to steer you to a pilot or company that specializes in the kind of ride you're looking for.

By now you've accomplished three things:

1) Decided what kind of balloon experience you want.

2) Found the provider that can do the best job of giving it to you.

3) Qualified, to the best of your ability, both

HOT AIR BALLOONING: TRUE FACTS

• A hot air balloon ride is the only form of flying that gives you tons of three-dimensional motion with almost no physical sensation of motion.

• A hot air balloon flight, done right, is completely exhilarating but not "scary."

• Hot air balloons must be registered with the FAA and undergo annual inspection by an FAA certificated inspection facility.

• Hot air balloon pilots are required by law to have at least one (of three) balloon pilots licenses: student, private or commercial.

• 99% of all commercial hot air balloon rides take place within a few hours of

the specific balloon you'll be flying in and the specific pilot who will be flying it.

Now it's time to focus on the goodies.

TRUE THRILLS

Here's how hot air ballooning stacks up in relation to the reward variables I've outlined for thrill sports:

Speed

Nearly all introductory balloon flights take place within a few hours of dawn or sunset—in winds less than five miles per hour. Winds stronger than that will deliver a ride that is more exciting than it is beautiful—especially on landing. The upper limit? Only a very few balloon pilots choose to fly in winds of 15 miles per hour or more. All know better than to take first-timers with them.

"Ballooning 101" is definitely the slowest of all the aerial adventures covered in this book. That's just one of the reasons it's so attractive to so many people.

Focus

In a balloon ride, time ebbs gently from present to past and future and back to present again. Leaving the ground in a hot air balloon tends to focus you on the present. You manage to stay very busy, thank you, alternating your gaze between the beautiful bag above and the disappearing ground below. Plus you've just got to shoot a few glances at the faces of your pilot and your fellow passengers. You are searching the moment, so to speak, for facial expressions that might mirror your own—expressions that reveal exhilaration, astonishment or even (per-

(perhaps)some anxiety.

About the time the noise of the first "burn" stops, your mind begins to drift. You search the past for experiences that come close to comparing to this brand new one. Simultaneously you project yourself into the future—at first nervously, along the path between your present location and a completely unknown landing area; and then boldly, into animated conversations with friends and loved ones on the ground. "It was fantastic!" you're telling them. "You've got to give this balloon stuff a try!"

When it's time to land, you shift gears back into the present. Once again your gaze flits back and forth between the beautiful bag above and all the possible obstacles on the approaching ground below. Expectant eye contact between you and the pilot, and you and the other passengers confirms mixed feelings all around. "Hope we land—soon and safe!" your eyes say to each other. "Why do we have to land at all?" say your hearts.

Your view of the world

With the possible exception of landing—which can be a very focused, here-and-now experience—hot air ballooning is as wide open as it gets. You see and feel the entire world laid out below and around you.

How does it compare to REAL life?

What makes a hot air balloon ride seem like such an other-worldly experience? That's an easy one. A hot air balloon is the only aircraft in which you experience dramatic three dimensional motion—without any sensation of motion at all. It is the only aircraft in which you can pretend that *you*—not the earth—are a rela-

dawn or sunset —when the winds are usually less than 5 mph.

- *Balloon pilots control the altitude of a hot air balloon by controlling the temperature of the air inside it. Because winds blow at different speeds and directions at different altitudes, a balloon pilot can (within limits) control speed and direction of a balloon.*

- *The safety record of hot air ballooning proves that it is at least as safe as flying in a commercial airliner, and much safer than flying in a private plane.*

tively fixed point in space—that the earth below is moving around in relation to *you,* rather than vice versa.

To put it another way: Imagine you are riding a hot air balloon inside an infinitely large plastic beach ball. If you're in any aircraft other than a hot air balloon, your senses will tell you, pointedly, that you and your craft are moving around inside the beach ball. In a hot air balloon the sensation of motion is caused by the beach ball moving up, down and all around—just for you.

How does it feel?

Why don't you feel any sense of motion as the balloon moves? Two reasons: First, because you ascend and descend so gradually in a hot air balloon there is virtually no "elevator effect"—no changes in "G" loading as a result of acceleration towards or away from the line of gravity. For the most part, your body cannot feel the rise and fall of a hot air balloon. Second, because you are drifting with the wind, it is just like you are a part of it. There is no sensation of motion in the air around you, and no whistle of the wind to let you know how fast you're moving.

In the utter calm and silence of a hot air balloon ride, in the absence of any of the normal gravitational sensations of motion, it's easy to pretend that you and your balloon—for this all too brief period of time—have physically merged with motion and gravity.

And *that* is something you can't get anywhere else in the world of adventure sports.

RESOURCES FOR DOERS AND DREAMERS

If you're intrigued by hot air ballooning and want to find out more about it before actually doing it, consult any of the following resources.

National and State Organizations

Balloon Federation of America (BFA): P.O. Box 400, Indianola, Iowa 50125. (515) 961-8809. Jim Swanstrom, Executive Director. Sharon Ripperger, Office Manager. General information, monthly publication (*Ballooning Magazine*), calendar of events. BFA's calendar includes dates and locations of all major ballooning events. If you want to be involved as an event volunteer, ask about the BFA Observer Corps.

There are a number of ballooning clubs in California. The larger ones are:

Southern California Balloon Association: 12345 Firethorn Street, Rancho Cucamonga, California 91739. Dale Wong, Membership Chairman. (714) 899-9844.

San Diego Balloon Association: P.O. Box 23390, San Diego, California 92123. Ed Rawley, President. (619) 560-1979.

Aeronaut Society: P.O. Box 14763, Oakland, California 94614. Yvonne Lyckberg, President. (510) 261-4222.

Pacific Coast Aeronauts: c/o Jeanne Anson, 200 Burnett Avenue, #102, Morgan Hill, California 95037. (408) 778-2842.

Napa Pilots' Association: c/o Steve Frattini, P.O. Box 2179, Yountville, California 94599. (707) 963-9133.

Books and Magazines

Ballooning Magazine: See BFA, above.

Balloon Life Magazine: Publisher: Tom Hamilton; editor: Glen Moyer. 2145 Dale Avenue, Sacramento, California 95815. (916) 922-9648.

The Balloon Book, Paul Fillingham. David McKay Co., New York. The history of ballooning plus "101 questions."

Ballooning: The Complete Guide to Riding the Wind, Dick Wirth, Jerry Young. Revised 1991, Random House. Excellent, beautifully illustrated volume. Covers ballooning technique and competition. Unfortunately, the resource guide at the end was not updated and is virtually useless.

Bags Up, Kurt R. Stehling. Playboy Press, 1975. A great collection of balloon adventures and "war stories."

Observation Points

You can see hot air balloons flying year round in most of the areas listed below. If you don't want to get out of bed before dawn—which you'll have to do to get in on the excitement of balloon inflation and launch—at least try to catch a balloon between "hops." That way you'll be able to see both the buzz of those getting off the balloon and the anticipation of those getting on.

Del Mar Coast: Coastal scenery just North of San Diego. Year round flights. One of the only sunset flight locations in the state.
See #1 on map page 142.

Temecula Wine Country: Southern California's answer to the famous Napa Valley. Year round sunrise flights.
See #2 on map page 142.

Rancho Cucamonga/Fontana: Year-round sunrise flights over vineyards, fields. Closest flying to the San Gabriel Mountains.
See #3 on map page 142.

Perris: Just east of Lake Elsinore. Southern California's "milk-run" over dry, scrubby farmland. Year-round sunrise flights.
See #4 on map page 142.

Chino: Year round sunrise flights from Prado Park. Park has two lakes, golf courses. Near site of 1984 Olympic equestrian center and shooting range.
See #5 on map page 142.

Palm Springs/Palm Desert: Sunrise and sunset flights over golf courses and hotels. Seasonal: October through May only.
See #6 on map page 142.

Lancaster/Palmdale: Desert north of Los Angeles. Year-round sunrise flights.
See #7 on map page 142.

Moorpark: Grassy area north of Los Angeles, west of Lancaster/Palmdale: Year round sunrise flights. Challenging to pilots because of terrain and weather.

See #8 on map page 142.

Merced/Fresno: Sunrise flights over San Joaquin Valley farmland.

See #9 on map page 142.

Monterey: The only coastal flying in Northern California. Sunset flights between Castroville and Salinas. Seasonal: October to March only.

See #10 on map page 142.

Sacramento: The Hidden Valley area is green year-round. Sunrise flights.

See #11 on map page 142.

Coloma: A unique flying area near Placerville. Sunrise flights over the heart of motherlode country, and over the South Fork of the American River.

See #12 on map page 142.

Tracy/Livermore: Western edge of California's central valley, next to Diablo Mountain Range. Vast agricultural area. On a clear day you can see from the Pacific Ocean to the Sierra Nevada Mountains. Sunrise flights. The Livermore end of this area is pretty much dead for ballooning. Development has made flying there difficult.

See #13 on map page 142.

Napa Valley: One of the most famous and heavily trafficked balloon flying areas in the world. Sunrise flights over vineyards and rolling hills, year round.

See #14 on map page 142.

Salinas Valley: Fertile agricultural area (vineyards, lettuce) just a short drive from Monterey. Sunrise flights.

See #15 on map page 142.

Santa Clara Valley: South of San Jose. A few companies fly from Morgan Hill, a few others fly from Hollister. Pretty agricultural country between coastal mountain ranges. Morgan Hill is rapidly developing, however, and Hollister is a little too windy. Sunrise flights.

See #16 on map page 142.

RESOURCES FOR DOERS

The providers listed below represent the cream of the crop among those who sell hot air balloon rides to the public. You will notice that most commercial balloon activity in California is concentrated in rural areas between San Diego and San Francisco. These areas offer the relatively flat, obstacle-free terrain, and the calm (sunrise, sunset) wind conditions necessary for safe balloon flight.

Commercial balloon operators avoid the northern and eastern parts of California for three reasons: mountainous terrain, windy conditions and a lack of large population centers to draw customers from.

Southern California

Adventure Flights, Inc., Lake Elsinore: (213) 651-5311. Call for address and directions. In business 15 years, Adventure Flights offers both sweetheart and group rides. Owner Jim Bilbrey flies mostly out of Perris. He guarantees that the balloons he flies are never more than a year old. That's because he's a distributor for Aerostar, one of the largest manufacturers in the country. He also books flights with independent contractors in Del Mar, Moorpark and Camarillo. FAA-approved balloon repair station.

See #4 on map page 142.

High Adventures Hot Air Balloon Flights: P.O. Box 7755, Mission Hills, California 91346. (818) 891-8864. In business seven years, owner Ian Kite gives both sweetheart and group flights in the Antelope Valley (Palmdale, Lancaster area) and Moorpark. Kite requires that pilots who work for him have a minimum of 350 hours as pilot in command of a hot air balloon.

See #8 on map page 142.

OZ Airlines, Moorpark: Call for address and directions. (213) 464-6487. In business seven years, owner Bruce Brinkerhoff offers sweetheart and group rides in the Moorpark area. He's a former Nevada State Champion (1985), and he and his main pilot, Frank Jones, have 21 years and nearly 3,000 hours experience under their belts.

See #8 on map page 142.

Desert Balloon Charters, Inc.: P.O. Box 2713, Palm Desert, California 92261. Call for directions. (619) 346-8575. In business 10 years. Sweetheart and group flights over Palm Springs, Palm Desert area between October and May. Owner John (The Balloon Tycoon) Zimmer has a 10-acre "Balloon Ranch," with a private picnic area—the only one of its kind in the state. Hotel pick-up. Help with hotel bookings. Company slogan: "Champagne, flight certificate, balloon pin, and TOO MUCH FUN!"

See #6 on map page 142.

Flight Odyssey Balloon Co.: 12345 Firethorn Street, Rancho Cucamonga, California 91739. (714) 899-9844. In business eight years. Owner and chief pilot Dale Wong has over 10 years experience in a variety of balloons. Caters to small groups (2-8 people), flies mostly on weekends. Sunrise flights in Rancho Cucamonga/Fontana area, Perris, and Prado Regional Park in Chino. Aerostar balloon dealer.

See #3 on map page 142.

Full of Hot Air Balloon Company: 13213 Harbor Boulevard, Garden Grove, California 92643. (714) 530-0110. In business five years. Owner Paul (Twinkletoes) Schaefer stands 6'2" and weighs 240 pounds. Schaefer, who earns his living elsewhere, is a sport hobbyist who flies passengers two to four at a time, Sundays only, out of Perris. Be forewarned: three couples have become engaged while riding in Schaefer's balloon.

See #4 on map page 142.

A Beautiful Morning Balloon Company: 1342 Camino Del Mar, Del Mar, California 92014. Call for directions.(619)481-6225. In business 13 years, this was one of the first outfits to offer sunrise and sunset balloon rides along the coast of Del Mar. Owner Jay Kimball was California State Balloon champion in 1988 and 1989. He also owns Napa Valley Balloon Company in Northern California.

See #1 on map page 142.

California Dreamin': P.O. Box 3016, Carlsbad, California 92009. (619) 438-3344. In business seven years. Owner David Bradley has been a pilot for 14 years. Specialty is large groups (4-8) per balloon. Private flights available. Sunrise flights in Temecula wine country. Sunset flights on Del Mar coast.

See #1 on map page 142.

Pacific Horizon: P.O. Box 8737, Rancho Santa Fe, California 92067. Call for directions. (619) 756-1790. In business 10 years. Owners Peter Gallagher and Hans Petermann are Del Mar locals and former hang glider pilots. Both have well over 1,200 hours in balloons. Del Mar sunset flights. Temecula wine country sunrise flights. Sweetheart flights available, but groups (six per balloon) are their specialty. One of the few providers to use Thunder and Colt balloons—a European-style design with a tall, rectangular basket. Office includes a gift shop.

See #1 on map page 142.

A Sky Surfer Balloon Company: 1221 Camino Del Mar, Del Mar, California 92014. Call for directions: (619) 481-6800. In business 12 years. Owners Tiemo and Conni von Zweck pioneered sport ballooning in the Del Mar area. Tiemo was among the first to demonstrate the feasibility of sunset flights, for which the area is famous. Sunrise flights in Temecula, and (seasonally) Palm Springs. One of the few big companies to own a small balloon for sweetheart flights. Beautiful theme balloons are designed by Tiemo and Conni. Office, with small gift shop, is also a famous studio for balloon art.

See #1 on map page 142.

Del Mar Balloons: P.O. Box 2103, Del Mar, California 92014. (619) 259-3115. In business 10 years. Head pilot and owner John Shirley has over 2,000 hours. One of the first commercial balloon operations in the Del Mar area. Sweetheart and group (6-8 per balloon) flights available. Distributor for Balloon Works. One specialty is balloon rides for adventurers confined to wheelchairs. Del Mar Balloons also works with the "Make-A-Wish-Foundation" in giving rides to children with life-threatening illnesses.

See #1 on map page 142.

Seventh Heaven Balloon Adventures: 28710-B, Las Haciendas, Suite 102, Temecula, California 92590. (800) 677-3600. Owner Brad Gagne, in business six years. Sunrise flights at Perris and Temecula. Evening flights in Palm Springs (seasonal) and Del Mar. Groups up to 20, sweetheart flights. Average four per balloon. Temecula flights feature a winery tour and champagne brunch.

See #2 on map page 142.

Air Affaire Enterprises: P.O. Box 23390, San Diego, California 92193. Call for directions (619) 560-1979. In business six years. Owner Ed Rowley was 1991 Nevada State Champion. Air Affaire's slogan is "elegance aloft." They bring white linen, candles and silverware to the traditional post-flight champagne brunch. This makes them an especially good resource for those with romantic intentions. Sunrise flights in Temecula. Sunset flights in Del Mar.

See #1 on map page 142.

Sunset Balloon Flights, Inc.: 2201 San Dieguito Drive #1, Del Mar, California 92014.

(619) 481-9122. In business six years. Owner Frank Reed was the first to cross the Alaska Range in a balloon. Specialty is sunset flights on Del Mar coast. With six balloons, two of which can carry 10 passengers, Sunset is the largest balloon company in the San Diego area. It also offers two services that no one else does: monthly flights in Dana Point (Orange County) and an on-location bungee jumping service called Balloon Bungee, Inc.

See #1 on map page 142.

Above All Balloon Charters: 30197 Deer Meadow Road, Temecula California 92591. Call for directions: (714) 694-6287. In business eight years. Owners David and Kimberly Lynch both serve as pilots, and with 800 and 400 hours respectively, they're both experienced. Sweetheart and group flights available in the Temecula wine country and on the Del Mar coast. Group flights (4-6 per balloon) in Perris. Specialty is personalized service ranging from airborne weddings to group balloon rallies.

See #2 on map page 142.

Teddy Bear Flights: 3830 Avenue Del Presedente #47, San Clemente, California 92672. (714) 498-0111. Dennis (Captain Teddy Bear) Biro has been in business only four years, but he's logged 2,000 hours in balloons over an 18-year period. One of the few companies to specialize in private and sweetheart flights, Teddy Bear gets most of its business from word-of-mouth referrals from satisfied customers. Sunrise flights in Perris and Temecula. The only company to include 360-degree in-flight photos with ride.

See #1 on map page 142.

Fantasy Balloon Flights: 83701 Avenue 54, Thermal, California 92274. (800) GO ABOVE. Owners Cindy and Steve Wilkinson have been in business 10 years. Sunrise and sunset flights daily in Palm Desert, in season. Sunrise flights in Temecula, sunset flights in Del Mar, year round. Six passenger balloons. Large groups and sweetheart flights. Will fly children. One specialty is balloon weddings.

See #6 on map page 142.

Northern California

Above The West Hot Air Ballooning: P.O. Box 2290, Yountville, California 94599. (800) 627-2759. In business five years. Sunrise Napa Valley balloon flights. "Mom and Pop" operation run by Nielsen and Carol Ann Rogers. Specializes in small groups (4-6) and sweetheart flights. Single flights typical, sometimes two hops. Sit-down champagne breakfast in a Yountville restaurant follows flight. Only company that provides transportation to Napa Valley from San Francisco hotels.

See #14 on map page 142.

Adventures Aloft: Box 2500 at Vintage 1870, Yountville, California 94599. (707) 255-8688. In business 20 years, this is one of the first Napa Valley balloon companies. Owner/head pilot Chuck Foster has over 4,500 hours in balloons and pilots for V.I.P. customers. All other pilots have at least 700 hours. Large groups (6-8 per balloon) and private parties.

See #14 on map page 142.

Balloon Aviation of Napa Valley, Inc.: Same address and owner as Adventures Aloft. (800)

367-6272. This is Chuck Foster's marketing vehicle for corporate groups and tour groups.

See #14 on map page 142.

Balloons By The Sea: 71 Myrtle Court, Salinas, California 93905. (Monterey area). (408) 424-0111. In business six years. Former skydiving world champion Mike Eakins has accumulated 860 hours in just six years of ballooning. Between October and March he offers the only sunset balloon flight in Northern California—between Castroville and Salinas. Year-round sunrise flights in Salinas, Monterey and Santa Clara Valleys, depending on conditions. Small groups, private parties and totally custom adventures are Eakins' specialty. He's looking into "helicopter hop ballooning" for those with money and imagination.

See #15 on map page 142.

Bonaventura Balloon Company: 133 Wall Road, Napa, California 94558. (707) 944-2822. In business eight years, owner Joyce Bowen specializes in small groups and unique services. Her flights start in the heart of the Napa Valley in the St. Helena-Rutherford area, and fly over the highest concentration of wineries and vineyards in the Valley. Weddings, combined activity trips (i.e. ballooning, cycling, wine tasting) and Bowen's famous "Stay and Fly" package—which includes a night at the beautiful Rancho Camus Inn in Rutherford—help set her apart from the crowd. *Balloon Life* magazine featured Bonaventura Balloon Company in its June 1991 issue.

See #14 on map page 142.

Napa Valley Balloons, Inc.: P.O. Box 2860,

Yountville, California 94599. (800) 253-2224. Owners Don Surplus, Jim Mattison, Kim Kleist and Jay Kimball have been in business for 12 years. Sunrise flights in Napa Valley. Launch from Domaine Chandon Winery. Catered picnic champagne brunch. Groups up to 90. Private flights available. Average of 6-8 passengers per balloon.

See #14 on map page 142.

Once In A Lifetime: 1458 Lincoln #12, Calistoga, California 94515. (707) 942-6541. Owner Stuart Rosen has been in business since 1984. Operates in northern part of Napa Valley out of vineyards of various wineries. Two sister companies: Napa's Great Balloon Escape: P.O. Box 4197, Napa, California 94558 (707) 253-0860; and Once In A Lifetime of Sonoma County: P.O. Box 1263, Windsor, California 95492 (707) 578-0580, which operates out of the Russian River Valley in Sonoma County.

See #14 on map page 142.

Sonoma Thunder Wine Country Balloon Safaris: 4914 Snark Avenue, Santa Rosa, California 95409. (800) 759-5638. Owner and chief pilot W. Scot van der Horst has been flying 20 years. He has operated in Sonoma wine country since 1979. Morning flights from Sonoma county to Mendocino. Coast sometimes visible, Russian River below. Redwoods to the west, geysers to the east. Romance flights for two, and groups up to six per balloon.

See #14 on map page 142.

Sierra Valley Balloons: P.O. Box 585, Merced, California 95341. (209) 723-0610. Mike Smith gives dawn flights over San Joaquin Valley farm country near Merced and Fresno. This is a small outfit, offering excellent, personal service.

See #9 on map page 142.

Coloma Country Inn: P.O. Box 502, Coloma, California 95613. Call for directions (916) 622-6919. In business eight years. Owners Alan and Cindi Ehrgott provide what many people call the best "bed and breakfast balloon experience" in the state. For less than $200 per person you get a night at the Inn, a dawn balloon flight over the heart of California's mother lode country, and a champagne breakfast back at the inn. When the wind's right, Alan will treat you to his patented "splash and dash" balloon dips into the South Fork of the American River. Reciprocal arrangements with a number of whitewater rafting companies make the Coloma Inn the happening place for adventurers who want both air and water on the same weekend.

See #12 on map page 142.

MountainAire Balloon Adventures: P.O. Box 1907, North Highlands, California 95660. (916) 348-8778. Owner Jeff Koch has been flying for years. He offers unique 2-4 person rides in the beautiful Hidden Valley area northeast of Sacramento. One flight per balloon per day. Very personalized service.

See #12 on map page 142.

Balloon Excelsior, Inc.: 1241 High Street, Oakland, California 94102. (415) 261-4222. Brent Stockwell and Christine Kalakuka. In business since 1970, Balloon Excelsior is the oldest full-service balloon company in the West. FAA certificated flight school since 1972, certificated repair station since 1974. No passenger rides.

PARASAILING

Crescent City
Yreka
Newell
Mt. Shasta
Alturas
Eureka
Redding
Red Bluff
Susanville
Chico
Fort Bragg
Ukiah
Yuba City
Santa Rosa
Placerville
South lake Tahoe
Sacramento
San Francisco
Oakland
Stockton
Sonora
Lee Vining
Yosemite
San Jose
Santa Cruz
Merced
Bishop
Monterey
Salinas
Fresno
Lone Pine
Visilia
Kettleman City
Death Valley Jct.
San Luis Obispo
Bakersfield
Santa Maria
Wheeler Ridge
Mojave
Baker
Barstow
Santa Barbara
Ventura
Palmdale
Needles
Los Angeles
San Bernardino
Santa Ana
Long Beach
Palm Springs
Oceanside
Escondido
Blythe
San Diego
El Centro
Yuma

Chapter Six

Parasailing

Norwegian beauty Rigmore Ask's 20th birthday party was a special one. Three girlfriends kidnapped her, blindfolded her and made her walk the plank—so to speak—right into a power boat run by **Newport Parasail** of Balboa Island.

Here's how it went:

RIGMORE WALKS THE PLANK: A Parasailing Surprise Party

"These people are *supposed* to be my friends," complained Ms. Rigmore Ask as she clutched at the arms of her companions and stumbled into a boat called *The Island Cruzer*. "But I think they're up to no good!"

Lisa Lobito (22), Sonja Ingebrighsen (20) and Nina Hetland (19) held their hands over their mouths and giggled as they watched their disoriented friend squirm in her seat. Boat driver Mike Perrin and owner Eddie Diruscio were in on the surprise. They handed Rigmore her lifejacket but offered no other clue.

"When can I take this blindfold off?" whined Rigmore. "I want to see what's going on too!" "Be patient!" "All in good time!" "Quit sniveling!" The chorus of razzing set off a wave of high-pitched laughter that ended only when Diruscio said the jig was up.

"I've got to launch into my spiel," said Diruscio. "First, about the sharks in these waters.

You ladies have nothing to worry about because they're all *man*-eaters!"

Once the uproar subsided, he continued. "You're here to go parasailing, Rigmore. You'll be flying in a parasail 300 feet above this boat. We'll probably dunk you in the ocean before we reel you back in. You can take the blindfold off —but only if you agree to go first!"

Rigmore and her friends could hardly contain themselves as Diruscio helped them don life-jackets and parasailing harnesses. "We've flown 350-pounders in these things," said Diruscio while he snugged each woman's safety belt, "so you all should be just fine."

Perrin sped into the wind while Diruscio deployed the parasail behind the boat. Everyone on board gasped as the brightly colored, round ascending canopy inflated and sprang to life. Rigmore wasted no time pouncing into the seat at the back of the boat. She sat down and looked up while Diruscio clipped her into the tightly reined parasail flying just overhead and behind.

Everyone on board gasped as the brightly colored, round ascending canopy inflated and sprang to life.

When both crewmen had visually confirmed that Rigmore was safely attached to the canopy, Perrin accelerated the boat, then activated the on-board hydraulic winch. As it reeled Rigmore out and up—to a position about 100 feet behind and 300 feet above the boat—Lisa, Sonja and Nina howled their approval. Wide-eyed and open-mouthed, Rigmore kicked her feet and waved her arms at her friends.

Half-way through the 10-minute flight, it was time for Rigmore's dunking. Perrin slowed the boat way down and the parasail started to descend. In the silence of the idling engine, Rigmore could be heard squealing her objection to the coming splashdown.

"Dunk her all the way!" shouted someone

on-board. "Dunk her again!" shouted another as a thrashing Rigmore went waist deep into the ocean. Perrin hit the throttle just enough to tease Rigmore into thinking she was on her way up—but then idled back again. Just before she went in for a second time he hit the throttle and she was saved.

Rigmore flew a few more minutes at the top of the line. Then Perrin and Diruscio reeled her back into the boat—just like she was a big flying fish. When she touched down on the back seat of the boat, Rigmore shrieked: "That was great!! That was fantastic!! I wanna go again!!"

But now it was Sonja's turn. Sonja bounced to the back of the boat while exchanging high-fives with her beaming friend. Rigmore had earned big points by going first. Sonja nailed down "The Noisiest Flier" prize on her ride. She was followed by Nina who won "The Funniest Expression on Launch" award, and Lisa who wowed them all by hanging upside down and taking her dunking head-first.

Parasailing is probably the closest thing to an amusement park ride that thrill sports have to offer. It's as simple as falling off a log.

On the way back to the dock Rigmore described her flight as "kind of like downhill skiing, only better." Lisa said she felt like she was "floating in a dream." Sonja liked the smooth feeling of "just hanging in the breeze," and Nina said: "I just felt so—free—up there!"

FIRST RIDE
(Cost: $30-$40 for a 10-minute ride)

Parasailing is probably the closest thing to an amusement park ride that thrill sports have to offer. It's as simple as falling off a log. That's because you have very little to do. Speed, altitude and direction control are built into the system itself. Your only responsibility is to sit back and enjoy the sights, sounds and sensations of flying.

The classic launch method—the kind you've probably heard about—has you taking off from a beach at the end of a fixed length tow rope. This kind of parasailing, known as the fixed line method, is popular in foreign resort communities like Acapulco, Mexico.

Parasails, unlike skydiving or paragliding canopies, are round instead of crescent-shaped. They are specifically designed to ascend smoothly when towed.

A successful launch in the fixed-line method depends on the boat driver's ability to co-ordinate his acceleration of the boat with your readiness to lift off under canopy. And, when the ride is over, the boat driver must swing in close to the beach *and* time his deceleration so that you and the parasail float safely onto the beach. Poor timing on the part of the driver can put you between a rock and a hard place. You have very little, if any, control over where you're going to land.

Fixed-line parasailing is not available in California.

Developers of the modern "direct method" described at the beginning of this chapter have eliminated the potentially dangerous transitions between beach and sky. Their feeling is: "Why mess with remote control when you can launch and land your customers from right inside the boat?"

Parasails, unlike skydiving or paragliding canopies, are round instead of crescent-shaped. They are specifically designed to ascend smoothly when towed. The canopy is attached to an on-board hydraulic winch. When the boat driver hits the gas, the winch gradually releases line, allowing the canopy to climb to an altitude of about 300 feet. You have nothing to do but sit back and enjoy the 7 to 15 minute ride. When your turn is up, the driver reels you back in to the same on-board seat or platform that you took off from. No guess, no mess.

All in all, modern parasailing is a fun ride that will give you a good gut-check on your appetite for true air sports like hang gliding, paragliding and sky diving. At the very least, it's a nice aerial view that's simply not available any other way.

MYTHS

All of the myths about this amazingly simple ride of passage are based on the usual assortment of negative speculation and rumor that plagues most incredibly fun activities that look more dangerous than they really are.

"If the tow-line breaks while I'm parasailing, I'm dead!"

Wrong. **The truth is:** If the tow line breaks while you're parasailing, you'll float gently down to the water and bob around in your life jacket for a minute or two. That's about how long it will take the boat to turn around and come get you.

"I have to be mature and in pretty good shape to parasail!"

Parasail operators like to put it this way: "If you can sit, you can parasail." Remember there's nothing you have to do up there. **The truth is:** Individuals who weigh as little as 70 pounds and as much as 275 pounds can parasail under the same canopy. As to maturity, get this: Parasail operators routinely strap toddlers as young as two years old into a special double harness which allows them to be accompanied by a parent. There is no upper age limit. If you're 90 (or more!)and you can sit, you can parasail.

"The ones who say they are terrified of heights are the ones who end up having the most fun. We just sit back and let them watch everybody else go first. When their turn comes they generally go for it, and they always have the biggest smiles on their faces when we reel 'em back in."

"I'm afraid of heights! No way can I parasail!"

Not according to most parasail boat drivers. To hear them tell it, **the truth is:** Parasailing might actually be a decent cure for those who are afraid of heights. Driver Mike Perrin of **Davey's Locker Parasailing** says: "The ones who say they are terrified of heights are the ones who end up having the most fun. We just sit back and let them watch everybody else go first. When their turn comes they generally go for it, and they always have the biggest smiles on their faces when we reel 'em back in."

Consult your shrink, of course, but if you're afraid of heights, parasailing just might be a quick and easy way to overcome that fear. And that will give you a great feeling of personal accomplishment.

"I can get eaten by a shark when they dunk me in the ocean in the middle of my parasailing ride!"

Well, yeah—but so what?! Thrills are thrills. Actually the chances of getting eaten by a shark are pretty slim—unless, of course, you've just seen *JAWS II* or had a recent encounter with that nasty plastic shark at Universal Studios.

TRUE CHILLS
(And how to avoid them)

The best part about parasailing is that you don't have to do anything but sit back and enjoy the ride. The worst part is that if something goes wrong once the ride starts, there is nothing you can do to save yourself. Your fate depends on the boat driver's skill and common sense.

Two parasailing fatalities happened when the

boat driver allowed a customer to take off his life jacket so his small child could sit on his lap. When the driver didn't slow down enough during the planned "splashdown," both father and child were knocked cold on impact with the water. Without lifejackets, they drowned.

Listen carefully: Pick your parasailing outfit carefully. Your life depends on it.

There are no licensing or regulating bodies in parasailing. Anybody can buy a parasail and anybody can buy a boat. And after they've slapped the two together, they can do anything they want to whomever they want. If they do it to you, you have absolutely no control over your own destiny.

Avoid parasailing "hobbyists" like the plague —unless you consider yourself an expert on boats, winches, towing dynamics, parasails and human nature.

Avoid parasailing "hobbyists" like the plague—unless you consider yourself an expert on boats, winches, towing dynamics, parasails and human nature.

Assuming that you confine your parasailing to professional commercial operators, your safety depends entirely on the care and quality of the equipment and the experience of your driver and crew.

Parasailing accidents are so rare that parasail operators don't even have a clever term for a fatal accident.

Parasailing does indeed get you up in the air, however, and as we've discussed, that's an inherently dangerous place to be. It's certainly reason enough to ask a few questions about the apparatus that will take you there and back. You also want to know something about the captain and his crew, since your life is in their hands.

MODERN PARASAILING: TRUE FACTS

• Parasailing, done right, is a convenient way for you to check out your appetite for real airsports like skydiving, hang gliding and paragliding.

• If you can sit, you can parasail. It's that simple. You don't have to do anything in a parasail except enjoy the ride.

• Commercial parasailing companies are the only ones required by law to have a U.S. Coast Guard captain driving the boat.

• There are no regulatory or licensing bodies governing private operation of parasails. That's reason enough to avoid non-commercial operators or "hobbyists" categorically.

Captain and Crew Considerations

The boat driver is the most important human component of a parasailing system. He controls the boat and the winch, which is exactly what controls your flight path and altitude under canopy. Because a parasailing boat driver takes passengers for hire, he must, by law, be certified by the U.S. Coast Guard as a licensed "captain." Don't even think about parasailing with an unlicensed driver.

Only one other crewman is required. That's the one who will supervise and assist you while you get in your harness, hook into the parasail, leave the boat under canopy and return to the boat under canopy. He also is the one who watches your shenanigans in the sky so the captain can focus some of his attention in the direction the boat is headed.

Here are some questions you should ask of your prospective parasailing captain:

Are you a Coast Guard licensed captain?

"Yes" is the only acceptable answer, and the driver should be able to produce and show his license.

How long has this company been in business?

Experience definitely counts, but relatively new companies may be O.K.—as long as they are experienced at driving a boat and operating a tow winch, and as long as they have experienced parasailing crew people handling the passengers.

How long have you been dragging people around the sky?

Again, experience counts but a relatively new

driver isn't necessarily cause for alarm. He does, after all, know how to handle a boat and has a captain's license to prove it. On the other hand, if both driver and crewman are "one-month wonders" in the world of parasailing, you'll want to look elsewhere.

Are we having fun yet?

Expect parasail drivers and crewmen to yuk it up. Part of the thrill of thrill sports is the perception—if not the actual fact—of DANGER. Competent commercial parasail operators don't have much real risk to peddle. If they make jokes about sharks, death and other disasters, it doesn't mean they take their jobs lightly. They're just trying to help you have more FUN.

Do you anticipate any wind or sea changes that might effect the operation?

No one flies in small craft warning conditions. What you really want to know is: Will the conditions give me a ride that matches my expectations? Early morning conditions are generally calmer and deliver a kinder, gentler ride. Stronger afternoon conditions deliver a slightly more thrilling ride.

Where and how do operations take place?

Right next to shore is definitely no good. An unclear, non-specific answer isn't much better. Your captain should know exactly where he's taking you. Your crewman should be able to explain how your ride will go.

Is this outfit insured?

Insurance is available for parasailing operators. Expect them to have an insurance policy in force.

• ***Every single commercial parasailing operation in California uses "the direct method" of parasailing — where a winch reels you out of and back into the boat under an already inflated canopy.***

• ***In parasailing, your safety is entirely in the hands of the boat driver. Make sure you pick a good one.***

Equipment Considerations

Once again: There are no governing bodies that supervise the manufacture, testing and inspection of parasailing equipment, per se. You pretty much have to trust parasail operators as business people to use good equipment and to maintain it properly.

Here are some questions you can ask which will permit a commercial parasailing company to prove to you that they do things right.

What kind of boat do you use?

The four primary manufacturers of "direct method" parasailing boats are Island Cruzer, Nordic, Skyrider and UFO. Some home-built parasailing boats are good, some aren't. There's no reliable way for you to tell the difference.

Can you tell me a little about your regular service intervals? For the boat? For the winch system?

Each boat, engine, drive system and winch system has different maintenance requirements and schedule. The captain should sound like he knows what he's talking about when he answers this question.

Most operators replace a rope every two months, or whenever a visual inspection reveals frays, nicks or heavy wear spots. Your best bet? Let someone else go first!

How often do you inspect/replace the tow rope?

This depends almost entirely on how much use the rope gets. Most operators replace a rope every two months, or whenever a visual inspection reveals frays, nicks or heavy wear spots. Your best bet? Let someone else go first! That way you can eyeball the rope yourself. Knots, duct tape, etc. are bad signs.

What kind of parachute/harness do you use?

The three main manufacturers of both parasails and parasail harness systems are: Waterchute (made in an FAA-certified loft in Perris, California), Waterbird (made in England) and Cloudhopper (distributed by a company in Utah). All commercial operations in California use one of the above. Waterchute parasails are especially modified for the special demands of winch towing, where the chute is constantly inflated and under stress.

How often do you inspect/replace the parasail and harnesses?

It's best if canopies are replaced every year. Every two years is O.K. if the canopy is in good shape. Loose stitching, patches, duct tape or frayed lines are bad signs. Visually inspect your personal harness to make sure it, too, is in good shape.

Are those water skiing-style lifejackets?

These are more comfortable than horse collar-style life vests. Your comfort is important.

Do you carry on-board all equipment required by law?

Radio, Coast Guard-approved flotation devices, fire extinguisher, first aid kit? Tool kit? Air horn? Check for all of these.

TRUE THRILLS

Here's how parasailing stacks up in relation to the reward variables I've outlined for thrill sports:

Speed

Slow to moderate. Depends on the conditions. Your first speed sensation can best be described as "hovering." Even though the boat will be moving forward through the water, you will be moving backward and upward in relation to the boat. The two motions kind of cancel each other out. It's fun seeing the wake of the boat and feeling like you're standing still in mid-air at the same time.

It's fun seeing the wake of the boat and feeling like you're standing still in mid-air at the same time.

Once at altitude, you'll notice that your visual sensation of speed will change dramatically depending on whether you're being towed into the wind, or along with it. When you're going with the wind, the water below will look like it's zipping by. When you're headed into the wind, the water below will barely drift by. The stronger the wind, the bigger this difference will be.

Play a little game with yourself. Halfway through your ride, start trying to tell which way the wind is blowing just by noticing your speed in relation to the water below.

Focus

Like hot air ballooning, parasailing gives you a nice blend of present, past and future. Until you get acclimated to the speed sensations described above, you will lock onto the present. Soon, the newness of what you're experiencing will be replaced by a nearly unconscious search of your past. You're looking for something to compare parasailing to—especially if you've never been hanging in mid-air before. Next, your mind travels down the tow line to your friends in the boat below. You start thinking about sharing your excitement with them, wondering if they'll have as much fun as you're having when their turn comes. Dunks, and the final reel-in, yank you back to the present.

The next thing you know, you're back inside

the boat relaying your experience and waving your hands around while the next thrill-seeker gets hooked up and reeled out.

Your view of the world

If you've done other airsports, parasailing will feel narrow and limited. That's because you're "flying" at the end of a rope, and you know darn well that you can only travel up and down in line with that rope. You also know that you can't move much from side to side.

On the other hand, if you've never, ever been suspended in mid-air, parasailing will feel more "wide-open" than anything you've ever done before. That's why parasailing is such a good appetizer for would-be hang glider pilots, paraglider pilots or skydivers. Parasailing will tell you—quickly, cheaply and conclusively—whether dangling in mid-air agrees with you or not.

If you've never, ever been suspended in mid-air, parasailing will feel more "wide-open" than anything you've ever done before.

How does it compare to REAL life?

Because of the different perspectives of different altitudes, and the strange new sensations of speed and motion, odds are good that parasailing will seem at least a little bit otherworldly to you. On the other hand, if you're a particularly adventurous type—or if you've done other airsports before—it might feel more like a slow-motion roller coaster ride, or a particularly interesting ferris wheel.

How does it feel?

Parasailing is like a playground swing ride—a playground swing on the end of a yo-yo string! Your hips feel the swing of the swing while your torso feels the pull of the string. Meanwhile this contraption in the air above you—or maybe it's that contraption in the water below you—drags you through thin air in all three dimensions of space.

RESOURCES FOR DOERS AND DREAMERS

Books and Magazines

There are no parasailing magazines. One book, however, is definitely worth owning if you want to know something about parasails, or any other kind of parachute, for that matter.

The Parachute Manual, Volume II, Dan Poynter. Para Publishing, P.O. Box 4232, Santa Barbara, California 93140-4232. (805) 968-7277. Everything you've ever wanted to know about all kinds of parachutes, including parasails.

Observation Points

Call any of the parasailing operators listed below for directions to their place of operation. Observation rides are available, space permitting.

RESOURCES FOR DOERS

Fixed line commercial parasailing operations have never found a place in California, primarily because of liability concerns among those who have jurisdiction over the beaches. The direct method, which allows operators to avoid the beach entirely, is relatively new. Consequently, there are very few parasailing operations in California—and there are none that have been in business longer than six years.

Parasailing Catalina: P.O. Box 2275, Avalon,

California 90704. (213) 510-1777. The first to offer direct-method parasailing in California. In business six years. Owners Guy Ciletti and Carole Anderson. Ciletti designed Island Cruzer Boats, which are manufactured in Corona. Waterchute canopies and harnesses. Year-round operations. Two locations on Catalina Island: Avalon and The Isthmus.

See #1 on map page 172.

Capo Beach Parasail, Inc.: 34675 Golden Lantern, Dana Point Harbor, California 92629. (714) 496-5794. Owner Bill Byrd has been in business three years. He also operates Capo Beach Jet Ski out of a nearby location. Sign up at Dana Wharf Sport Fishing. Operates year-round out of Dana Point Harbor. Nordic boat. Waterbird chutes and harnesses. Charters and private parties.

See #2 on map page 172.

Newport Parasail: 400 Main Street, Balboa, California 92661. (714) 673-1434. Island Cruzer boats, Waterbird chutes and harnesses. Owner Eddie Diruscio has been in business three years. Shop is on historic Balboa Pavillion. Year-round operations take place in ocean outside Newport Harbor.

See #3 on map page 172.

Pacific Parasail, Inc.: P.O. Box 1216, Santa Cruz, California 95061. (408) 423-3545. In business two years. Owner Ian McIntyre uses an Island Cruzer boat, and Waterbird chutes and harnesses. Year-round operations from Santa Cruz Municipal Wharf. Shop is on the wharf.

See #4 on map page 172.

San Diego Parasailing Adventures: 1641 Quivira Road, San Diego, California 92109. (619) 223-4-FUN. Don Correia is the general manager. In business two years. Nordic boat, Waterbird chutes and harnesses. Year-round operations between Crystal Pier and the Jetty in Mission Beach. Office at Seaforth Boat Rentals, Mission Bay. The only operation in San Diego. Experienced captains.

See #5 on map page 172.

Skyrider Parasailing of Long Beach, Inc.: 320 Pine Avenue, Suite 503, Long Beach, California 90802. (213) 493-4979. Owners Bill, Bob and Caroline Kimball have been in business two years. They have the only Skyrider boat on the west coast. This system features an unique recliner seat on a sled. It carries two people without harnesses. You don't get wet unless you want the operators to "skip" you. No dunking. Waterbird parachutes. Year-round operations from two locations (Seaport Village and Shoreline) in Long Beach. Call for directions.

See #6 on map page 172.

South Shore Parasailing: Box 11436, Tahoe Paradise, California 96155. (916) 541-7272. In business five years. Owner Ari Makinen uses a UFO Premium Parasail Boat and U.S. Parascending chutes and harnesses. Operates on South Lake Tahoe. Summer months only: beginning of June to middle of September. Ari's daughter Eva is a licensed boat captain.

See #7 on map page 172.

Skydiving

Crescent City
Yreka
Newell
Mt. Shasta
Alturas
Eureka
Redding
Red Bluff
Susanville
Chico
Fort Bragg
Ukiah
Yuba City
Santa Rosa
Placerville
South lake Tahoe
Sacramento
San Francisco
Oakland
Stockton
Sonora
Lee Vining
Yosemite
San Jose
Merced
Santa Cruz
Bishop
Monterey
Salinas
Fresno
Lone Pine
Visilia
Kettleman City
Death Valley Jct.
San Luis Obispo
Bakersfield
Santa Maria
Wheeler Ridge
Mojave
Baker
Barstow
Palmdale
Santa Barbara
Ventura
Needles
Los Angeles
San Bernardino
Santa Ana
Palm Springs
Long Beach
Oceanside
Escondido
Blythe
San Diego
El Centro
Yuma

Chapter Seven
Skydiving

It had to happen. In the process of researching a book on nine thrill sports, there had to be at least one moment when things didn't go exactly as planned. That moment happened on my first tandem skydive, when the chute opened—but not quite right.

MALFUNCTION: The Author Survives a Scare

No kiddin', there I was, thought I was gonna die!

Me and Mike, the skydiving instructor who was buckled to my back, had just plummeted about 8,000 feet in less than a minute. The reassuring opening shock of our monster tandem canopy had just brought a smile to my lips. That's when I heard Mike say the one word I'd hoped I'd never hear while dangling underneath an inflated bag of nylon.

"Uh-oh!"

I couldn't believe my ears. My certified, qualified and highly experienced tandem skydiving instructor had just said: "Uh-oh!"

My certified, qualified and highly experienced tandem skydiving instructor had just said: "Uh-oh!"

I mean, there we were, drifting peacefully through space after nearly a minute of exhilarating, eye-watering 120-mile-per-hour free-fall and this guy strapped to *my* back is muttering "uh-oh" under his breath. I glanced at the altimeter on my wrist. We were a good 4,500 feet off the deck.

I'm an experienced thrill sport expert. I instinctively knew that Mike's two-syllable assessment of our current situation had something to do with the lazy but definite right turn we seemed to be stuck in. Calmly, with every intention of being as helpful as I could possibly be, I asked the only intelligent question I could think of.

"Yo! Mike!," I blurted. "You didn't just say 'uh-oh' did you?!"

Mike, who is Australian, picked that moment to call me "mate." I knew it was his way of saying that our fates had just become irrevocably intertwined. "We've got a bit of a problem, mate!," said Mike. "Our right side steering lines are tangled at the slider."

"Does that mean we can only turn right?" My inquiring mind wanted to know. "How we gonna land if this thing is spiraling us to the right?"

"We can't," said Mike. "We have to see if we can fly straight without stalling. If we can we'll stick with this canopy. Otherwise we'll have to cut away and go to our reserve."

We'd have to suffer through another mind-bending free-fall while we waited for the reserve—our last remaining parachute—to open and open properly. If it didn't, the stop at the end of our ride would be a sudden one—caused by the ground.

"RESERVE?!" The word sent shivers down my spine. Going to our reserve meant we'd first have to get rid of our main chute. Then we'd have to suffer through another mind-bending free-fall while we waited for the reserve—*our last remaining parachute*—to open and open properly. If it didn't, the stop at the end of our ride would be a sudden one—caused by the ground.

"We got some time," said Mike. "Let's try to fix this one."

"Yeah, let's!" I agreed. "What can I do?"

Mike told me to pull down on the left riser until we were flying straight. I did what he said while he tried to jerk the right side lines loose. In the meantime I got us going straight all right—but at a speed that Mike said may or may not be

■ *Mark Appling comes "off the rock" above Emerald Bay at Lake Tahoe*

Left page:

- *Just before the BOING...the first drop of a bungee ride, as the cords stretch to their limit before flinging the thrill-seeker back into the air*

This page:

- ***Right:*** *Parasailer prepares for take-off from a speed boat at Newport Beach, with canopy inflated and trailing behind*

- ***Below right:*** *Greg Stiles soars over Tahoe National Forest in his paraglider*

- ***Below:*** *Yvonne Gaines leads Headstone Rock in Joshua Tree—a good introduction for novices*

Left page:

- *Skydiver exits the plane with a wave and a smile—about to head for the ground at 120 miles per hour*

This page:

- ***Top:*** *Combining buoyancy and balance, sea kayaking appeals to those who want a very personal water adventure*

- ***Above left:*** *River kayaker hits the rapids alone, using body motion and a paddle to make it through the whitewater*

- ***Above right:*** *Hot air balloon aloft over Lake Tahoe—the destination is irrelevant; the trip is everything*

This page:

- ***Left:*** *River rafters negotiate Cherry Creek in California, working in unison to follow the route through the rapids*
- ***Below:*** *Beginner takes a tandem ride in a hang glider...all the experience of soaring with the birds, without all the instruction*

Right page:

- *Pure freedom...Ken Holbert hang gliding near Torrey Pines, using gravity as his engine*

- ***Right:*** *A novice paraglider pilot experiences his first few feet of flight on a training hill near Hemet*
- ***Below:*** *The joy of a first-time bungee jumper over the Feather River in California*

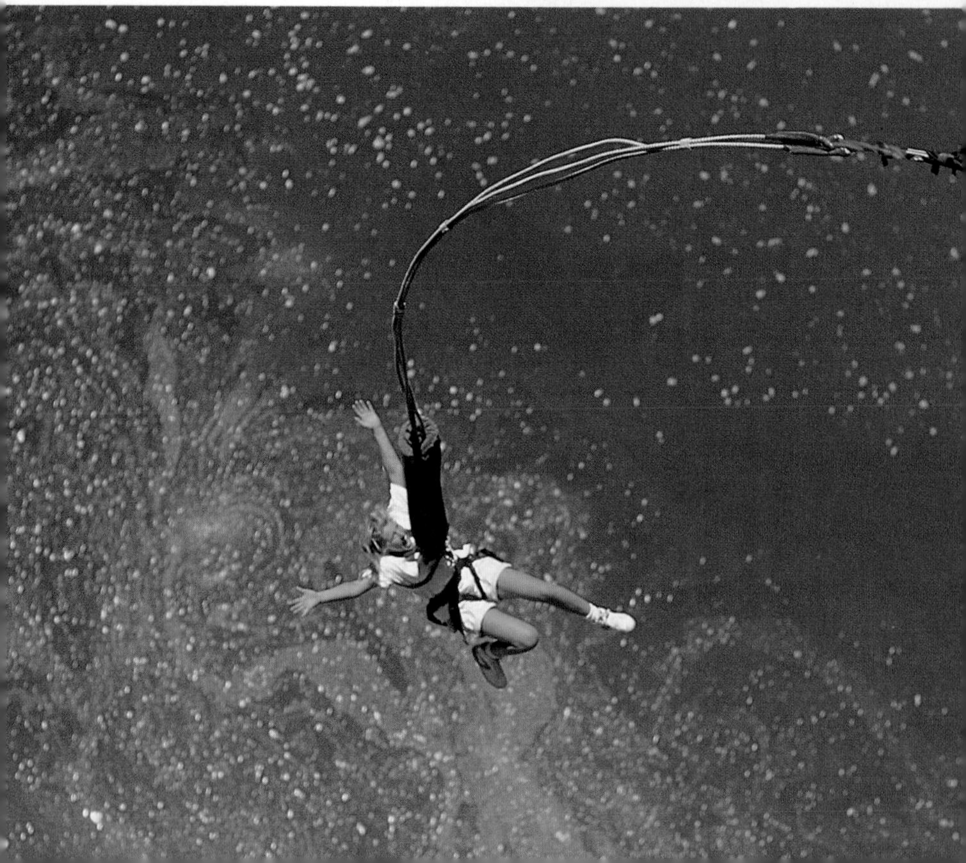

good enough to bring us to earth under full control.

"We still got time," said Mike. "I'll keep trying." Mike's apparent unhappiness with our current canopy was beginning to concern me, especially since the altimeter on my wrist said we were only 2,500 feet off the deck.

"Uh—Mike," I said. "You havin' any luck? We're getting kind of low!"

Mike offered bad news and good news. The risers were still tangled and they were damned well going to stay that way. The good news was that we weren't going to have to play our last card.

"We'll stick with this canopy," said Mike. "We can make it fly straight and our descent rate isn't too bad. We should be all right. But you're really going to have to help me flare [pull down hard on both sets of risers] on landing."

I quickly confessed to Mike that I REALLY LIKED what he said and how he said it. The smile returned to my lips and got bigger and bigger as we approached the ground. Mike's professional judgement had been right-on. We were flying straight and our landing would be spectacularly uneventful.

Mike offered bad news and good news. The risers were still tangled and they were damned well going to stay that way. The good news was that we weren't going to have to play our last card.

Several feet off the deck, Mike yelled: "Pull hard! Now!" So that's what I did. We were down! No jolts. No steps. I was so happy I burst out laughing.

"So how'd ya like THAT?!" Mike's boss yelled at me as he ran over to help us pack up. Good old Don was fully expecting to bathe in the excited babbling of yet another satisfied customer.

"We had a MALFUNCTION, Don!," I shot back, my eyes blazing with the thrill of what felt like a close call. "It was WONDERFUL!! Thanks for the freaking ride!"

Postscript

Don and Mike discussed the malfunction while I walked around bragging to everyone in sight. Me and Mike had looked death in the eye, I said, and WE WON. The truth was, the malfunction was not that big a deal. Hell, we didn't even get to throw our perfectly serviceable, professionally packed reserve parachute. I felt cheated! I wanted to try again!

FIRST RIDE
Cost: first static—about $140, first tandem—about $150, AFF—about $300)

Two of the three current methods for introducing newcomers to skydiving deliver nearly a full minute of supervised free-fall before chute deployment. The only one that doesn't is the venerable old "static-line" technique.

Most people think it's crazy to jump out of a perfectly good airplane. What makes such a quintessential leap of faith irresistibly attractive to skydivers is the breathtaking 120-mile-per-hour free-fall that follows.

Two of the three current methods for introducing newcomers to skydiving deliver nearly a full minute of supervised free-fall before chute deployment. The only one that doesn't is the venerable old "static-line" technique. Odds are great that your mental image of skydiving is based on static-line techniques.

Static Line

"What do they do to first time skydiving victims?" you might ask. "That's an easy one! I heard they hook their parachute rip-cords to a clothesline inside an airplane, then make 'em jump out—all alone—at low altitude (about 2,500 feet)! Those poor slobs get about one miserable second of free-fall before a nylon line jerks their chute open! And if the chute doesn't open correctly, they get to deal with it by themselves! Plus they have to find the landing area and land without help too!"

Granted, static-line jumps are still offered by many skydiving schools. They're even still popular among those who cherish the solo experience above all else, and some who are committed to becoming card-carrying skydivers. But, these days, a vast majority of first-time, one-time skydiving adventurers opt for either accelerated free-fall or tandem. Both deliver the awesome rush of free-fall the first time out.

Accelerated Free-Fall (AFF)

At about $300 a pop, this is definitely the most expensive way to try skydiving. That's because you need two instructors per student. And what do these instructors do? They dive right alongside you when you leap solo at 12,000 to 13,000 feet. With an instructor on each side, you get hands-on help in stabilizing your body during free-fall. The instructors stay right with you until it's time to deploy your chute. Following deployment, radio contact enables them to coach you through any problems throughout your flight, approach and landing.

Accelerated free-fall starts with a five-hour ground school. That's so you'll know what to do in the extremely unlikely event that both your instructors get struck by lightning on the way out of the airplane. Although AFF is primarily an advanced teaching technique for those who eventually want to jump solo, United States Parachute Association (USPA) statistics indicate that an AFF jump is the safest way to go for a first-timer. Some say that's because the extensive ground school forces you to think like a pilot from the word go.

Tandem

Half as many instructors translates to half the cost. For about $150, you can jump tandem from an altitude of 12,000 to 13,000 feet your first time out. Like accelerated free-fall, tandem gives you almost a full minute of free-fall. You're securely buckled to the front of the instructor. He or she carries a huge, two-person main chute on his back. The rip-cord is on the front of your harness. Following free-fall, he signals for you to pull the cord. If you seize up or pass out, he pulls it for you. You get to help steer the canopy on approach. And you've got to help apply the brakes on landing.

Tandem skydiving is almost like doing it yourself. You have responsibilities up there! But—if you blow it—there's a pro on board to bail you out.

Tandem skydiving is almost like doing it yourself. You have responsibilities up there! But —if you blow it—there's a pro on board to bail you out.

Don't make the mistake of considering a tandem jump a roller-coaster ride. Pay attention in ground school, as if you're quite sure your instructor is destined to pass out up there, leaving you in charge.

MYTHS

Skydiving myths are as abrupt as the sport itself. Like most myths, skydiving myths come from one of two sources: true facts blown way out of proportion, or uninformed "common sense" laced with negative speculation.

Let's start with the biggest of all myths:

"If my parachute doesn't open properly, I'm dead—right?"

Wrong. **The truth is**: If your *reserve* parachute doesn't open *at all*—or if you don't throw it in time—you're dead. But consider the levels of protection you have to go through to get to that point.

First, you deploy your main parachute. Maybe one time out of several hundred it doesn't deploy perfectly. That's called a malfunction, and only about three percent of them can be attributed to equipment problems or bad luck. The rest result from "pilot error." That can be anything from failing to pack your main chute properly to choosing to pull your rip-cord before you've stabilized your body in free-fall. Those are the kinds of things that happen to skydivers who are careless. They almost never happen to people who have placed themselves in the hands of USPA certified instructors.

Sometimes a malfunction is uneventful. That means you can fix it or (as I found out in my jump) land safely in spite of it. But let's say you can't. That's when you get rid of (cut away) your main chute and deploy your reserve chute. USPA statistics indicate about one in 800 main chute deployments have to be cut away. Reserve chutes, by law, must be packed and inspected regularly by an FAA licensed parachute rigger. Reserve chute malfunctions are almost unheard of in the world of skydiving.

According to USPA Director Paul Sitter, the man who composes fatality reports for the organization, skydiving's fatality rate is about one per 100,000 jumps. And that figure includes stupid mistakes as well.

"The wind—not the skydiver—controls the canopy once it's deployed."

This myth is based on the maneuverability and performance limitations of old-style round parachutes. They had a vertical descent rate of 17 to 23 feet per second and a constant forward speed of about eight miles per hour. You could steer them some and slow them down some but, in a gross sense, it was the breeze that wafted you into the landing area from altitude. No one uses those things anymore.

The truth is: Modern "square" or "parafoil" parachutes are completely controllable and have a much wider performance envelope than the round chutes they replaced. Vertical speed is controllable between zero and 18 feet per second and horizontal speed is controllable between zero and 25 miles per hour. You can land on a dime and get nine cents change.

Skydivers have a term for bull's-eye landings. The call them "dead centers."

You can land on a dime and get nine cents change.

Dead center disks used to be 10 centimeters wide—about as wide as a softball. A skydiver by the name of Dwight Reynolds (U.S. Army Parachute Team: Golden Knights) landed on one of those 105 consecutive times. The new five centimeter disk—about the diameter of a golfball—has proven to be more challenging. The unofficial consecutive dead center record for the smaller target currently stands at 10.

Controllable? Yeah, they're controllable.

"So how hard do I hit? I heard landing in a parachute is like jumping off the top of a two-story building!"

Once again, old-style round parachutes are the source of this belief. But the "buckle-yer-knees" era of skydiving touchdowns is long gone. And so are most of the ankle and knee injuries that used to befall first-time static-line students who didn't hit right. Modern para-foils don't drop out of the sky. They fly towards the ground until you bring them to a dead stop with a well-timed landing flare.

The truth is: Landing in a modern skydiving parachute is a lot like magically appearing on the ground.

"I won't be able to breathe in free-fall!!"

So? What's your point? Even a weenie can hold his breath for 50 seconds! JUST KIDDING! Of course you can breathe in free-fall. Who knows where that myth came from.

"I'd have to be crazy to jump out of a perfectly good airplane!"

Some wise-guy skydivers will look you in the eye when you say that and gasp: "Man, you should see some of the airplanes we jump out of!!" **The truth is:** Airplanes are just elevators. Skydivers wouldn't think of jumping out of them if there were another way to get to altitude.

Wise-guy skydivers will look you in the eye and gasp: "Man, you should see some of the airplanes we jump out of!!"

When it comes to skydiving, "craziness" is personally defined. It all depends on your own personal gut-level assessment of skydiving's obvious risks and obvious rewards.

TRUE CHILLS (And how to avoid them)

There's no getting around it. When you're in mid-air and heading straight for the ground at 120 miles per hour, you're in a dangerous position. Your safety depends entirely on two bags of nylon (your main chute and your reserve chute), plus your ability to make sure that one of them stops your fall before the ground does.

If the ground stops your fall, skydivers will look at each other and say: "Did you hear that [so and so] *'bounced'* yesterday?!"

At the introductory level only three things can cause you to "bounce" at the end of a skydive:

1) Poor instruction.
2) Bad bags of nylon (poorly designed or improperly packed parachutes).
3) Your own ignorance or stupidity.

It is your responsibility to select an introductory experience that provides state-of-the-art instruction on state-of-the-art equipment.

Instructor/School Considerations

In the world of skydiving, state-of-the-art instruction is defined by the United States Parachute Association (USPA). The USPA not only certifies three levels of instructors, they also certify schools and drop zones (the places where you can skydive) as well.

It is your responsibility to select an introductory experience that provides state-of-the-art instruction on state-of-the-art equipment.

Make sure you select a USPA-certified school that operates out of an USPA-certified drop zone. Make sure the person who will be teaching you has the minimum USPA instructor ratings for your choice of static-line, AFF or tandem.

Traditional instructor ratings for static line or AFF:

USPA Jumpmaster: Pre-jump training and student jump supervision.

USPA Instructor: Qualified to present the first-jump course and to supervise a training program and its personnel.

USPA Instructor/Examiner: Qualified to supervise and administer a jump program.

The USPA does not have a tandem instructor certification in place. Therefore, in addition to traditional certification, tandem instructors must also have certification proving that they are operating in accordance with the FAA "Tandem Exemption." Essentially that means they have been trained in tandem procedures by either Strong Enterprises or the Relative Workshop, the two Florida-based manufacturers who are authorized by the FAA to produce tandem equipment and train tandem instructors.

If you go to an USPA-approved school in an approved drop zone, you will not encounter an instructor who does not have the minimum qualifications. If you want to qualify your instructor *beyond* minimum standards, meet with him personally and ask the following questions:

How long has this school been in business?
Insist on at least two years.

How many jumps do you have?
Tandem or AFF instructors must have at least 500 individual jumps before they can apply for an instructor rating. What you want to know is: How many *tandem or AFF* jumps has your instructor had? (25 seems like a fair minimum, in my opinion!)

Have you ever had an accident involving a passenger or student?
If yes, ask about the circumstances: Was it a screw-up or an honest mistake?

How many times have you had a malfunction? Gone to a reserve canopy? With a student?
(Ask about the circumstances!)

Your life is in the hands of the person who will supervise your first skydive. Don't be shy about asking that person anything you want.

Equipment Considerations

The Federal Aviation Administration (FAA), working cooperatively with the USPA, also participates in the regulation of skydiving equipment, activities and procedures.

The FAA issues a Technical Standards Order (T.S.0.) for all reserve canopies and harnesses used in the United States. T.S.0.'d parachutes have been tested to standards written by members of the Parachute Industry Association (PIA) under the auspices of the Society of Automotive Engineers (SAE) for approval by the FAA. Parachute testing focuses on structural integrity, reliability and rate of descent under maximum load.

Your life is in the hands of the person who will supervise your first skydive. Don't be shy about asking that person anything you want.

T.S.O. standards for tandem parachutes are currently under development. Tandem skydiving is currently permitted under the FAA Tandem Exemption referred to above. The two manufacturers who have the most experience designing and producing tandem canopies are: Strong Enterprises of Orlando Florida and the Relative Workshop of DeLand, Florida.

Commercial pilots and private pilots flying for skydiving operations must follow all pertinent FAA regulations (FAR 105, FAR 91). While some clubs use private pilots to take their people to altitude for a jump, a commercial pilot's license is the industry standard.

FAA-certified parachute riggers are the only people allowed to pack reserve canopies. Reserve canopies must be inspected and repacked every 120 days, in accordance with FAA regulations and the manufacturer's instructions.

A main canopy can be packed by the person using it, an FAA licensed rigger, or a person under the supervision of an FAA licensed rigger.

You may have noticed that your main canopy —the one you'll be throwing first—does not have to be T.S.O.'d through the FAA. You can trust your provider to select, maintain and correctly use a main canopy with a proven safety record.

Here are some questions you can ask that will allow your school/instructor to prove to you that they are worthy of your trust.

Who makes the main parachutes that you use for student jumps?

American manufacturers set the standard for the world in sport parachutes. Your main parachute should be made by one of the big five: Strong Enterprises, Precision Aerodynamics, Para-Flight, Glide Path International or Performance Design. (Performance Design manufactures the tandem chute that Relative Workshop has an FAA Tandem Exemption for).

What size parachutes do you use for student jumps?

Most schools have three sizes of canopies for individual jumps:

• 280 square foot, 7-cell canopies are for people who weigh 90 to 125 pounds.

• 288 to 292 square foot, 9-cell canopies are for 120 to 180 pound jumpers.

• 340 square foot, 9-cell canopies are for people who weigh 180 to 250 pounds.

Slightly larger chutes should be used if the drop zone is at high altitude.

MODERN SKYDIVING: TRUE FACTS

• *You can get nearly a minute of exhilarating free-fall on your very first skydive. And you won't be alone.*

• *While on any skydive—static-line, AFF or tandem—think and act as if you are the only one on earth who can be relied upon to save your life.*

• *All skydiving schools should be affiliated with the USPA, and all their instructors should be certified. But you should definitely interview the instructor you plan to go up with—because your life is in his or her hands.*

• *Modern skydiving reserve parachutes and harnesses must pass airworthiness standards specified by the FAA.*

How old is the main canopy that I will be jumping with?

Under ideal conditions, a parachute is good for about 1,000 jumps. If the parachute is regularly exposed to sun and dirt, especially during repacking, it is good for about 500 to 600 jumps.

Do you have a certified FAA rigger working here?

FAA certified riggers are required by law to keep detailed records on all the chutes they repack. Don't be afraid to ask to see the repacking card for the reserve chute you'll be wearing.

Can I see the chute I'll be jumping with?

You can tell a lot about the care and maintenance of a parachute just by looking at the pack it's in. Frayed, fading cloth, duct tape and dirt on the outside don't bode well for the inside.

Is the reserve chute automatic activating device (AAD) calibrated annually and maintained by the factory that produced it?

The AAD is designed to deploy your reserve at "last-chance" altitude if your main hasn't been deployed. Yes is the only good answer.

Do you provide a radio? Altimeter? Helmet?

All are indications of a professional school.

Good skydiving schools will welcome the opportunity to show you concrete evidence that they do things right.

TRUE THRILLS

Here's how skydiving stacks up in relation to the reward variables I've outlined for thrill sports:

Speed

The dive itself is raw speed, pure and simple—the most basic rush thrill sports have to offer. But it's the speed reversals that really get you. When you exit the airplane you go from zero to 120 miles per hour STRAIGHT DOWN in just seconds. The acceleration to "terminal velocity" simply takes your breath away, mainly because you think you're about to die. But once you stabilize in free-fall, it's like speed slows down. You say to yourself: "Wow! I've never gone so fast this slow before!"

Right about then, it's time to throw your chute and the speed sensation becomes "Wow! I've never slowed down this fast before!" and the next thing you know, you're floating through space like a bubble. It all happens in less than a minute, and you're left dangling under a canopy wondering, "How many time zones did we go through?! Is this the same planet?"

• Modern skydiving canopies are fully controllable and can be landed softly on a dime with nine cents change.

• Skydiving free-fall is the purest rush thrill sports have to offer.

Focus

Present. Definitely present. Although having your life pass before your eyes when you step out of the plane is kind of like a quick dance with the past. And envisioning all the things you'll never get to do if you die (while waiting for the canopy to open) is kind of a future trip. But—no—skydiving is definitely a here-and-now sport.

Your view of the world

It's hard to describe an 8,000-foot, 120-mile-per-hour plunge through space as anything but extremely focused. But towards the end of free-fall you start to look around and enjoy the wide-open feel of things. Chute deployment feels like you've just been yanked blindfolded up a 300-foot chimney. Finally, the ride into the landing zone under canopy is as wide-open and three-dimensional as it gets.

How does it compare to REAL life?

Again, it's the reversals. You go from the secure world of an airplane cabin, to a world of hard speed and deafening wind, to an unbelievably soft and noiseless world underneath a beautiful canopy.

How does it feel?

Skydiving is all butt, eyes and ears—with a little bit of stomach thrown in so you can really feel the reversals described above. It's your butt, mainly, that jumps out of the airplane. It's also what "hurts so good" during and after the opening shock of your parachute. Your eyes widen, get watery, blink, blink again and stare. Your ears don't know what the hell is going on from one second to the next. And your stomach tells you you're gonna die at least three times in a minute and a half. Oh yeah, plus you get to breathe hard. Any questions?

RESOURCES FOR DOERS AND DREAMERS

If skydiving sounds like a kick to you, but you'd like to learn more about it before jumping out of an airplane, consider the following resources.

National Organizations

United States Parachute Association (USPA): 1440-P Duke Street, Alexandria, Virginia 22314. (703) 836-3495. General information on ratings, service, certification, membership. Monthly publication is *Parachutist Magazine.*

Books and Magazines

Parachuting, The Skydiver's Handbook, Dan Poynter, 1989. Para Publishing, P.O. Box 4232, Santa Barbara, California 93140-4232. This is the most definitive text on skydiving for basic to intermediate level enthusiasts. Detailed, accurate, entertaining. $19.95. (800) PARAPUB.

Skydiving, a Dictionary, Bill FitzSimons. Fodderstack Press, P.O. Box 38, Flint Hill, Virginia 22627. Humorous.

Parachuting's Unforgettable Jumps III, Howard Gregory. Howard Gregory Associates, 640 The Village #209, Redondo Beach, California 90277. A historical view of both airborne and sport jumping.

Skies Call, Andy Keech. Skies Call, P.O. Box 57238, Washington, D.C. 20037. Three volumes of outstanding color photos by a gifted parachuting photographer.

The Parachute Manual, Volume II, Dan Poynter. Para Publishing, P.O. Box 4232, Santa Barbara, California 93140-4232. (805) 968-7277. Everything you've ever wanted to know about all kinds of parachutes.

Parachuting Manual with Log, Dan Poynter. Para Publishing, P.O. Box 4232, Santa Barbara, California 93140-4232. (805) 968-7277. Pocket-sized first jump course/logbook. Excellent illustrations, crammed with essential information. Least expensive way ($2.50) to learn lots about skydiving.

Parachuting Manual with Log for Accelerated Free Fall, Jan Meyer. Para Publishing, P.O.Box 4232, Santa Barbara, California 93140-4232. (805) 968-7277. Basic essentials of learning to skydive via the AFF method.

Parachutist Magazine: See USPA listing under Organizations.

Skydiving Magazine: P.O. Box 1520, DeLand, Florida 32721.

Observation Points

Call any of the drop zones or schools listed below. Most will allow non-participants to sit in on a ground school and/or observe their skydives from the ground. Observation rides—where you go up in the airplane and watch people take the leap—are available, space permitting, for a fee ranging from $8 to $24.

RESOURCES FOR DOERS
USPA Certified Drop Zones/Schools

California City Sky Dive Center: California City Municipal Airport, California City, California 93505. (800) 2-JUMP-HI. Static-line, tandem, accelerated free-fall. Observation rides available for $8 to 16. Non-participants welcome in ground school. Bob and Judy Celaya run the place, Bob in the air and Judy on the ground. New hangar, clean bathrooms and showers. Camping facilities available.

See #1 on map page 190.

Cy Perkins Parachute Center: Skylark Airport, Lake Elsinore, California 92330. (714) 674-

1299. Static-line, tandem, accelerated free-fall. The birthplace of Southern California sky diving. Club president is parachute manufacturer Gary Douris of Freeflight Enterprises. Welcomes all experienced skydivers and first-timers. First-timers referred to Sky Diving Adventures.

See #2 on map page 190.

Perris Valley Skydiving: 2091 Goetz Road, Perris, California 92572. (714) 657-9576. These folks control the drop zone at Perris Valley Airport. All skydivers welcome. Refers beginners to Perris Valley Skydiving School.

See #3 on map page 190.

Perris Valley Skydiving School: Perris Valley Airport, Perris, California 92570. (800) 832-8818. Tandem and accelerated free fall. Observation rides may be available for $20. Non-participants welcome in ground school, space permitting. Jump groups of 4 to 40. Jeff and Sherry Jones operate the school. Family in business over 30 years. Pool and snack bar, camping (tent space) showers and bathrooms.

See #3 on map page 190.

San Diego Airsports, Inc.: 13531 Otay Lakes Road, Jamul, California 91935. (619) 421-0968. Static-line, tandem. Small outfit owned and operated by Don Mumma. This is the only skydiving school in San Diego. Uses Cessna 206 which is too small to permit observation rides.

See #4 on map page 190.

Skydiving Adventures, Inc.: Hemet-Ryan Airport, Hemet, California 92546, and Skylark Airport, Lake Elsinore, California 92330. (800) 526-9682. Tandem, static-line, accelerated free-fall. Don and Robin Balch own and operate. Don, who has been jumping since 1964, was one of the first to get enthusiastic about tandem jumping. Tandem instructor/examiner. Observation rides for non-participants ($16.) Non-participants welcome in ground school. The Balch's goal in life is to get everyone hooked on skydiving, so watch out. Gear sales and service. Reserve repacks available. Camping free, RV hook-ups available at nominal charge. Showers and bathroom. Snacks.

See #5 on map page 190.

Sport Parachuting School: 16145 Victory Boulevard, Van Nuys, California 91406. (818) 994-0711. Static-line, tandem referrals, accelerated free-fall. Bill Reed gives a free ground school at the only sky diving outfit based in L.A. He does his jumping at the California City Drop Zone.

See #6 on map page 190.

Madera Parachute Center: Madera Airport, 4130-D Aviation Drive, Madera, California 93637. (209) 673-2688. Static-line, tandem, accelerated free-fall. Dave and Nita Gilbert operate by appointment only. Observers welcome. Call for seasonal hours and directions.

See #7 on map page 190.

Sky Dance Skydiving: 24390 Aviation Avenue, Yolo County Airport, Davis, California 95616. (916) 753-2651. Skydiving heavyweights Dan O'Brien and Ray Farrell own and operate the premier skydiving operation serving the Bay Area—the first school in the state to offer tandem jumps. Ray is a master rigger, an instructor/examiner, and one of the few instructors in the country qualified to train tandem instructors under the auspices of the FAA Tandem Exemption. Dan is an accomplished competitive skydiver. Static-line, tandem, accelerated free-fall.

See #8 on map page 190.

Skydive Paso Robles, Inc.: 4990 Wing Way, Paso Robles Municipal Airport, Paso Robles, California 93446. (805) 239-3483. Owner Deborah Stephens' school services California's central coast. Good year-round weather. On airport landing zone. Bunk beds and showers in the hangar make this one of the most convenient drop zones around for travelers. Static-line, tandem, accelerated free-fall. Observers welcome. Call for seasonal schedule.

See #9 on map page 190.

Skydiving West: Office: 439 Santa Monica Street, Los Banos, California 93635. Drop zone: Mendota Airport, Mendota. (209) 655-DIVE. Owner J. R. Taylor is open every weekend 9 AM to sundown. Dives by appointment only. Observers welcome. Country diving in the heart of the San Joaquin Valley. On-site showers, camping available at the airport. Static-line, tandem, accelerated free-fall.

See #10 on map page 190.

The Parachute Center: P.O. Box 423, Acampo, California 95220. (209) 369-1128. Owner Bill Dause has some philosophical differences with the USPA. He also has 15,000 jumps, the second most in the country, and operates an excellent school. He is, however, an USPA member and certified instructor. Static-line, tandem, accelerated free-fall. Operates seven days a week out of Lodi Airport. See #11 on map page 190.

Air Adventures West: 25637 South Lake Road, Taft, California 93268. (800) 423-8908. This full-service parachute center has been open for about a year at this location. The school is not USPA-affiliated but all instructors and personnel are USPA certified. Owners Bill and Kay Jones have jumped 100,000 students over 30 years with no fatalities. Bill designed the collegiate skydiving scoring system which bears his name. Located 35 miles east of Santa Barbara, this drop zone features grass packing areas, shade, camping and real bathrooms. Tandem and accelerated free-fall.

See #12 on map page 190.

Skydive Eureka: Somoa Airport, Eureka, California 95501. (707) 445-8681. At this time, owners Roger and Kim Mullis do introductory tandem jumps only. But what jumps they are. You exit the plane 9,000 feet over beautiful Northern California coastline and land in a field near the ocean. Serious beginners are referred to Skydance Skydiving in Davis, The Parachute Center in Lodi, or The World's Greatest Drop Zone in Southern Oregon.

See #13 on map page 190.

The World's Greatest Drop Zone: 30902 Redwood Highway, Cave Junction, Oregon 97523. (503) 592-2874. Open two years. Located at Illinois Valley Airport between Grants Pass, Oregon and Crescent City on the Northern California coast. Owner Ken Spiva gives tandem and accelerated free-fall jumps to Northern Californians and Southern Oregonians alike. Beautiful scenery, modern conveniences. Spiva owns a couple of large planes, including a DC-3. Excellent place to observe "relative work" (multiple-person formation jumping).

See #14 on map page 190.

Bay Area Skydiving: Byron, California. (510) 634-7575. Closest drop zone to the Bay Area. Owner Jani (Yah-nee) Bango had a chance to re-open the old Byron drop zone. He jumped on it. Jani is a young pup by skydiving standards, but he used to fly for Deborah Stephens at Skydive Paso Robles, so he has plenty of experience. Static, tandem, accelerated free-fall.

See #15 on map page 190.

Hang Gliding

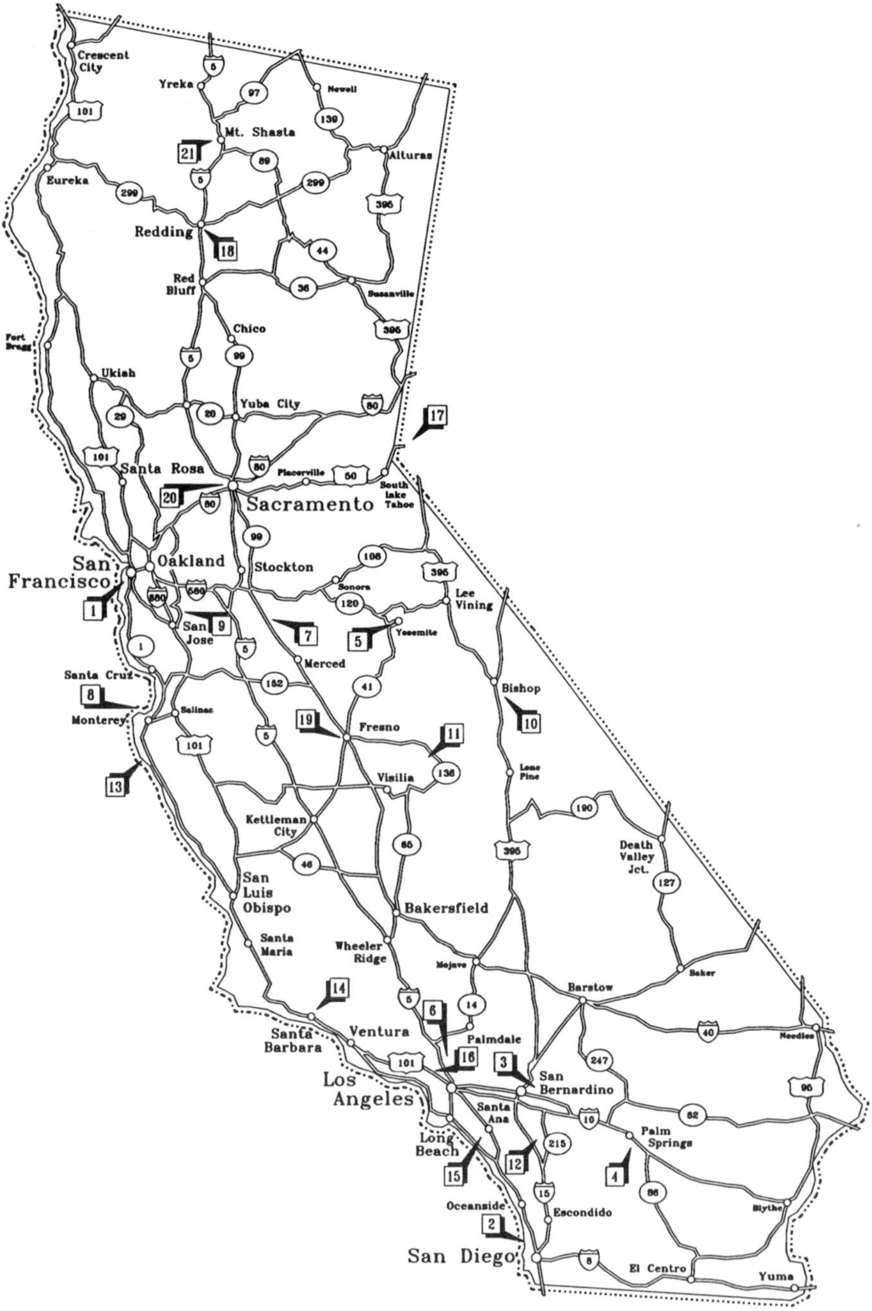
Crescent City
Yreka
Newell
Mt. Shasta
Alturas
Eureka
Redding
Red Bluff
Susanville
Fort Bragg
Chico
Ukiah
Yuba City
Santa Rosa
Placerville
South lake Tahoe
Sacramento
San Francisco
Oakland
Stockton
Sonora
Lee Vining
San Jose
Yosemite
Merced
Santa Cruz
Bishop
Monterey
Salinas
Fresno
Lone Pine
Visalia
Kettleman City
Death Valley Jct.
San Luis Obispo
Bakersfield
Santa Maria
Wheeler Ridge
Mojave
Baker
Barstow
Santa Barbara
Ventura
Palmdale
Needles
Los Angeles
San Bernardino
Santa Ana
Palm Springs
Long Beach
Oceanside
Escondido
Blythe
San Diego
El Centro
Yuma

CHAPTER EIGHT

HANG GLIDING

JIM SKELTON'S LIFE WAS FOREVER CHANGED by his two-stage introduction to hang gliding. Skelton, who lives in Redlands, California, tells his story:

BUNNY HOP—THEN FLY UNITED: Jim Skelton's Trip Through Time and Space

"I had always wanted to try hang gliding—ever since I saw some 'crazy maniac' jump off a highway turnout in Palm Desert, California. I'll never forget it: Just a few moments after he launched, I was watching him soar overhead with the birds!

"A few years passed. Then one night, coming out of my favorite restaurant, I walked right into a hang gliding advertisement on the tailgate of a green Ranchero pick-up. The sensations of watching that guy in Palm Desert came back to me in a rush. I was shocked. I thought to myself: 'How many times do I have to be hit in the face with this before I actually do it?' I called **High Adventure Hang Gliding** that same night.

"I thought to myself: 'How many times do I have to be hit in the face with this before I actually do it?'"

"I blurted two years worth of questions into the phone: 'Where? When? How much? How high? How safe?' I wanted to know!

"Diane McKenzie patiently answered all my questions. She explained how her husband Rob starts people out with a day of instruction at a very small 20-foot training hill. The second lesson would be a high-altitude tandem flight from Crestline, a 3,200-foot mountain in the San Bernardino mountain range.

"The next day I was out at Rob's Pepper Avenue training hill learning how to control a hang glider. We worked most of the day on flat ground. Rob ran alongside telling me what to do. Finally, at the end of the day, Rob told me I was ready to fly by myself from the top of the 20-foot slope.

"Just feeling my feet leave the ground was an overwhelming experience. The glider literally picked me up off the ground and I flew!"

"I started running just like I'd been running all day long. I was just a few steps down the slope when I realized my legs were waving in space. I was in the air! It didn't matter that I was only two feet off the ground. Just feeling my feet leave the ground was an overwhelming experience. The glider literally picked me up off the ground and I flew!

"I couldn't even imagine doing anything in a hang glider that felt better than that first little hop. Boy, was I wrong.

"The day of my first tandem flight I can honestly say I was the most excited person in the world. Rob and I would hook into the same glider and fly together to the landing area 3,200 feet below. Rob explained that my first job was to run at his side—kind of like at the training hill—while he launched the glider. After that he'd let me fly the glider for several minutes before he took over again for our approach and landing.

"We set up the glider and pre-flight inspected it. Then we did a practice run to make sure we wouldn't trip over each other on launch.

"Our launch was smooth. The next thing I knew, I felt like a bird. I heard myself say 'I can't believe I'm flying!' I said it again and again. I couldn't believe that my feet were so far off the ground—that I was completely at the mercy of this fantastic flying contraption, and Rob McKenzie's flying abilities.

"As we flew away from the hill, the open space between my feet and the ground got bigger and bigger until it turned into a whole new world. It was fantastic! The only sound was the sound of the air flowing past us. I felt like I was right in the center of everything—like time was standing still just for me. The only thing on my mind was: 'Me! Flying!' It was like total freedom, total immersion in the moment.

"After a few minutes, Rob finally got my attention long enough to convince me to take control of the glider. Under his guidance, with thousands of feet between us and the ground, I learned how simple it is to control a hang glider: Shift your weight to the left, the glider turns left; shift your weight to the right, the glider turns right. I could fly this thing!

"The best part is I still get that same feeling—total freedom, total immersion in the moment—every single time I fly."

"My first tandem flight convinced me that flying would be in my life forever. Just three weeks later, I did my first high-altitude solo flight on my own equipment. I've been flying three times a week ever since.

"The best part is I still get that same feeling—total freedom, total immersion in the moment—every single time I fly."

FIRST RIDE
(Cost: $75-$125 bunny slope, $90-$135 tandem, $150-$225 both)

If one or the other of Jim Skelton's adventures sounds intimidating to you, remember this: You don't have to do both. Beginner hang gliding pilots have a choice of how they want to learn.

Bunny slope training starts out with you

running on flat ground. You're attached to an exceptionally stable glider that floats overhead. Your instructor runs alongside as you learn the basic "start," "stop" and "turn" controls of the glider.

In this way, you can learn how to take off, maneuver and land without ever leaving the ground. To put it another way, modern teaching techniques make it so you don't actually have to fly until *after* you've learned how.

A bunny slope day culminates with you confidently and competently launching from a shallow slope. You'll fly a few feet off the ground and land safely on your own two feet.

Modern teaching techniques make it so you don't actually have to fly until after you've learned how.

Bunny slope training is ideal if you want to pilot your own aircraft (at a very low altitude!) before you trust body and soul to some strange contraption and some grinning stranger who promises you the ride of your life. Just a few hours on a bunny slope gives you confidence in hang gliding equipment. It also gives you a gut-level conviction that hang gliders really do work as advertised, with you—not the wind—in total control.

On an introductory **tandem flight,** you and a specially trained instructor both hook into a large two-person hang glider. A breathtaking 15- to 60-minute high altitude flight from a mountain, hill or cliff follows. The instructor performs the launch, and then, much like a drivers' education instructor, he or she turns the glider over to you while still retaining the ability to control it himself. Towards the end of the flight, the instructor takes control again for the landing approach and landing.

An introductory tandem flight will immerse every last ounce of your being in thin air. You get actual, real-life, high-altitude exposure to the silent, swooping sensations that hang glider pilots rave about. Best of all, if you choose your resource in accordance with the guidelines in this book, you get it safely—under the direct, hands-on supervision of a professional, certified instructor.

Neither a tandem ride or a bunny slope lesson, you will notice, calls for any of the do-or-die, now-or-never life-threatening shenanigans that everyone yammers about every time you bring up the subject of hang gliding. And in both cases, you are only called upon to do what—down deep—you really yearn to do in the first place: fly free like a bird in the sky above.

Neither a tandem ride or a bunny slope lesson, you will notice, calls for any of the do-or-die, now-or-never life-threatening shenanigans that everyone yammers about every time you bring up the subject of hang gliding.

MYTHS

Expect to encounter some or all of these objections from your loved ones the instant you announce your intention to "just give hang gliding a try."

By all means stick the noses of your loved ones directly into this MYTH section. If they hear what they want to hear first, *maybe* they'll pay attention long enough to read the truth. And the truth *might* make them think twice about having you thrown in the looney bin for even thinking about hang gliding.

"Isn't hang gliding a "Do or Die, Flop or Fly" proposition?!"

Most people think that anyone who gets within 100 yards of a hang glider will eventually face a momentous, gut-wrenching decision: one that offers only one positive consequence.

"Sure, you might luck into an exhilarating flight," your mom might say in reference to this moment, "but what if you crash and die, or—worse yet—chicken out in front of all your friends?"

The truth is that hang gliding's "do or die" instructional days are long gone. As you have seen from Jim Skelton's tandem flight, you are basically along for the ride the first time out—just as you would be if you signed up for a tour of the Grand Canyon in a sight-seeing plane.

As far as bunny slope training goes, a competent modern hang gliding instructor would never knowingly ask you—or require you—to do anything you don't feel prepared to do. "The first time I left the ground, I was totally prepared for it," says Skelton. "Still, it was the most exhilarating moment of my life—I was in control! I was flying!"

By the time you are allowed to fly on your own, you will be confident and eager to progress. Your anxiety will be the good kind—the kind that keeps you focused and ready to meet the new challenge at hand.

By the time you are allowed to fly on your own, you will be confident and eager to progress. Your anxiety will be the good kind—the kind that keeps you focused and ready to meet the new challenge at hand.

"Don't hang gliders immediately plummet and crash when the wind stops?!"

Most people think that the wind powers hang gliders. Because the wind is a fickle and unpredictable source of power, it stands to reason that a person's chances of emerging alive and unscathed from a hang glider flight are—as folk legend Bob Dylan might say—"blowin' in the wind."

The truth is that gravity, not the wind, powers hang gliders. And what's more constant, more reliable, than gravity?

Here's how it works: A hang glider, like all aircraft, is an airfoil. As such it flies only when air is moving over its wing at a certain minimum rate. Until the advent of paragliders (see next chapter), hang gliders were the only aircraft on the face of the earth light enough and slow enough to be foot-launched by human beings. A hang glider weighs between 50 and 80 pounds and will fly at an airspeed as low as 20 miles per hour.

Gravity is the engine in a hang glider. It causes the glider to move downward through whatever air mass it is in. The downward motion caused by gravity pulling on the combined weight of the glider and the pilot gives the glider its minimum airspeed—no matter what the pilot is doing, and no matter what the wind is doing.

Gravity is the engine in a hang glider. It causes the glider to move downward through whatever air mass it is in. The downward motion caused by gravity pulling on the combined weight of the glider and the pilot gives the glider its minimum airspeed—no matter what the pilot is doing, and no matter what the wind is doing.

Wind is only a problem to a hang glider pilot if it is blowing too strong (more than about 25 miles per hour), if it is too turbulent, or if it is blowing in a direction that prevents the pilot from launching and landing straight into it. Launching and landing into the wind assures that the glider will be going as slow as possible in relation to the ground. Push a paper airplane straight into the wind and it will glide gently to the ground. Toss it with the wind and it will crash into the earth at least as fast as the wind blows—probably faster.

Yes, a hang glider can climb away from the ground. But only when its pilot locates and maneuvers into a mass of air that is moving upward faster than the glider is moving downward through it. A hang glider ALWAYS moves downward through whatever air mass it is in. It moves downward at a minimum rate of 200 feet per minute (fpm). A hot air mass (known as a thermal) that moves away from the ground at 500 fpm will carry a hang glider away from the ground at a rate of 300 fpm.

Add it up: air mass moving 500 fpm away from ground, minus glider moving 200 fpm down through air mass = glider moving away from ground at 300 fpm.

"So the wind doesn't power a hang glider. But it does seize control of the glider whenever it wants —doesn't it?"

Those who think that hang glider pilots can't control the speed and direction of a hang glider are arguably crazier than the very hang glider pilots whose sanity they question.

The truth is (once again) that gravity—in the form of the pilot's body weight—allows a hang glider pilot to control his craft. In fact, a hang glider pilot can totally control the speed and direction of a hang glider—*if* he is smart enough to fly a properly designed hang glider in suitable weather conditions. Contrary to popular belief, "flyable" conditions are easy to identify. In such conditions there are really no such things as "mystery winds" of the type that slap down jet airliners in thunderstorms.

To control the speed of a hang glider, you shift your weight forward (to go faster) or rearward (to go slower). You control direction by shifting your weight right (to go right) or left (to go left.)

The glider goes where your body weight tells it to go. It's that easy.

The bottom line? Even crazy people know that stepping off into thin air without any clue as to your fate or destination would be no fun at all. Even crazy people know better than to launch into a thunderstorm.

Common sense!

"Shift your weight!? You gotta be kidding! What happens when your arms get tired?!"

Many people have this terrifying image of a wide-eyed, white-knuckled hang glider pilot hanging on for dear life. They want to know how a person can blithely shift weight around when every ounce of arm and hand strength must be devoted to hanging onto the hang glider.

Their concerns would be justified—*if* a hang glider pilot were attached to the glider primarily by his arms and hands.

But, **the truth is**, a hang glider pilot is suspended from the hang glider in a hammock-like device called a harness. The pilot's weight is supported entirely by the harness which is attached, via carabineer, to the center of gravity (CG) of the glider. The CG is a point near the center of the wing that is carefully calculated by hang glider designers. It's the one point on the glider that will allow you to change the speed and direction of the glider simply by shifting your weight forward or aft, or side to side.

A hang glider pilot is suspended from the hang glider in a hammock-like device called a harness. The pilot's weight is supported entirely by the harness, which is attached, via carabineer, to the center of gravity (CG) of the glider.

You don't, as they say, "hang onto" the triangular bar underneath a hang glider. It is not designed to support weight. It is called a control bar because its primary function is to give you something to pull and push against as you shift your weight around.

"If a hang glider breaks in mid-air while I'm on a high altitude tandem flight, I'm dead—right?"

Wrong. **The truth is:** All hang glider pilots carry a parachute. A tandem instructor carries a real big one and he knows how to use it—if he has to. Odds are overwhelming that he won't have to. Thanks to the hard work and success of

MODERN HANG GLIDING: TRUE FACTS

• Your first hang gliding experience, whether you take a bunny slope lesson or a tandem ride, is no more dangerous than taking a ride in a Cessna—if you're careful enough to pick a good school and a good instructor.

• Most modern instructors are certified. You should never take a lesson from one who is not certified even if he claims to be "certifiable."

• Modern hang gliders are thoroughly tested for structural integrity and aerodynamic stability. Most modern equipment is certified. Don't hook-in to equipment that is not certified even if someone claims it is "certifiable."

the Hang Glider Manufacturer's Association (HGMA), structural failures of certified hang gliders are almost unheard of these days. However, if one should occur—or in the extremely unlikely event of a mid-air collision—your pilot will simply deploy his great big parachute and the two of you will float safely to the ground.

"Yeah, well, so how do those hang glidin' fools breathe up there?"

Get real!

The truth is: Hang glider pilots breathe like everyone else—only a little harder. That's because they're excited. They are, after all, having a *great* time up there.

TRUE CHILLS
(And how to avoid them)

Fatal hang gliding accidents are almost unheard of among beginners and novices—especially the ones who learn to fly from qualified professional instructors. Most of the hang gliding fatalities you hear about are intermediate or advanced pilots who fly conditions and/or equipment that they aren't ready for.

Still, it is possible to get killed in a hang glider your first or second time out. Here's how: One eager young pilot taught himself basic launch and landing skills in smooth conditions at a 50-foot training hill in the Midwest. He came to Southern California to fly Crestline, a 3,200-foot mountain he had read about in a magazine. He compounded his already risky situation by launching into a strong wind. The combination of high altitude and turbulent air was too much for him. He panicked, became disoriented, and died when he crashed his glider downwind into the mountain about 50 feet below launch.

Another young woman ALMOST lost her life when she trusted the wrong pilot to give her an introductory tandem ride. The pilot, who had never given a tandem ride before, carefully attached her to the glider before launch. Unfortunately he forgot to attach himself as well. Three steps into launch he fell away from the glider and landed, unharmed, in some bushes a few feet below take-off. Imagine the woman's terror as she flew off alone without a clue in the world as to what to do next. Fortunately, the air was smooth and the glider was slow and stable. With nervous trial and error, and a little luck , she was able to control the glider well enough to "land" in a field below without breaking her neck.

The only way you can get hurt or killed in a hang glider is via fast, hard contact with the ground. Hang glider pilots call it "going in."

At the introductory level, there are only three things that can cause you to "go in" in a hang glider:

- Poor instruction.
- Poor equipment.
- Poor judgement (includes carelessness).

Poor judgement leads directly to poor instruction on poor equipment—which greatly increases your chances of "going in." Again: It is your responsibility to select an introductory experience that provides state-of-the-art instruction on state-of-the-art equipment.

- *With modern instruction you will learn how to start, stop, and turn a hang glider before you even leave the ground.*

- *You—not the wind and not blind fate—control the speed and heading of a hang glider.*

- *You—not your instructor and not your friends—are the final authority in all "fly/don't fly" decisions.*

- *A vast majority of the people who try hang gliding do not become fully trained hang glider pilots. They just walk away from the experience with a memory that will last a lifetime.*

If you select an instructor that hasn't bothered to earn all the USHGA instructor certifications required for the type of instruction you are receiving, you're misplacing your trust.

Instructor/School Considerations

In the world of hang gliding, state-of-the-art instruction is defined by The United States Hang Gliding Association (USHGA). The USHGA offers the following certifications for those who teach others to fly hang gliders.

USHGA Basic Instructor: Qualified to teach training slope lessons.

USHGA Advanced Instructor: Qualified to teach training slope lessons and high altitude flying skills—except tandem.

USHGA Tandem Instructor: Qualified to take people with no hang gliding experience on tandem flights. Pilots with USHGA Tandem I or Tandem II ratings can take only other USHGA rated pilots on tandem flights. All of the resources listed in this chapter provide USHGA certified instruction.

If you select an instructor that hasn't bothered to earn all the USHGA instructor certifications required for the type of instruction you are receiving, you're misplacing your trust.

Equipment Considerations

Once you have selected a certified instructor, trust him or her to use a glider that is certified by the HGMA.

Thanks to the concern and dedication of the HGMA, most modern American hang gliders are subjected to extensive testing for structural strength and aerodynamic stability. Strength testing assures that the glider is strong enough to stay in one piece throughout all normal (and some abnormal) flight maneuvers. Believe it or not, a pilot would have an easier time breaking a Cessna in mid-air than he would a hang glider. Aerodynamic stability testing assures that the glider's flight characteristics—its natural tendency to fly straight and stay right side up—match the skill level of the pilot it is designed to carry.

Each manufacturer is responsible for testing its own gliders. Documentation of that testing is then reviewed by an HGMA committee. If the committee accepts the documentation as complete, it issues a "Certificate of Compliance" to the glider's manufacturer.

If you have any doubts about the certification status of a hang glider, simply ask your carefully selected certified instructor: "Hey, has the HGMA issued a Certificate of Compliance on this thing yet, or not?!"

If he says "No" or, worse yet, "I dunno," renew your search for an instructor worth trusting your life to.

One exception: Some schools use equipment that is specially modified for use on their specific bunny slope. By installing smaller frame parts, they make the glider lighter and easier for you to lug around. These gliders are perfectly safe as long as they are used only on the bunny slope under the supervision of a certified instructor.

TRUE THRILLS

Here's how hang gliding stacks up in relation to the reward variables I've outlined for thrill sports:

Speed

Hang gliding is a moderately paced thrill

If you like the sound of running briskly off a hill on takeoff, or skimming silently across the ground at about 25 miles per hour, you'll like hang gliding.

sport. It's neither blazing nor pokey. Gliders cruise at about 25 miles per hour and can go as fast as 50 miles per hour. The pilot controls speed changes which, done properly, are smooth as opposed to radical or choppy. If you like the sound of running briskly off a hill on takeoff, or skimming silently across the ground at about 25 miles per hour, you'll like hang gliding. Yes, you can slow them down to zero miles per hour on landing, as long as you land into the wind.

Focus

Whether you're up or down, happy or sad, an introductory hang gliding experience will rivet you in the present moment like you wouldn't believe. The act of flying—the mere idea of controlling your own destiny in mid-air—will give you a fresh new perspective on the tired old phrase "here and now."

Your view of the world

Spatially speaking, hang gliding is wide-open. You fly untethered. The glider will go exactly where you make it go. There is no cockpit around you. Whether you're two feet off the ground at a bunny slope, or thousands of feet in the air on a tandem flight, you can't be any more out there in the breeze than you are in a hang glider.

How does it compare to REAL life?

Your first "bunny hop" in a hang glider will make you think you've discovered a new dimension. Your first tandem flight will feel more like a whole new world.

How does it feel?

If you've ever wanted to feel like a bird, see like a bird, climb, cruise or soar like a bird, hang gliding is as close as you'll get to it in this lifetime. After you've relaxed about halfway through your introductory tandem ride, focus on your backside for an instant. The hang glider you're hooked into will feel like part of your spine.

Whether you're up or down, happy or sad, an introductory hang gliding experience will rivet you in the present moment like you wouldn't believe.

RESOURCES FOR DOERS AND DREAMERS

If you're intrigued by hang gliding, and want to find out more about it before actually doing it, consider any of the following levels of involvement.

National Organizations

United States Hang Gliding Association (USHGA): P.O. Box 8300, Colorado Springs, Colorado 80933. (719) 632-8300. General information on ratings, services, certification, membership. Monthly magazine. Of special interest is *Hang Gliding Magazine Special New Pilot Edition.*

Books and Magazines (can be ordered from the USHGA)

Right Stuff for New Hang Glider Pilots, Erik Fair. ($8.95) This book entertains while it informs. Though primarily aimed at people already enrolled in hang gliding lessons, the book also gives outsiders an inside look at some of the zanier aspects of hang gliding's off-beat culture.

Manbirds, Maralys Wills. ($9.95) A rich chronicle of hang gliding's early history. Also a personal look at one pioneer family's life and death encounter with hang gliding.

Hang Gliding For Beginning Pilots, Peter Cheney. ($29.95)Thorough and well- illustrated, this book is the best written resource available to the beginner hang glider pilot.

Flying Conditions, Dennis Pagen. ($7.50) Dry but informative. The only book on wind and weather as it effects hang glider pilots.

Hang Gliding Flying Skills, Dennis Pagen. ($9.95)Very technique-oriented. For beginner to intermediate pilots.

Hang Gliding Magazine: 6950 Aragon Court #6, Buena Park, California 90620. (714) 994-3050. Editorial submissions and inquiries only. Direct all other inquiries to the USHGA. Many think that editor Gil Dodgen produces the best publication in sport aviation. It's the official voice of the USHGA.

Observation Points

The following places offer the most consistent and spectacular observation points in the state of California. You can observe from either the point of take-off (launch site) or the landing area (LZ or landing zone).

Hang glider pilots everywhere shower love, affection, and heartfelt gratitude on anyone who will drive them and their vehicles to a launch site. After watching your pilot launch, you simply drive his or her car down to the landing area so he or she doesn't have to hitch-hike back up to retrieve it after a hard day of flying. Don't be shy. Just sing out, "Anyone need a driver?" and you'll be treated like royalty by everyone within earshot. And don't worry about pilots bumming your car for the ride up. They'll want you to drive their cars, with their specially-built racks for carrying hang gliders. Here are some prime locations for just watching or for volunteering to be a driver:

Fort Funston (San Francisco): Excellent coastal cliff soaring. Training. From Highway 1 take Skyline Boulevard (Highway 35) north. Drive three miles, then U-turn at John Muir Drive. Entrance to Fort Funston is 1/4 mile back. Call Chandelle (415-539-6800) or Air Time of San Francisco (415-759-1177) for conditions report.

See #1 on map page 216.

Torrey Pines (San Diego): The only other great coastal cliff soaring site in the state. From Interstate 5 take Genesee Avenue West. Go straight past the light on top of the hill. The road becomes North Torrey Pines Road. Go right on Torrey Pines Scenic Drive. Store is a double-wide trailer with windsock. Call Torrey Pines Flight Park (619-452-3202) for conditions report.

See #2 on map page 216.

Crestline (San Bernardino): Mountain soaring. Take Highway 18 out of San Bernardino to Crestline exit. Stop in downtown Crestline to ask directions to "Teddy Bear" launch site. Call High Adventure (714-883-8488) for conditions report.

See #3 on map page 216.

Vista Point (Palm Desert): Foothill soaring. Take Highway 74 out of Palm Desert. Drive to the scenic turnout about three miles up-hill.

Call Upward Bound (619-322-9214) for a conditions report.

See #4 on map page 216.

Glacier Point (Yosemite National Park): Scenic glide. Take Glacier Point Road to Glacier Point Parking Area. A limited number of pilots are permitted to launch between dawn and 8 AM, usually between June and September. Call Yosemite Ranger Station and ask for the "hang gliding ranger."

See #5 on map page 216.

Kagel Mountain (Sylmar, L.A. area): Mountain soaring. Go to Sylmar Flight Park landing area. You'll need a four-wheel-drive vehicle to get to launch. From Interstate 405 go to Interstate 210 East. Exit on Hubbard Street North (left) to Simshaw right. Go to the end of Simshaw, left on Gridley to end of the road. If you want to get to launch (and be a big hit too), volunteer to be a driver.

See #6 on map page 216.

Lake McClure (Coulterville, Modesto area): Hill soaring. Sensitive site, limited access. Call Ultraflight Hang Gliding Systems (209-874-1795) for information and directions. Nearby Bird Road (I-5 and Highway 132) and Don Pedro (off 132) are also good observation points, according to Ultraflight's Will Brown.

See #7 on map page 216.

Marina Beach (Marina): Sand dune training and low-cliff coastal soaring, depending on conditions. From Highway 1 in Marina take Reservation Road to Marina State Beach. Call Western Hang Gliders (408-384-2622) for a conditions report.

See #8 on map page 216.

Ed Levin Park (San Jose): Coastal mountain gliding and soaring. This state park is a great place to picnic and watch hang gliding. From Interstate 680 take Calaveras Boulevard/Highway 237 East to Downing Street. Go left into Ed Levin State Park. Call Mission Soaring (408-262-1055) for information.

See #9 on map page 216.

Owens Valley (Bishop): Wilderness mountain soaring. The Owens Valley is a mecca for advanced hang glider pilots. Numerous launch points throughout the valley attract cross-country hang glider pilots from all over the world. Flights of 100 to 200 miles are not uncommon. Cross-country pilots are especially grateful to those who volunteer to drive retrieval vehicles. Call Owens Valley Soaring (619-387-2623) for details.

See #10 on map page 216.

Dunlap (outside Kings Canyon National Park): Foothill soaring. 40066 Millwood Road, Dunlap, California 93621. (209) 338-2422. Dunlap Valley Lakes R.V. Park is owned and operated by two hang glider pilots named Dave and Connie Bowen. Located just to the west of Kings Canyon Park, Dunlap is a great place to kick back in your camping rig and watch hang glider pilots fly down from the mountains above. Open year-round. Facilities include store, showers, laundry, etc.

Directions: From Fresno take Highway 180 East to the small town of Dunlap. Go right on Dunlap Road, then, a few miles later, left on

Millwood Road.
See #11 on map page 216.

Elsinore (Lake Elsinore): Mountain soaring. From I-5 take Ortega Highway (74) to Lake Elsinore. Landing area is near intersection of Ortega Highway and Grand Street. Local Elsinore pilots ("The E Team") are the zaniest group of fliers in the state.
See #12 on map page 216.

Big Sur (Plaskett Creek Campground): Coastal mountain gliding and soaring.
See #13 on map page 216.

RESOURCES FOR DOERS

The resources listed below are the cream-of-the-crop in their respective areas. Please note: You cannot rent hang gliding equipment unless you are a trained pilot. All schools, however, provide equipment for lessons.

Although there are a number of club-level or independent certified instructors in California, the best instructors gravitate toward the established schools and dealers. Hang gliding training, like whitewater kayak training, is very site specific. The best schools and dealers have the best training areas and their programs are specifically designed to use those training areas in the safest possible way.

Hang gliding instruction is also a matter of skill and timing. That means you want to take instruction from an instructor who teaches regularly—one whose skill and timing are as fine-tuned as Jose Canseco's home run swing. You're far more likely to find that at an established school/dealership.

If you find an independent certified instructor who has access to a regular training site, and he or she teaches at least 10 students a year, you might have something. Ask to observe a lesson. If what you see matches the descriptions of bunny slope and tandem training that you read at the beginning of this chapter, the instructor is probably a competent one.

The following resource guide includes only the schools, dealerships and instructors that meet these two criteria: 1)Access to a regular training site. 2) Instructors that either teach a minimum of 10 students a year or refer students to someone who does.

Southern California

Hang Glider Emporium: 613 North Milpas, Santa Barbara, California 93103. (805) 965-3733. In business 17 years. Ken de Russy is one of the best and most experienced instructors in the state. His nearby training site, "The Mesa" is perhaps the best training hill in the state. Full service retail store is run by Ken and his wife Bonnie Nelson. Tandem flights referred to qualified local pilots.

Directions: Highway 101 to Milpas Street. Go six blocks towards mountains. Store is on left.

See # 14 on map page 216.

Hang Gliding Center: 4206 K Sorrento Valley Boulevard, San Diego, California 92121. (619) 450-9008. John and Aimee Ryan's full service retail store features a convenient training hill right next door. Bunny slope and tandem training. The place to go in San Diego if you aspire to become a fully trained pilot.

Directions: From Interstate 805, exit west on

Sorrento Valley/Mira Mesa Boulevard. Right on Sorrento Valley Boulevard. Go about a half-mile to last building in industrial park.

See #2 on map page 216.

Hang Flight Systems: 1202 M East Walnut, Santa Ana, California 92701. (714) 542-7444. Located next door to Wills Wing, the largest manufacturer of hang gliders in the U.S. Dan Skadal and crew usually know about new equipment and techniques before anyone else. Full service retail. Bunny slope and tandem training.

Directions: Interstate 5 to 1st Street (E). Left on Grand. Immediate right on Walnut. Left into parking area. Unit M is at end on right.

See #15 on map page 216.

High Adventure Hang Gliding: 4231 Sepulveda Street, San Bernardino, California 92404. (714) 883-8488. Rob and Diane McKenzie operate a full service retail store out of their living room and garage. Rob, who helped write the USHGA's standards for tandem instruction is, without question, the most accomplished tandem pilot in the nation. A unique specialty is teaching non-hearing students how to fly. Bunny slope training too.

Directions: From Interstate 215 North, take Highway 30 East. Exit north on Waterman Avenue. West on 40th Street, then right on Sepulveda. House/store is two blocks on right.

See #3 on map page 216.

Torrey Pines Flight Park: 2800 Torrey Pines Scenic Drive, La Jolla, California 91342. (619) 452-3202. The only place in Southern California for legal coastal ridge soaring. Also the only hang gliding shop in the state with a restaurant on premises (The Cliff Hanger Cafe). On-site bunny slope training, tandem training. Excellent place to observe hang gliding. Separate number (619) 457-9093 gives recorded wind velocity and direction.

From Interstate 5, take Genesee Avenue west. Go straight at light on top of hill. Road becomes North Torrey Pines Road. Right on Torrey Pines Scenic Drive.

See #2 on map page 216.

Windsports International: 16145 Victory Boulevard, Van Nuys, California 91406.(213) 474-3502. In business for 17 years, Joe Greblo and wife Kris run one of the best full-service hang gliding centers in the world. Joe has been instrumental in helping the USHGA develop training standards. He's also the guy you see flying in most of the small truck commercials. Windsports instructors teach every day except Monday and offer both group and private lessons. Directions: From Interstate 405 exit west on Victory Boulevard. Go about 1/2 mile. Store is on right.

See #16 on map page 216.

Upward Bound: P.O. Box 1175, Palm Desert, California 92261. (619) 322-9214. Scott Smith doesn't teach much but his favorite flying site, Vista Point, is one of the best places in Southern California to witness hang gliding first hand. He'll point you in the right direction for whatever you want. Call for directions.

See #4 on map page 216.

Northern California

Air Time of San Francisco: 3620 Wawona Street, San Francisco, California 94116. (415) 759-1177. Full service retail hang gliding near Fort Funston, the premier coastal soaring site in Northern California. Specializes in bunny slope training. Tandem by referral to qualified pilots. Training hill is just minutes from shop. Directions: From Highway 1 go west on Sloat Boulevard. Right on 47th, one block to Wawona.

See #1 on map page 216.

Chandelle Hang Gliding Center: 488 Manor Plaza, Pacifica, California 94044. (415) 359-6800. Chandelle has been serving the sport aviation community in the Bay Area since 1973. Full service hang gliding. Main man Andy Whitehill specializes in private and semi-private instruction. Training hill is at the base of Fort Funston cliff, just minutes from shop. Primary instructors offer tandem flights. From Highway 280 take Highway 1 South. First exit in Pacifica is Manor Drive. Store is in Manor Plaza at end of off-ramp.

See #1 on map page 216.

Mission Soaring: 1116 Wrigley Way, Milpitas, California 95035. (408) 262-1055. Full-service hang gliding. Pat Denevan and crew offer one of the best pilot training programs in the state. It is geared especially for those who want to make hang gliding an avocation. Bunny slope training. Tandem flights available. From Interstate 680 take Calaveras Boulevard/Highway 237 West. Go left at Hillview Street, then left at Los Coches. Los Coches becomes Sinclair Frontage Road. Shop is on corner at Wrigley Way.

See #9 on map page 216.

Western Hang Gliders: Marina State Beach, Highway 1 and Reservation Road, Marina, California 93933. (408) 384-2622. Soft sand, gentle slope and consistent wind make the Marina Beach training dune one of the best in the state. Full service hang gliding with an emphasis on easy bunny slope training. Tandem flights available. Proprietor Jim Johns has 11 years on site as state-approved concessionaire. From Highway 1, take Reservation Road to Marina State Beach.
See #8 on map page 216.

Hang Gliding Connection: 1887 O'Conner Avenue, Redding, California 96001. (916) 241-6974. Phil Sergent teaches basic lessons, plus he can tell you about some beautiful flying sites in the Redding area. Call for information.
See #18 on map page 216.

Hang Gliding Hanger: 6785 North Wilmington, Fresno, California 93711. (209) 264-7627. Brothers Tim and Dan Fleming don't teach. No training hills. But they'll be happy to tell you where to go for learning and observing. Call for information.
See #19 on map page 216.

Owens Valley Soaring: 5201 Westridge Road, Route 2, Bishop, California 93514. (619) 387-2673. The Owens Valley is a premier flying area for advanced pilots. Still, Kevin Klinefelter manages to introduce a few new people to the sport every year. Call for information.
See #10 on map page 216.

Pilots' Supply: (Sacramento area) 2766 Mojave Court, Cameron Park, California 95682. (916) 677-4953. Brad Hilliker only teaches a few people a year. But he knows the hang gliding scene and will be happy to point you in the right direction. Call for information.

See #20 on map page 216.

Silent Flight: P.O. Box 1206, Mt. Shasta, California 96067. (916) 938-2061. Dave Thomason and Candice Smith run the top hang gliding resource in the top part of the state. Full service. Bunny slope and tandem instruction. Call for information.

See #21 on map page 216.

Ultraflight Systems: (Modesto area) 13155 Snowflower Drive, Waterford, California 95386. (209) 874-1795. Will Brown offers basic instruction, sales and service. He'll tell you where to go for tandem instruction. Directions: From Modesto, go east on Highway 132 (towards Yosemite) to the town of Waterford. Turn left onto Tim Bell Street. Make the second right onto Snowflower Drive.

See #7 on map page 216.

Adventure Sports: 3650 Research Way #25, Carson City, Nevada 89706. (702) 883-7070. Owners Ray Leonard and Jackie Danskin bought the hang gliding/paragliding portion of a 10-year-old business (High Sierra Sports) two years ago. Ray has been flying hang gliders for 17 years, paragliders for two. A full half of Ray and Jackie's customers are from California, particularly the Bay Area, Sacramento and Tahoe. Full service shop: lessons, sales, service, repairs. Ray teaches/flies at any of 12 local sites, depending on conditions. Call for unique video site guide which might inspire you to travel to Nevada.

See #17 on map page 216.

PARAGLIDING

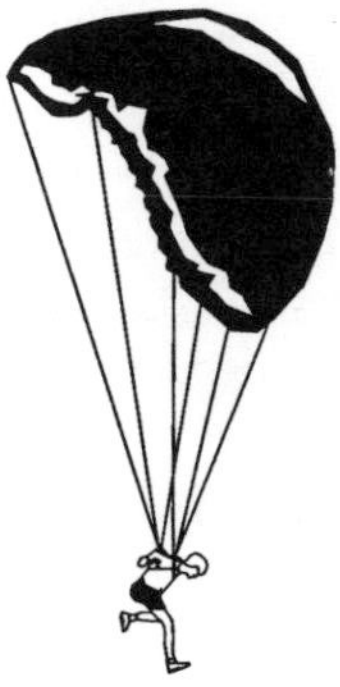

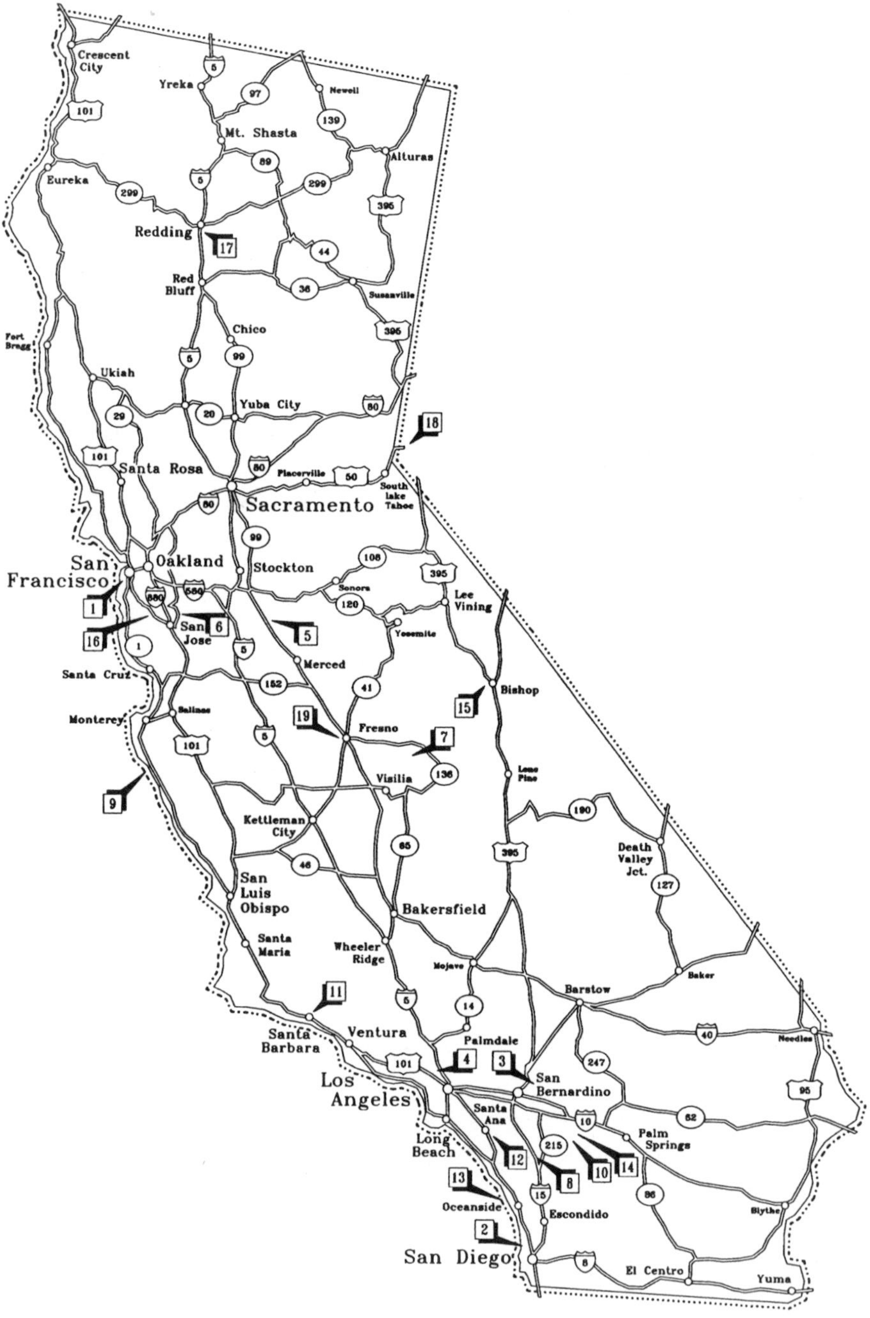

Crescent City
Yreka
Newell
Mt. Shasta
Alturas
Eureka
Redding
Red Bluff
Susanville
Chico
Ukiah
Yuba City
Santa Rosa
Placerville
South lake Tahoe
Sacramento
San Francisco
Oakland
Stockton
Sonora
Lee Vining
Yosemite
San Jose
Merced
Santa Cruz
Monterey
Salinas
Bishop
Fresno
Visilia
Lone Pine
Kettleman City
Death Valley Jct.
San Luis Obispo
Bakersfield
Santa Maria
Wheeler Ridge
Mojave
Baker
Barstow
Santa Barbara
Ventura
Palmdale
Needles
Los Angeles
San Bernardino
Santa Ana
Palm Springs
Long Beach
Oceanside
Escondido
Blythe
San Diego
El Centro
Yuma

CHAPTER NINE

PARAGLIDING

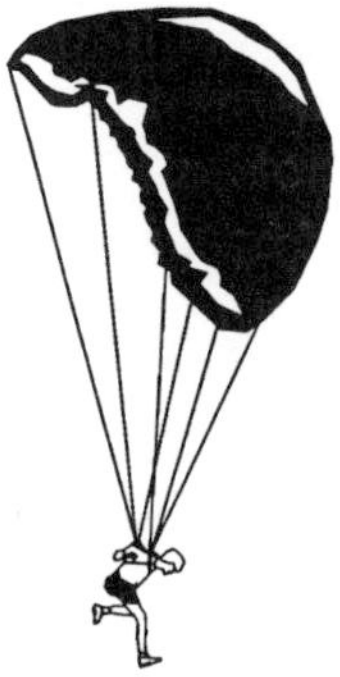

LISA BEARD LEARNED TO FLY A PARAGLIDER by learning to trust the man who was showing her how. She tells her story:

LOW AND SLOW: Lisa Beard's Encounter With Trust

"Steve and I were already friends when I decided I really wanted to learn how to fly a paraglider. When I first met him about three years ago, he took me on a tandem flight in a hang glider. It was like discovering a whole new world.

"Steve is part-owner and head designer of a company that manufactures hang gliding and paragliding equipment. He's an expert pilot plus he's patient enough to teach others how to fly. At the time we went hang gliding together, Steve hadn't yet gotten the paragliding end of his business off the ground. He could only offer to teach me hang gliding.

"But I really wasn't interested in learning to fly a hang glider. The wing looked heavy and awkward to me, and I had no desire to lug it up and down a hill—even a small one. I could also tell that it was real easy to land hard in a hang glider if your timing [of a landing flare] was less than perfect.

"I really wasn't interested in learning to fly a hang glider. The wing looked heavy and awkward to me, and I had no desire to lug it up and down a hill—even a small one."

"Though Steve and I were dating at the time, and he was obviously interested, I pretty much kept him at bay. I've always had a hard time building up the kind of trust you need to have in a guy before you enter into a serious relationship with him. We stayed in touch, though, while I dated around. In the meantime, Steve concentrated on learning everything he could about paragliders so his company could produce them.

"The more he got into paragliding, the more excited I got listening to him talk about it. Even though I was dating another guy at the time, Steve said he'd be willing to teach me as a friend. I quickly agreed to go out to the training hill with him.

"It was a real eye-opener. Unlike hang gliders, paragliders are extremely light and slow and *soft.* By watching others run on flat ground and down the shallow slope at the Gilman training hill, I realized that it's almost impossible to 'blow' a landing in a paraglider, and even if you do, there are no hard metal parts to hurt you if you crash into them. Steve apparently realized that I was ready to give it a try because all of a sudden he handed me a paragliding harness and said: 'Let's go!'

"My voice said: 'I'm not ready! I want to watch some more!'—but my excitement must have been stronger than my apprehension. The next thing I knew, I was trotting along flat ground and being tugged upward by a beautiful canopy that floated overhead. Steve held me down by the waist while he told me how to control the paraglider. I felt like a puppet in the hands of a puppeteer. For instance, when the wing drifted right, Steve would tell me to pull down on the lines on the left side until it straightened out. It was so simple! Before I knew it, I was controlling the canopy myself without him telling me what to do.

"The next thing I knew, I was trotting along flat ground and being tugged upward by a beautiful canopy that floated overhead."

"That's about the time he told me I was ready for my first flight from the top of the gently sloped 25-foot hill. It was also about the time that I realized how much trust I had placed in this guy and how *maybe* he was more than just a friend after all.

"My first flight was absolutely wonderful! As soon as I left the ground I shrieked: 'Wow, I'm a bird! What do I do now?!' Everyone, Steve included, was laughing when I landed on my own two feet a few seconds later. Even though I had gotten only about three feet off the ground, I knew I was hooked. I think it was that quiet, floating feeling that got to me more than anything. It's a peaceful feeling you can't really get anywhere else."

Author's postscript: Lisa Beard and Steve Pearson have decided to glide through life together. As this book goes to press, they are engaged to be married.

FIRST RIDE
(Cost: $65-$125 per day)

If you want to give paragliding a try, you must commit to a solo experience. There are no legal resources for tandem rides at this time, and there's no real need for tandem instruction in paragliding. That's because solo flying skills sufficient to get just a few feet off the ground are very simple to learn. You can easily learn enough to get safely off the ground, if not by the end of your first day on a bunny slope, at least by the end of day two or three.

"My first flight was absolutely wonderful! As soon as I left the ground I shrieked: 'Wow, I'm a bird! What do I do now?!'"

Note that some paragliding instructors do offer tandem rides, but these are not legal and not even all that fun. Since paragliding is so slow and controlled, a tandem ride is not nearly as exciting as it is in hang gliding or skydiving. You might as well go to the effort to learn how to do it yourself the first time.

Soft, light, simple and slow are the best words to describe your first day underneath a paraglider. Short of the "reel 'em out, reel 'em in" sport of parasailing, paragliding is the simplest way on planet earth for you to commit sport aviation.

If you're looking for a one-day experience—a short, sweet taste of flying like a bird—you can't beat a day on the bunny slope with a qualified paragliding instructor. You will experience the heady sensations of flight quickly, safely and easily.

Short of the "reel 'em out, reel 'em in" sport of parasailing, paragliding is the simplest way on planet earth for you to commit sport aviation.

But be forewarned: The simplicity and exhilaration of skimming along the ground in a paraglider may magically transform you. You may decide that you're not a "one-day pumpkin" after all. You may decide that you're a bona fide sky prince or princess, capable of conquering heaven itself in your new-found wing.

MYTHS

The worst paragliding myths are the ones that will lead you to believe that the sport is brainlessly simple, that it is merely a joy-ride rather than a serious form of aviation.

Allow your loved ones to read this myth section. It will prove to them that you appreciate and understand the dangers associated with any form of aviation—no matter how many magazines, newspapers or junk-journal TV shows describe it as "the piece-of-cake air sport everyone's been waiting for."

"If I can launch and land a paraglider, I can

safely fly it any time I want, any where I want, in any conditions I want."

Listen carefully. Heaven (or the hospital) is exactly where you'll end up if you allow yourself to be deluded by the initial ease of paragliding. Launch and landing skills—as easy as they are to learn in paragliding—are just the tip of the iceberg. You also need to accumulate enough knowledge, wisdom and judgement to survive a career in sport aviation.

The bottom line? If your first or second day on the bunny slope gets you hooked on paragliding, make absolutely sure you stick with your qualified instructor until you both agree that you're ready to progress to higher flight. And then make absolutely sure you know your limitations—especially in terms of the conditions and locations you are prepared to fly.

"Because paragliding is the easiest to learn form of sport aviation, it must also be the safest."

The truth is: Because the skills it demands are simple to learn and master, paragliding has the *potential* to be the safest form of sport aviation—especially here in America where our "risk management" conscious legal system acts to severely restrict the number and location of flying sites. American flying sites, because they are precious and few, tend to be regulated by the flying buffs (experienced hang glider and paraglider pilots) who use them. Regulation effectively closes these sites to unqualified pilots which in turn greatly improves the sport's safety record.

In Europe, where paragliding has been extremely popular for many years, it's a far different story. As practiced in Europe, paragliding is the least safe form of sport aviation.

European paraglider pilots throw themselves off any piece of unregulated public or private property they happen to stumble upon. No one stops them because the European legal system does not permit them or their families to sue everyone in sight when they get themselves hurt or killed. Consequently, European hang glider pilots—whose safety record is far superior to that of their paragliding friends—routinely look on in amazement as over-confident people with three or four days of paragliding training under their belts launch from dangerous mountain locations into dangerous weather conditions.

"Paragliders are parachutes, right? Doesn't that mean they just kinda fall out of the sky, that I don't have much control over where they go?"

Paragliders are direct descendants of the modern parafoil or square parachutes that skydivers now use. They are legitimate airfoils that glide like any other unpowered flying wing. The better beginner canopies can fly about five feet forward for every one foot of vertical descent.

Paragliders are direct descendants of the modern parafoil or square parachutes that skydivers now use. They are legitimate airfoils that glide like any other unpowered flying wing. The better beginner canopies can fly about five feet forward for every one foot of vertical descent. Old-style round skydiving parachutes are the ones that pretty much just fall out of the sky. No one uses those things anymore.

Control of forward versus vertical speed is easy in a paraglider. You control it with "brake lines" that are attached to the rear edge of the paraglider. You hold the right side lines in your right hand and the left lines in your left hand. If you want to slow your forward speed and increase your downward speed you pull both sets of lines part way down. If you want to stop the paraglider (it's called a landing!), you pull both sides all the way down.

You also use the brake lines to control the direction of a paraglider. If you want to go right, you pull the right side brake lines down part-way. The right side of the paraglider slows down while the left side keeps flying at the same speed and—voila!—you have a right turn. Pulling the left side lines part way down gives you a left turn.

The truth is: Paragliders are ridiculously simple to control. Because paragliders fly so slowly, and because you can maneuver them so precisely, you can easily land on a dime in a paraglider—and get nine cents change.

"Paragliders are soft bags of dacron or nylon cloth, for cryin' out loud! If they collapse in mid-air, I'm a dead duck, right?"

At the introductory level, this is not an issue. That's assuming, of course, that you've placed yourself in the hands of a qualified instructor. No responsible instructor will permit you to fly at a bunny slope in wind conditions that could cause a partial or complete collapse of your paraglider—or in wind conditions that could yank you higher in the air than you'd care to fall.

Paragliders are ridiculously simple to control. Because paragliders fly so slowly, and because you can maneuver them so precisely, you can easily land on a dime in a paraglider—and get nine cents change.

At high altitude, a canopy collapse does indeed spell trouble. Any combination of turbulent weather conditions and pilot ignorance/stupidity can cause a canopy collapse to occur. That's why all paraglider pilots who fly at altitude carry a back-up parachute with them. It gives them a second chance in case they mess up.

The truth is: Paragliders are indeed more subject to weather-induced or pilot-induced collapse than hang gliders, sailplanes or airplanes. Even moderately turbulent weather conditions that a modern hang glider can handle without any problems can deflate a paraglider either in part or in whole, either for a split second or for far too long. A paraglider is, after all, a cleverly designed bag of cloth with strings attached. It has no more shape than a wadded up dish towel—until it is filled with air.

Don't tackle soaring conditions until someone who knows something agrees with your assessment that you're ready to progress.

The bottom line is that you—as an entry level paraglider person who has just decided to take up paragliding as a hobby following a particularly inspirational day of training at a bunny slope—should stick to calm or very mild conditions. Don't tackle soaring conditions until someone who knows something agrees with your assessment that you're ready to progress.

TRUE CHILLS (And how to avoid them)

A paraglider is an aircraft. The only way you can come to harm in a paraglider—or any other aircraft—is via fast, hard contact with the ground. Sound familiar? Yes, it's exactly what I said about hang gliding. The same applies here.

Paragliders haven't been around long enough for paraglider pilots to come up with a fancy term for a fatal accident. If they had any imagination, however, they would probably call it "pounding in."

At the introductory level, there are only three things that can cause you to "pound in" in a paraglider:

- Poor instruction.
- Poor equipment.
- Poor judgement (includes carelessness).

As is the case with hang gliding, poor judgement leads directly to poor instruction on poor equipment—which greatly increases your chances of getting killed. It is your responsibility to select an introductory experience that provides state-of-the-art instruction on state-of-the-art equipment.

The evidence indicates that the people who are most likely to die while paragliding are the ones who, for one reason or the other, are fooled by the apparent simplicity of the sport—the ones that assume they are capable of flying conditions, places or equipment that they simply aren't ready for.

The evidence indicates that the people who are most likely to die while paragliding are the ones who, for one reason or the other, are fooled by the apparent simplicity of the sport.

One expert hang glider pilot in the Bay Area had no trouble at all learning how to launch, soar and land a paraglider at Fort Funston. He knew the coastal cliff flying site like the back of his hand from hundreds of hours of hang gliding. He died after landing his paraglider on a ledge on the face of the cliff. He fell from his precarious perch and hit his head on a rock. Was he trying to take advantage of the fact that paragliders are so slow and maneuverable that they can be landed in places where hang gliders can't? Was he trying to save himself a long walk up from the beach below? No one knows for sure.

A beginning paraglider pilot in Washington state—one who had done thousands of skydiving jumps—apparently felt that his skydiving experience qualified him to teach himself how to fly a paraglider. Without professional supervision, he selected a paraglider that was more difficult to fly than the more stable and collapse-resistant Class I canopies recommended for beginners. After launching from an easy site in moderate conditions, he experienced a minor wing collapse on one side. This put him in a turn back toward the hill.

For a number of reasons, skydiving canopies don't have partial collapses nearly as often as

MODERN PARAGLIDING: TRUE FACTS

- *You will probably get a few feet off the ground during your first day of bunny slope training. But even if you don't, you'll have an enormous amount of fun learning how to inflate your canopy and control it properly while you moon-walk along flat ground.*

- *Your first day of paragliding is no more dangerous than taking a ride in a Cessna —if you're careful enough to pick a good school and a good instructor.*

- *You should never take a lesson from an instructor who is not APA/USHGA "certified" even if he claims to be "certifiable."*

paragliding canopies. Because this skydiver hadn't been taught how to handle a partial collapse in a paraglider, he didn't perform the relatively simple maneuver for re-inflating his wing. He never regained control and flew straight back, downwind, into the hill—and died.

Whether you're new to sport aviation or not, the best way to avoid a fatal accident in paragliding is to stay well aware of what you don't know—and don't ever be fooled by the ease and apparent simplicity of paragliding. It is a serious form of sport aviation and it can kill you in a hot second if you let it.

Instructor/School Considerations

In the world of paragliding, state-of-the-art instruction is cooperatively defined by The American Paragliding Association (APA) and The United States Hang Gliding Association (USHGA).

The USHGA's involvement in the domestic paragliding scene is a long story that boils down to this: Hang glider pilots and paraglider pilots, whether they admit it or not, are soul-mates. Both groups fly silent, foot-launchable soaring aircraft. Pilots from both groups get the same gleam in their eyes when they recount their aerial exploits.

On a more practical level, hang glider pilots and paraglider pilots must inevitably share the same precious flying sites. Both groups know that competitive squabbles over the use and regulation of flying sites only serve to attract negative attention from already nervous landowners and bureaucrats. That's why paragliding people and hang gliding people have embraced one another, albeit with varying degrees of enthusiasm.

Consequently the USHGA has agreed to adopt the APA's pilot proficiency rating system and instructor certification system. As a first-time paragliding student, you are considered a candidate for a Class I pilot rating. Make sure the person who is teaching you has the following minimum qualifications:

•An APA/USHGA Class I Pilot Rating. (Class II is a more advanced rating.)

•An APA/USHGA Instructor Rating.

If you select an instructor who hasn't bothered to earn these ratings, you're misplacing your trust.

Equipment Considerations

Once you have selected a certified instructor, you pretty much have to trust him or her to use properly designed equipment that is suitable for a totally inexperienced pilot such as yourself. Unfortunately, there is no domestic equivalent of the Hang Glider Manufacturer's Association (HGMA) in paragliding.

Three European certification standards exist, two of them through hang gliding associations

•Swiss Hang Gliding Federation (SHV)

•German Hang Gliding Federation (DHV)

•ACPULS: an association of European paraglider manufacturers, headquartered in France

The testing standards for all three organizations are continually evolving. Generally speaking, a manufacturer who wishes to certify a paraglider must subject it to a series of tests which prove that it meets specified minimum criteria for strength, flight stability and performance. The tests must also demonstrate that the canopy can recover from stalls and collapses

• Most modern paragliders are tested for strength, aerodynamic stability, and ability to resist spontaneous collapse due to turbulence. "Type I" certified canopies are the only kind suitable for beginners because they are more likely to recover from collapse without special action on the part of the pilot.

• With modern instruction you will learn how to start, stop and turn a paraglider before you even leave the ground.

• You—not the wind and not blind fate—control the speed and heading of a paraglider.

while in the hands of a pilot whose skill level it is designed for.

Paragliders that pass Level I certification requirements are the only ones suitable for beginner pilots. Generally speaking, a Level I canopy should not take any special skills to fly safely, and it should recover from a collapse without any special control input from the pilot. Also, a Level I canopy is more resistant to spontaneous collapse as a result of turbulence.

Paragliders that pass Level I certification requirements are the only ones suitable for beginner pilots.

If a certified instructor tells you that you're special—that he'd like to train you on his own personal (more advanced) Level II or Level III canopy—tell him to take a hike. Then find another certified instructor. Look for one who teaches on a suitable Level I paragliding canopy. Look for one who has personally flown that canopy, one who maintains and cares for that canopy as if it were a cherished child.

TRUE THRILLS

Here's how paragliding stacks up in relation to the reward variables we've discussed for thrill sports:

Speed

Paragliding is pokey compared to hang gliding but zippy compared to most hot air balloon rides. Paragliders cruise along in a very narrow speed range (15-25 mph compared to 20-50 mph for a hang glider). If you like the sound of trotting off a hill on takeoff, or floating silently across the ground at about 15 mph, you'll like paragliding.

Focus

Paragliding is definitely a present-focused

activity. But paragliding delivers a kinder, gentler here-and-now experience than, say, hang gliding. Whereas hang gliding rivets you in the present, paragliding simply requires your full attention.

Even if you're just two feet off the ground at a bunny slope, your brain will register "wild blue yonder" every time.

Your view of the world

Spatially speaking, paragliding is every bit as wide-open as hang gliding. You fly untethered, in total control. There is no cockpit around you. Even if you're just two feet off the ground at a bunny slope, your brain will register "wild blue yonder" every time.

How does it compare to REAL life?

The first time a paraglider pulls you (by your rear end) into mid-air, you'll think you've discovered the third dimension of space for the first time. And when you touch down following your first flight, the world around you will seem brighter and crisper than the one you left behind.

How does it feel?

When you touch down following your first flight, the world around you will seem brighter and crisper than the one you left behind.

Imagine sitting on a swing at a playground. Instead of swinging, you're just kind of rocking gently back and forth. Your toes barely touch the ground, and your hands loosely grip the chains that rise to the beam that supports your seat. Now imagine that, in the blink of an eye, you can magically transform the playground into an open vista of sky, the chains into gossamer "risers," and the supporting beam into a beautiful, billowing canopy. In another blink, you start floating towards the horizon and—suddenly, to your indescribable delight—you notice that your toes are no longer touching the ground.

RESOURCES FOR DOERS AND DREAMERS

If paragliding sounds intriguing to you, but you want to find out more about the sport before actually doing it, look to any of the following resources for information:

National Organizations

American Paragliding Association (APA): 25 Goller Place, Staten Island, New York 10314. (718) 698-5738. General information on ratings, service, certification, membership. Monthly publication devoted exclusively to paragliding.

United States Hang Gliding Association (USHGA): P.O. Box 8300, Colorado Springs, Colorado 80933. (719) 632-8300. General information on ratings, services, certification, membership. Monthly magazine mostly devoted to hang gliding with some paragliding coverage.

Books and Magazines

Paragliding: A Pilot's Training Manual, Mike Meier. ($19.95) This comprehensive, well-written volume is, without question, the best resource available for those who think they might want to take up paragliding. It covers everything from aerodynamics to equipment to weather to state-of-the-art instructional technique. The author, a leading figure in sport aviation for nearly two decades, periodically revises the book to keep it current. Available through Wills Wing, Inc. (714) 547-6366.

Flying Conditions, Dennis Pagen. ($7.50) The

only book available on wind and weather as it effects paraglider and hang glider pilots. Available through USHGA.

Paragliding Flight, Dennis Pagen. ($19.95) Well-illustrated. Covers a wide range of topics including instructional technique, history, basic aerodynamics and basic micrometerology.

The Parachute Manual, Volume II, Dan Poynter. ($49.95) Para Publishing, P.O. Box 4232, Santa Barbara, California 93140-4232. (805) 968-7277. Everything you've ever wanted to know about all kinds of parachutes.

Paragliding: The Magazine, the official voice of the American Paragliding Association. 3314 West 11400 South, South Jordan, Utah 84065. (801) 254-7455. Editor: Fred Stockwell. Published six times a year and loaded with great color pictures and articles of interest to pilots from beginner to advanced.

Observation Points

The following places offer the most consistent and spectacular observation points in the state of California. You can observe from either the point of take-off (launch site) or the landing area (landing zone or LZ).

Paraglider pilots usually land at the bottom of the hill or mountain they launch from. Consequently you will be very popular indeed if you volunteer to drive them and their backpackable paragliders to the top of the flying site. Your generous offer saves them the trouble of a car retrieval trip back up the hill at the end of a flying day. You'll be rewarded with the royal treatment and a bird's-eye view of your pilot's launch into the wild blue yonder.

Fort Funston (Bay Area): Excellent coastal cliff soaring. Training. From Highway 1 take Skyline Boulevard (Highway 35) North. Drive three miles, then U-turn at John Muir Drive. Entrance to Fort Funston is 1/4 mile back. Call Chandelle (415-539-6800) or Air Time of San Francisco (415-759-1177) for conditions report.

See #1 on map page 244.

Torrey Pines (San Diego): The only other great coastal cliff soaring site in the state. From Interstate 5 take Genesee Avenue West. Go straight past the light on top of the hill. The road becomes North Torrey Pines Road. Go right on Torrey Pines Scenic Drive. Store is a double-wide trailer with a windsock. Call Torrey Pines Flight Park (619-452-3202) for conditions report.

See #2 on map page 244.

Crestline (San Bernardino): Mountain soaring. Take Highway 18 out of San Bernardino to Crestline exit. Stop in downtown Crestline to ask directions to "Teddy Bear" launch site. Call High Adventure (714-883-8488) for conditions report.

See #3 on map page 244.

Kagel Mountain (Sylmar, L.A. area): Mountain soaring. Go to Sylmar Flight Park landing area. You need a four wheel drive vehicle to get to launch. From Interstate 405 go to Interstate 210 East. Exit on Hubbard Street North (left) to Simshaw right. To end of Simshaw, left on

Gridley to end of road. If you want to get to launch (and be a big hit too), volunteer to be a driver.

See #4 on map page 244.

Lake McClure (Coulterville, Modesto area): Hill soaring. Sensitive site, limited access. Call Ultraflight Hang Gliding Systems (209) 874-1795) for information and directions. Nearby "Bird Road" (I-5 and Highway I-32) and "Don Pedro" (off 132) are also good observation points, according to Ultraflight's Will Brown.

See #5 on map page 244.

Ed Levin Park (San Jose): Coastal mountain gliding and soaring. This state park is a great place to picnic and watch hang gliding. From Interstate 680 take Calaveras Boulevard/Highway 237 East to Downing Street. Go left into Ed Levin State Park. Call Mission Soaring (408-262-1055) for information.

See #6 on map page 244.

Dunlap (Outside Kings Canyon National Park): Foothill soaring. 40066 Millwood Road, Dunlap, California 93621. (209) 338-2422. Dunlap Valley Lakes R.V. Park is owned and operated by two hang glider pilots named Dave and Connie Bowen. Located just to the west of Kings Canyon Park, Dunlap is a great place to kick back in your camping rig and watch hang glider and paraglider pilots fly down from the mountains above. Open year-round. Facilities include store, showers, laundry, etc. Directions: From Fresno take Highway 180 East to the small town of Dunlap. Go right on Dunlap Road, then, a few miles later, left on Millwood Road.

See #7 on map page 244.

Elsinore (Lake Elsinore): Mountain soaring. From I-5 take Ortega Highway (74) to Lake Elsinore. Landing area is near intersection of Ortega Highway and Grand Street. Local Elsinore pilots (The E Team) are the zaniest group of fliers in the state.

See #8 on map page 244.

Big Sur (Plaskett Creek Campground): Coastal mountain gliding and soaring.

See #9 on map page 244.

Soboba: Look for the big "S" on the side of the mountain outside of the Southern California town of Hemet.

See #10 on map page 244.

RESOURCES FOR DOERS

Schools and Retail Outlets

The resources listed below are the cream-of-the-crop in their respective areas. Please note: You cannot rent paragliding equipment unless you are a trained pilot. All schools, however, provide equipment for lessons.

Although there are a number of club-level or independent certified instructors in California, the best instructors gravitate towards the established schools and dealers. Paragliding training —like whitewater kayak training—is very site specific. The best schools and dealers have the best training areas and their programs are specifically designed to use those training areas in the safest possible way.

Paragliding instruction is also a matter of skill and timing. That means you want to take instruction from an instructor who teaches regularly—one whose skill and timing are fine-tuned. You're far more likely to find that at an established school/dealership.

If you find an independent certified instructor who has access to a regular training site, and he or she teaches at least 10 students a year, you might have something. Ask to observe a lesson. If what you see matches the description of beginners' training that you read in this chapter, the instructor is probably a competent one.

The following resource guide includes only the schools, dealerships and instructors that meet these two criteria: 1) Access to a regular training site. 2) Instructors that either teach a minimum of 10 students a year or refer students to someone who does.

Southern California

Hang Glider Emporium: 613 North Milpas, Santa Barbara, California 93103. (805) 965-3733. Like everyone else in the U.S., Ken de Russy is relatively new to paragliding. But he's been one of the best hang gliding instructors in the state for 17 years, and paragliding is easier to teach than hang gliding. Also, "The Mesa" is the best training hill in the state. Full service retail store is run by Ken and his wife Bonnie Nelson. Lessons and sales. Take Highway 101 to Milpas Street. Drive six blocks towards the mountains. Store on the left.

See #11 on map page 244.

Hang Gliding Center: 4206 K Sorrento Valley Boulevard, San Diego, California 92121. (619) 450-9008. John and Aimee Ryan's full service retail store features a convenient training hill 20 minutes away. The place to go in San

Diego if you aspire to become a fully trained pilot. Lessons and sales. From Interstate 805 exit west on Sorrento Valley/Mira Mesa Boulevard. Right on Sorrento Valley Boulevard. Go about a half-mile to the last building in the industrial park.

See #2 on map page 244.

Hang Flight Systems, Santa Ana: 1202 M East Walnut, Santa Ana, California 92701. (714) 542-7444. Located next door to Wills Wing, one of the largest manufacturers of paragliding systems in the U.S., Dan Skadal and crew usually know about new equipment and techniques before anyone else. Full service retail. Lessons and sales. Take Interstate 5 to 1st Street (E). Left on Grand. Immediate right on Walnut. Left into parking area. Unit M is at end on right.

See #12 on map page 244.

High Adventure Hang Gliding: 4231 Sepulveda Street, San Bernardino, California 92404. (714) 883-8488. Rob and Diane McKenzie operate a full service retail store out of their living room and garage. Rob is one of the most accomplished tandem hang glider pilots in the nation. Look for him to pioneer tandem teaching techniques for paragliding as well. A unique specialty is teaching non-hearing students how to fly. Full service. Lessons and sales. From Interstate 215 North, take Highway 30 East. Exit North on Waterman Avenue . Go west on 40th Street, then right on Sepulveda. House/store is two blocks on right.

See #3 on map page 244.

Torrey Pines Flight Park: 2800 Torrey Pines Scenic Drive, LaJolla, California 91342. (619)

452-3202. The only place in Southern California for legal coastal ridge soaring. Also the only paragliding/hang gliding shop in the state with a restaurant on premises (The Cliff Hanger Cafe.) Lessons and sales. Excellent place to observe paragliding. Separate number (619) 457-9093 gives recorded wind velocity and direction. From Interstate 5 take Genesee Avenue West. Go straight at the light on top of the hill. Road becomes North Torrey Pines Road. Right on Torrey Pines Scenic Drive.

See #2 on map page 244.

L.A. Paragliding (Windsports International): 16145 Victory Boulevard, Van Nuys, California 91406. (213) 474-3502. Although paragliding is relatively new to this country, you can count on Joe Greblo and Ted Boyse to offer a comprehensive, "safety-first" paragliding program. They've got the 17-year legacy of Windsports International (see hang gliding) to live up to. From Interstate 405, exit west on Victory Boulevard. Go about 1/2 mile. Store is on right.

See #4 on map page 244.

Airjunkies: 151 Tamarack Avenue, Carlsbad, California 92008. (619) 720-9775. Ken Baier's one-man show is kind of like a mom and pop store—without mom and without the store. Bunny slope training is at the base of Little Black Mountain. Lessons and sales. Interstate 5 to Tamarack west. One mile down on south side.

See #13 on map page 244.

Sky Dance Paragliding Company of Southern California: Headquartered in Encinitas, California (800) 845-4337. Scott Griffith owns and operates this one-of-a-kind "on the move" paragliding school. Scott takes groups of customers on seven-day paragliding instructional safaris. You start with the basics at a small dune in San Diego and finish with a high altitude flight either at Big Sur or Soboba (near Hemet in Southern California.) Scott also offers private instruction in addition to the tour groups which have had as many as 30 people in them. Call for directions and information.

See #13 on map page 244.

Accelerated Flight: P.O. Box 1226, Del Mar, California 92014. (619) 481-7400. Fred Lawley is one of the most experienced paragliding instructors in the state. He got in early, when the sport first came over from Europe in the late 1980s. Lessons and sales. Call for directions.

See #13 on map page 244.

Aerial Action: 12701 Gridley Street, Sylmar, California 91342. (818) 367-7210. Bob England (an Englishman) has been paragliding for six years and has a 63-mile flight under his belt. He's run his school out of his home for three years. Believe it or not, that makes him the oldest paragliding school in the L.A. area. In addition to offering certified instruction, Bob is the national distributor for APCO paragliders, which are made in Israel. Call for directions.

See #4 on map page 244.

Airtek: 425 Bonair Street, Suite 4, La Jolla, California 92037. (619) 454-0598. Marcus Salvemini. In business for three years, Airtek is the oldest paragliding school in San Diego. Lessons and sales. Airtek also manufactures equipment. Call for directions.

See #13 on map page 244.

Compact Wings: 1271 Avenida Floribunda, San Jacinto, California 92583. (714) 654-8559. Cary Mendes is an accomplished aviator. He has instructor licenses for helicopters, airplanes and hang gliders. He bagged it all for his main love —paragliding. Lessons and sales. Annual tours to Switzerland. Call for directions.

See #14 on map page 244.

Northern California

Air Time of San Francisco: 3620 Wawona Street, San Francisco, California 94116. (415) 759-1177. Full service retail paragliding near Fort Funston, the premier coastal soaring site in Northern California. Specializes in bunny slope training. Training hill is just minutes from shop. From Highway 1, go west on Sloat Boulevard. Turn right on 47th Avenue; one block to Wawona.

See #1 on map page 244.

Chandelle Hang Gliding Center: 488 Manor Plaza, Pacifica, California 94044. (415) 359-6800. Chandelle has been serving the sport aviation community in the Bay Area since 1973. Full service paragliding. Main man Andy Whitehill specializes in private and semi-private instruction. Training hill is at base of Fort Funston cliff, just minutes from shop. Directions: From Highway 280 take Highway 1 South. First exit in Pacifica is Manor Drive. Store is in Manor Plaza at end of off-ramp.

See #1 on map page 244.

Mission Soaring: 1116 Wrigley Way, Milpitas, California 95035. (408) 262-1055. Pat Denevan and crew offer one of the best hang gliding training programs in the state. Their paragliding program, under development at this writing, promises to be just as good. From Interstate 680 take Calaveras Boulevard/Highway 237 West. Go left onto Hillview Street, then left onto Los Coches. Los Coches becomes Sinclair frontage road. Shop is on corner at Wrigley Way.

See #6 on map page 244.

Hang Gliding Hanger: 6785 North Wilmington, Fresno, California 93711. (209) 264-7627. Brothers Tim and Dan Fleming don't teach, but they'll be happy to tell you where to go for learning and observing. Call for information.

See #19 on map page 244.

Owens Valley Soaring: 5201 Westridge Road, Route 2, Bishop, California 93514. (619) 387-2673. The Owens Valley is a premier flying area for advanced pilots. Still, Kevin Klinefelter manages to introduce a few new people to the sport every year. Call for information.

See #15 on map page 244.

Bay Area Paragliding Club: P.O. Box 3012, Moss Beach, California 94038. (415) 728-0938. Jack Hodges and David Sondergeld are the driving forces behind the premier paragliding club in the state. Although BAPC offers no formal lesson program, they do maintain a current referral list to area schools and instructors. Services include a monthly newsletter (*Ridge Runner*) and club meetings on the first Wednesday of each month. Meetings include videos, updates on the club's current efforts to promote safe paragliding, and an opportunity to meet local pilots. Everyone is welcome and there is no pressure to "sign up." Write for directions to meeting and more information.

See #1 on map page 244.

A Place of Wings: 1484 Falcon Court, Sunnyvale, California 94087. (408) 736-1222. Owner Gregg Pujol has been teaching paragliding in the Bay Area since 1988. More than 10 years of hang gliding make him an experienced member of the sport aviation community. Gregg's program features full-day lessons (instead of the industry norm of 1/2 day) and a four to one (maximum) student to instructor ratio. He teaches at Marina Beach, Fort Funston or Concord, depending on the season. Call for more information and directions.

See #16 on map page 244.

Vertical World Systems: P.O. Box 1632, Bishop, California 93515. (619) 873-8367. Proprietor Mark Axen has been paragliding since 1986 and hang gliding since 1975. Axen teaches both paragliding and hang gliding, from beginning to advanced levels. Although he offers year-round instruction, training in the summer months is between dawn and 10 AM due to the strong wind and thermal conditions that develop after mid-morning. Sales, service and repairs. Shop located at Bishop Airport. Take Line Street east out of Bishop. Follow the signs to Bishop Airport.

See #15 on map page 244.

Pro Design: 1600 East Cypress Avenue #8, Redding, California. (916) 222-4606. John Yates distributes and services Pro Design paragliders and paragliding harnesses from Yates Mountaineering Shop in Redding. Although he does some basic instruction, his specialty is organizing paragliding excursions for trained pilots. From I-5 in Redding, go east on Cypress. Go about two miles to Yates Mountaineering, on the north side of Cypress.

See #17 on map page 244.

Ultimate High Paragliding: Redding, California. (916) 472-3058. John Yates and Yates Mountaineering refer most basic instruction to Patrick Blackburn. His specialty is training paraglider pilots from the ground up.

See #17 on map page 244.

Ed Pitman Paragliding School: P.O. Box 188, Shasta, California 96087. (800) 759-7468. Ed Pitman has been flying paragliders for five years and teaching for three. As an APA (American Paragliding Association) Examiner, he is qualified to train other instructors. Ed's site situation is unique. He has a commercial use license for Whiskeytown National Recreation Area—the only such license in the country. He is especially well set-up for advanced training because he can coach his students through advanced canopy collapse maneuvers over the friendly waters of Whiskeytown Reservoir and Lake Shasta. Instruction by appointment only . Call for information and directions.

See #17 on map page 244.

Adventure Sports: 3650 Research Way #25, Carson City, Nevada 89706. (702) 883-7070. Owners Ray Leonard and Jackie Danskin bought the hang gliding/paragliding portion of a 10-year-old business (High Sierra Sports) two years ago. Ray has been flying hang gliders for 17 years, paragliders for two. A full half of Ray and

Jackie's customers are from California, particularly the Bay Area, Sacramento and Tahoe. Full service shop: lessons, sales, service, repairs. Ray teaches/flies at any of 12 local sites, depending on conditions. Call for unique video site guide which might inspire you to travel to Nevada. From Route 395 in Carson City, take Hot Springs Road (one way) to Research Way (right).

See #18 on map page 244.

KAYAKING

Crescent City
Yreka
Newell
Mt. Shasta
Alturas
Eureka
Redding
Red Bluff
Susanville
Chico
Fort Bragg
Ukiah
Yuba City
Santa Rosa
Placerville
South lake Tahoe
Sacramento
San Francisco
Oakland
Stockton
Sonora
Lee Vining
Yosemite
San Jose
Merced
Santa Cruz
Bishop
Monterey
Salinas
Fresno
Lone Pine
Visilia
Kettleman City
Death Valley Jct.
San Luis Obispo
Bakersfield
Santa Maria
Wheeler Ridge
Mojave
Baker
Barstow
Santa Barbara
Ventura
Palmdale
Needles
Los Angeles
San Bernardino
Santa Ana
Palm Springs
Long Beach
Oceanside
Escondido
Blythe
San Diego
El Centro
Yuma
1
2
3
4
5
6
7
8
9
10
11
12
13
14
15
16
101
5
97
139
89
299
395
44
36
99
20
29
80
50
108
120
580
880
41
152
136
190
65
46
127
14
40
247
95
10
62
215
15
86
8

CHAPTER TEN

KAYAKING

IF WATER IS YOUR ELEMENT AND YOU WANT to merge with its flow, kayaks are the only way to go. Rafts are fun, but they merely bob along on top of the water like a cork. You're shoved through the rapids like so much driftwood. Only the brute force of your paddle or the thrashing of your swim fins gives you control.

Kayaks, on the other hand, merge you—hips to water—with just the right blend of buoyancy and balance. Your lower body is encased from the waist down in an elegant plastic shell. Flick your hips and dip your paddle, just so, and you'll dart precisely where you want to go.

You don't even have to like whitewater to enjoy kayaking. Sea kayaks have boomed in popularity along the California coast. Sea kayaks—longer and faster than their river-running counterparts—zip through calm water or ocean swells equally well. Because of their versatility, sea kayaks appeal to a wide range of water-loving adventurers. Snorkelers, bird watchers, campers, photographers, trekkers, fishermen, scuba divers, surfers and even marina-bound brunch-nuts all take advantage of the increased range of operations offered by sea kayaks.

Whether you do it on a river, ocean, lake or bay, kayaking is simply the most efficient, most personal form of boating known to man.

Whether you do it on a river, ocean, lake or bay, kayaking is simply the most efficient, most personal form of boating known to man. All river kayaks and most sea kayaks enclose your lower body in a sealed cockpit. They are directly descended from the watercraft used by ancient Aleuts and Greenlanders thousands of years ago.

Kayaking takes a little finesse, but not much strength. With some structured practice of basic strokes and easy-to-learn water rescue techniques, you can learn enough about whitewater kayaking in two days to get you safely down a solid Class II rapid under professional supervision. And just four hours of sea kayaking instruction is enough to get you out cruising, unsupervised, with friends on an inland bay.

The key, in both cases, is to get competent instruction from a qualified kayak instructor. A pro knows how to structure your experience for maximum fun and safety.

With some structured practice of basic strokes and easy-to-learn water rescue techniques, you can learn enough about whitewater kayaking in two days to get you safely down a solid Class II rapid under professional supervision. And just four hours of sea kayaking instruction is enough to get you out cruising, unsupervised, with friends on an inland bay.

BIG DADDY AND LITTLE MAMA REVISITED: Our Gang Conquers The Powerhouse Run

Sometimes it's easier, and it's always more fun, to seize command of your own destiny in the company of classmates whose ineptitude matches your own.

Especially when you squirm into a kayak for the first time and wonder how on earth you'll manage to keep the thing right side up, much less get it through a menacing gang of rapids on the afternoon of the following day. A little reassurance goes a long way in that situation, and the timid squirmings of *all* your classmates on the first day of kayak school is reassurance enough.

Tom Moore runs a kayak school out of Kernville. He had just informed the ten of us that our current inability to tell a bow from a stern meant nothing. In less than 36 hours, we would all be qualified novice kayakers, capable of navigating the infamous Powerhouse Run on the Upper Kern River. The Powerhouse Run is a solid Class II, partial Class III stretch of whitewater just North of Kernville. It has widened the eyes of many a neophyte kayaker—especially those who have already made the run on a raft and declared it "no big deal."

Our group included Doug, a middle-aged oil executive; Dave, a young petroleum engineer; a recently married young man named Paul; a couple from Balboa Island (Bob and Kathy) and their yappy little dog, Sara Lee; a daughter/father team named Jessica and Dennis; and two young lovers from L.A. named Todd and Rebecca.

Most of us had never set foot in a kayak before, and the rest of us had no more than a few hours of kayaking under our belts. Yet, here we all were on a hot Saturday morning, lured by the promise of an actual whitewater kayak run on Sunday afternoon. That was the goal Tom had sworn us to when we signed up for lessons, and that was the goal that his "Beginner Kayaking 101" course was designed to accomplish.

Most of us had never set foot in a kayak before, and the rest of us had no more than a few hours of kayaking under our belts. Yet, here we all were on a hot Saturday morning, lured by the promise of an actual whitewater kayak run on Sunday afternoon.

Tom and his assistant Kim started us off with a series of stretching exercises. Although control starts at the hips in a kayak, it's the arms and shoulders that sweep through the air to apply paddlestrokes. Cold, stiff muscles and joints are more vulnerable to pulls and strains, Tom told us, than warm, loose ones.

Finally, it was time to get into the kayaks. The first part of our lesson would take place in the calm waters near the river bank. First, we learned how to get into our kayaks without capsizing them. Next, we learned how to seal off the small cockpit opening with the neoprene skirts attached to our waists. Then, before we got down to strokes, it was time to learn the most basic and important kayaking skill of all.

"You have to know how to do a wet-exit," said Tom. "It's easy to get out of a kayak, even when you're upside down and under water. All you have to do is yank your spray skirt loose, then bend forward at the waist. Then, keeping your legs straight, grasp the sides of the open cockpit and push up and back with your arms. Gravity takes care of the rest."

Wet-exits are a piece of cake. But they are also a pain in the neck. An open, empty kayak immediately fills with river water, and you have to drag it (and yourself) over to the bank, empty it out, re-board the silly thing, and re-attach your spray skirt.

We had already practiced the skirt removal and exit push while sitting in the boats on dry land. It was surprisingly simple, really, and we all got the hang of it quickly. None of us knew it at the time, but we'd be practicing wet-exits all day long—whenever we abandoned smooth, precise control of our kayaks in favor of what Tom and Kim called "gorilla kayaking," or the equally popular "seize maneuver."

"Gorilla" kayakers use brute strength when timing and finesse would work better. "Seizers" do nothing at all when just one deft stroke could easily save the day. Both gorillas and seizers, whether they like it or not, spend much of the day practicing wet-exits.

Wet-exits are a piece of cake. But they are also a pain in the neck. An open, empty kayak immediately fills with river water, and you have to drag it (and yourself) over to the bank, empty it out, re-board the silly thing, and re-attach your spray skirt. The hard part is paddling back to your smirking classmates.

Once Tom and Kim saw that we could all handle the wet-exit, they let us in on a little secret. "Now that you know you can do it," Tom said, "the good news is that you probably won't have to. Kim and I are going to show you the

Eskimo rescue."

Without warning Kim purposely capsized his kayak. Instead of immediately scrambling out of the cockpit, however, Kim hung upside down —underwater—and ran his hands back and forth over the exposed bottom of his boat. Tom paddled towards Kim until the bow of his kayak covered the area where Kim was waving his hands. Kim simply grabbed the bow and used it as leverage to flip himself right-side up. His spray skirt was still attached when he popped up. He was cooled off, smiling and ready to go.

"The secret is 'hang-time,'" Tom shouted to us. "Just relax, hold your breath and hang there. *Somebody* will save you!" Tom reminded us that, as normal human beings, we could probably hold our breath for 10 to 30 seconds as long as there was no panic in the equation. He also reminded us that as soon as we got tired of waiting for help, we could launch into a wet-exit.

Since we all agreed that a wet-exit was worth avoiding, we started an unofficial "hang-time" contest that would last the rest of the weekend.

We spent the rest of the day Saturday—between wet-exits and Eskimo rescues—learning basic strokes, how to "ferry" across moving water while facing upstream, how to do "S-turns" downstream, and how to put it all together in "eddy" turns which would allow us to get out of the meat of a rapid and over to the calm waters next to the river bank.

Rebecca, Bob, Dennis and Jessica did the best job of blending power and finesse while the rest of us gravitated towards either gorilla or seize tactics.

Sunday morning we did more of the same. Practice, practice, practice. A night of sleep and cogitation had done wonders for us. We weren't perfect by any means, but we were more relaxed and better able to enjoy each others' company. Collectively, however, we shook in our neoprene booties in anticipation of our upcoming encounter with a rapid called "Big Daddy" near the top of the Powerhouse Run.

Just before we left our practice site, we practiced "Eskimo rolls." Mastery of this classic kayaking maneuver allows you to paddle and twist your way back to right-side-up from an upside-down position. Experienced kayakers make it look incredibly easy, capsizing on purpose, then popping back up immediately and effortlessly.

Of course, there was no way any of us were going to master the Eskimo roll. That would require several days of practice. But for the purposes of our graduation run, we didn't really need the roll. All of us except Kathy and Doug were comfortable with wet-exits. Tom and Kim would be standing by ready to provide their friendly bows for Eskimo rescues whenever we went over.

Before we knew it, we were at put-in—the place above town where we would get in our kayaks and head downstream for "Big Daddy." There were several more rapids as well—just waiting out there for a chance to "slime" or "hammer" each and every one of us.

Doug and Kathy elected to take the inflatable kayaks that Tom and Kim keep on hand for people who aren't completely comfortable with their kayaking skills. It's almost impossible to capsize an inflatable kayak and they provide a fun ride that blends many of the best parts of kayaking and rafting. Dave and Paul weren't nuts about tackling the hairier rapids after just a day and a half of training, but they made it just fine by going directly behind Tom and Kim. They simply duplicated their instructor's path through the rapids.

Rebecca, at 105 pounds sopping wet, turned out to be the best kayaker among us. She was the only one of us that had a clean run with no capsizes. She was proof positive that kayaking requires substantially more grace than power. Even her boyfriend Todd—a middle-of-the-pack putz along with the rest of us—had to admit that Rebecca was our ace.

As for me, Tom and Kim said I was the best gorilla kayaker they had seen in months: I won the coveted hang-time award without so much as breaking a sweat. Kim was laughing when he shook my hand afterwards. He said he was pretty sure I had set an unofficial Kern River record for "upside-down kayaking," Powerhouse-style.

Flow Considerations

Nothing is more critical to safe, fun whitewater kayaking than knowing how much water is flowing down the river, month to month, day to day, hour to hour, instant to instant. The same stretch of the same river can provide a totally enjoyable beginner's run at one volume of flow, and turn into either a crashing bore or total death at another.

Nothing is more critical to safe, fun whitewater kayaking than knowing how much water is flowing down the river, month to month, day to day, hour to hour, instant to instant.

Flow comes from one of three main sources: water run-off from rains, run-off from melting snow-packs high in the mountains above the river, or specifically timed releases of water stored behind upstream dams. That's why flow changes from year to year, season to season, day to day, even instant to instant.

The amount and kind of whitewater you will encounter on a kayak run are determined by flow, overall steepness of the river bed, the shape of the river bed (at all points along the stretch that's being run), and the nature of the obstacles in the river bed at all points along the run. River people have developed a rating system which helps them—and you—determine if a river is likely to give you a safe, fun ride that is appropriate for your level of experience.

Here's the internationally accepted whitewater rating system:

Class I Whitewater: Moving water with small waves. Few or no obstructions.

Class II Whitewater: Easy rapids with waves. Wide, clear channels that are obvious without scouting from shore prior to running the rapid. Some maneuvering required.

Class III Whitewater: Rapids with high, irregular waves that are capable of capsizing a boat. Narrow channels that may require complex maneuvering and/or scouting from the shore.

Class IV Whitewater: Long, difficult rapids with constricted passages that often require precise maneuvering through very turbulent water. Scouting from shore often necessary. Conditions may make rescue difficult.

Class V Whitewater: Extremely difficult, long and very violent rapids with highly congested routes that nearly always must be scouted from shore. Rescue conditions are difficult, and mishaps can mean a significant hazard to life.

Class VI Whitewater: Many consider Class VI whitewater unrunnable. Even the proverbial experts admit that they are at significant risk when they tackle this stuff.

Generally speaking, graduates of competent whitewater kayaking schools are capable of safely running stretches of river that include Class II and Class III whitewater.

FIRST LESSON
(Cost: $65-$100 per day)

At the very least, learn the basics of kayaking from a professional instructor. Kayaking skills and attitudes must be built from a solid base, block by block, in a sequence that is appropriate to the river or body of water where the lesson is taught.

For example, **Sierra South**—the outfitter who provided the group lesson described above—tailors their program to the structure and spacing of the rapids, plus the normal seasonal flows on the Kern River. Another river would require a different program.

Sea kayak instructors, on the other hand, usually teach basic lessons on flat, calm water. A standard four- or five-hour calm water lesson is enough to get you ready for unsupervised calm-water paddling with friends.

River kayaks and most sea kayaks have this much in common: They are both enclosed cockpit vessels. Wet-exit techniques and water rescue techniques are critical to your safety in all forms of enclosed-cockpit kayaking.

River kayaks and most sea kayaks have this much in common: They are both enclosed cockpit vessels. Wet-exit techniques and water rescue techniques are critical to your safety in all forms of enclosed-cockpit kayaking.

Also, basic paddling skills, although simple, require some coordination between hips and upper body. It's the kind of coordination that is best acquired through structured, professionally supervised practice.

Keeping in mind that each training program will be a little different, here's what you should expect from an introductory kayaking lesson.

Sea kayaking on calm water

Typically requires one-half day on flat water in groups of two to ten, with a student/instructor ratio of no greater than six to one. Student to instructor ratios are particularly important in kayaking—especially if your whole group is in the water at the same time. Safety, not personalized instruction, is the most important issue here. If there is only one instructor for 10 students, you definitely don't want to be the third or fourth one yelling for help at any given time.

Student to instructor ratios are particularly important in kayaking—especially if your whole group is in the water at the same time. Safety, not personalized instruction, is the most important issue here.

The pre-lesson "ground school" will familiarize you with the equipment being used, the goals of your lesson and the steps you will be taking to achieve those goals. Emphasis will be on safety in the water and control of the kayak. After adjusting all equipment to fit your body, expect to practice boat entry and wet-exit on dry land.

The initial part of your time on the water is spent practicing basic paddlestrokes for forward and rearward propulsion, turning strokes, and the bracing strokes that help you stay right-side up. You also will learn how important side-to-side hip movements are to kayak control and how to coordinate those movements with paddlestrokes to maximum effect.

After you get a feel for basic controls, you will practice wet-exits and at least two different kinds of "sea rescue." The former teaches you how to get out of your kayak when it capsizes. The latter shows how you and one or two others can drain your capsized boat, then stabilize it so that you can climb back inside. Sea kayakers don't have the luxury of flopping over to a river bank to get themselves back together.

"Whitewater" kayaking on calm water

Most people start their whitewater kayaking careers by practicing basic paddle skills and the Eskimo roll at a pool. If you have your strokes down and the roll mastered before signing up for a bona-fide whitewater course, you'll be ahead of the game in both skill and confidence. Some schools and some branches of The Sierra Club offer Eskimo roll classes at a number of pools throughout the state. (See resource guide at the end of this chapter.)

Sea kayaking in the ocean

Typically requires one day of instruction in groups of two to ten, with a student/instructor ratio of no more than six to one. Before you tackle ocean kayaking, you should have a four-hour basic calm water lesson under your belt.

You can expect to review all the ground covered in a basic lesson before you're ready to take on the following: theory and technique of entering and exiting the ocean through surf; reading ocean conditions—tides, currents, waves, rocks and surf; paddling techniques in wind and waves; deep water solo rescues; trip planning; charts, tide tables, navigation, equipment checklists and first aid.

Forget length of class and cost variables when picking a whitewater kayaking school. What you really want to know is: How exactly do these people propose to transform you from a total neophyte into a kayaker who is capable of running the pre-specified stretch of whitewater?

Whitewater kayaking lessons

Whitewater kayaking lessons, as you already have heard, must be specifically tailored to the river in which they are taught. Cost, both in terms of time and money, will vary widely. The goal, however, is always to get you to a point where you can run a pre-defined stretch of mild-to-moderate whitewater safely—with a smile on your face.

Forget length of class and cost variables when picking a whitewater kayaking school. What you really want to know is: How *exactly* do these people propose to transform you from a total neophyte into a kayaker who is capable of running the pre-specified stretch of whitewater?

You can count on going through most of the following steps in a beginning whitewater kayak course:

• Course preview, including statement of goal and specification of steps you will take to achieve it; safety talk; equipment familiarization, fitting and adjustment.

• Stretching exercises on river bank at calm-water practice site.

• River bank practice of boat entry and wet-exit technique.

• Practice of basic strokes, body lean and bracing strokes in calm water

• Practice of wet-exits in calm water.

• Practice of wet and dry rescue techniques in calm water.

• Practice of upstream paddling, cross-stream ferrying, bracing in moving water, and turning into and out of eddies.

• Learning to "read water" and understand river currents.

• Introduction to Eskimo roll techniques.

• Graduation run along pre-specified stretch of Class I, II or III whitewater.

Whitewater tandem kayak rides

Tandem rides in "two-holer" kayaks are now available on the Powerhouse Run of the Upper Kern River. You'll be able to sit in the front cockpit and enjoy the view and sensation of kayaking while your guide in the rear cockpit does all the work. Call Tom Moore at **Sierra South** and ask about getting a ride with him or one of his guides on his new "Tupolino Duo." No experience necessary.

MYTHS

Kayaking does indeed require some skill. It also compels you to respect the power and beauty of water. But the idea that kayaking is hard and dangerous is a major myth. **The truth is:** It's easy to learn safe novice-level kayaking attitudes and skills. And flopping out of an upside-down kayak is almost as easy as falling out of bed.

"I heard kayaks go upside-down in a heart-beat!"

Kayaks don't go upside down on their own. It's the human inside a kayak that *controls* it into an upside-down position in a heartbeat. But the same human also can apply simple controls to keep it right-side-up. All schools teach you a combination of hip movements and "bracing" paddlestrokes which allow even novice kayakers to recover completely from near-capsize positions. **The truth is:** The Eskimo roll is proof positive that kayaks can be flicked and stroked to an upright position at will.

Kayaks don't go upside down on their own. It's the human inside a kayak that controls it into an upside-down position

MODERN KAYAKING: TRUE FACTS

•Kayaking is like merging your hips to the surface of the water. It's the most personal, most efficient form of boating known to man.

•Basic sea kayaking skills, including "wet-exits" and sea rescue techniques, can be learned in one 4-hour session. After that you'll be able to paddle, unsupervised, with friends, on calm water.

•Basic river kayaking lessons must be specifically tailored to the stretch of river that will be run on "graduation day." Consequently they vary widely in cost and length of time.

"Yeah, but if I do get upside-down in a kayak in cold, hard water, I know I'll be scared. Isn't fear and a sealed cockpit a deadly combination?"

It's not really deadly, but it sure isn't much fun. That's why kayak school is recommended for beginners. Kayak instructors know how to help you gradually deal with and control your natural fear of being upside-down underwater. Once you realize that there isn't much to fear, your mind is free to tell your body to perform the few simple steps it takes to remove yourself, quickly and cleanly, from the cockpit.

The truth is: Gravity and your own survival instincts will get you out of a kayak cockpit even if you're scared out of your gourd. Your exit will be easier and much more fun, however, if you just "chill out."

"Yeah, but if I hit my head on a rock while I'm underwater, I'm dead, right?"

It's true you could hit your head on a rock in whitewater. But if you're wearing a helmet and a life-jacket, there really isn't much to worry about—especially in Class II or III whitewater, and especially if you're under the supervision of an instructor.

"Kayaking is a lonely, solitary, 'man vs. nature' form of boating."

While you and your kayaking group certainly aren't "in the same boat," kayaking is very much a group experience. This is especially true at beginning levels where a team of students learn together under the supervision one or more instructors. **The truth is:** Kayaking is a great example of the maxim, "There is safety in numbers." Even expert kayakers stay in groups of two or more.

"If I want to try kayaking, I have to be mentally and physically 'tough' enough to learn complex skills that require great strength. Otherwise I'll crumble under the pressure."

Wrong. All you need to learn basic kayaking skills is enough desire to carry you through a few awkward moments during the first few hours of your first lesson. After that, you'll quickly see that the skills required aren't that complex, even though mastering them takes practice. You'll also find that finesse is far more valuable than power, and that worst-case scenarios such as capsizing or looking foolish in front of others are really quite manageable.

The truth is: You don't have to be particularly brave, strong, fit, or good under pressure to learn basic kayaking skills. Just bring the same level of concentration and focus that you would bring to any exciting new challenge in your life and you'll be fine.

"Kayaking, like whitewater rafting, is purely seasonal. You can only kayak in the spring and summer because that's when the rivers get water from melting snow in the Sierra Nevada Mountains."

Say this to a sea kayaker and he or she will look you in the eye and say: "Snow-melt? Run-off? We don't need no stinkin' snow-melt run-off!"

The truth is: You can sea kayak all year round in California. The ocean, bays, marinas and some lakes all offer year-round sea kayaking.

•While kayaking isn't complex or physically difficult, it does require certain skills and attitudes if it is to be done safely. These are best learned from a qualified whitewater kayak school.

•Closed cockpit kayaks are direct descendants of the boats used by ancient Aleut Indians and Greenlanders 6,000 years ago.

•There are two main kinds of closed cockpit kayaks: Whitewater kayaks are short and easy to turn. Sea kayaks are longer and travel faster in a straighter line.

•Kayaking requires more finesse than power. You don't have to be especially brave, skillful, or fit to learn basic kayaking skills and attitudes.

You just have to do a better job of guarding against hypothermia in the winter months.

Whitewater kayaking, of course, is generally limited to spring, summer and early fall, although some California rivers do offer year-round whitewater to those who are willing to take greater precautions against hypothermia.

TRUE CHILLS
(And how to avoid them)

The most common term for a fatal accident in kayaking is "hypothermia."

The most common injuries are arm and shoulder dislocations, or tendonitis as a result of poor paddling technique.

Hypothermia

If you get too cold, you die. It's that simple. The good news is that you don't have to get too cold. As one river expert puts it: "Hypothermia is the killer of the unprepared."

Any competent kayaking instructor will give you the following list of suggestions on how to avoid hypothermia on your river trip:

Hypothermia Busters

1) Always wear your life-jacket. It protects you from heat loss at your core.

2) Don't wear cotton clothes. Wet cotton makes you colder.

If you get too cold, you die. It's that simple. The good news is that you don't have to get too cold.

3) Wear wool clothes or, better yet, clothes made with synthetic materials like Polypropelyne that are specifically designed to protect against heat loss when wet.

4) Wear a wetsuit or a drysuit when appropriate. Ask your guide if he thinks one is appropriate.

5) Wear shoes or, if it's colder, neoprene

booties. You can lose a lot of heat from your feet.

6) Wear a helmet. A helmet, like a life-jacket, does double duty. Besides protecting you from a whack on the head by a rock or paddle, it also prevents heat loss from your head.

Also, keep the following facts in mind: The danger of hypothermia increases at high water levels; during spring snowmelt; when the water is cold; at high elevations; and in the rainy season when the days are short and air temperatures are as low as water temperatures.

A good rule of thumb is: When the air and water temperatures *combined* are less than 120 degrees Fahrenheit, the chances of hypothermia are much greater.

Arm, Shoulder, Wrist Injuries

A kayak paddle is a lever that pries against the water. If you fail to follow the few simple rules of leverage, you can suffer dislocations to the arms and shoulders, muscle strains and tears, and tendonitis in your shoulder, elbow and wrist joints.

For instance, if your arm is in a position above and behind your head, and any significant force —like a big hunk of whitewater—is applied to the blade of your paddle, you're looking at a dislocated shoulder.

Don't think you're immune to injury while stroking along on flat water. Sea kayakers are especially vulnerable to over-use injuries such as tendonitis if they fail to position their hands and wrists properly when grasping the paddle.

Pay close attention to your instructors when they warn you about the dangers of poor paddling technique.

Don't think you're immune to injury while stroking along on flat water. Sea kayakers are especially vulnerable to over-use injuries such as tendonitis if they fail to position their hands and wrists properly when grasping the paddle.

Instructor/Guide Considerations

A qualified professional instructor or guide will give you the best possible first kayaking experience. If you go kayaking under the supervision of a beer buddy, or a relative who has had one kayaking lesson, you are creating your own risk.

The American Canoe Association (A.C.A.) has the only widely recognized training standard for whitewater kayak instructors. Look for an instructor who is trained to A.C.A. standards. An A.C.A sea kayak instructor rating exists, but it is not yet widely recognized.

Here are some questions you can ask of your prospective kayaking school or guide:

How long has the school been in existence?

How many years of paddling does the instructor have under his or her belt. Two years is adequate, more is better. Less warrants further investigation.

Does the training program have depth and breadth?

There should be no program gaps which force you to take a lesson that is too challenging or not challenging enough. Remember FUN is one of your goals, too.

Is the training program coordinated with the body of water on which it is taught?

Ask about specific goals and the steps you will take to reach them.

Is the school insured?

Insurance is available. Be skeptical of a program that hasn't purchased liability insurance.

Are all instructors current in first aid, advanced first aid and C.P.R. training?

Yes is the only acceptable answer. Advanced life-saving credentials are another good sign.

Is the school/instructor active in local clubs/trade associations?

You're looking for someone who is committed to kayaking as a lifestyle as well as a business.

Beyond that, it's always a good idea to talk to your kayak instructor, either on the phone or in person. What you really want to know is: "Do I like this person? Is this someone I can have a little fun with out on the water—while he or she is teaching me how to kayak?"

Equipment Considerations

As a beginner, the best way to assure that you'll have good kayaking equipment is to select a qualified professional kayak school to give you your first kayaking experience.

That's because there are no regulations regarding the design, manufacture, distribution and sale of kayaking equipment. You, as a consumer, have no reliable means to distinguish bad equipment from good—unless you place yourself under the guidance of a licensed, insured kayaking school.

You, as a consumer, have no reliable means to distinguish bad equipment from good—unless you place yourself under the guidance of a licensed, insured kayaking school.

Licensing and insurance tend to go hand in hand with good equipment.

Sea kayaking is a little bit different. Some operators are subject to licensing standards of the agency that has jurisdiction over the body of water they use, but others—especially those that operate in the ocean—aren't. The following are questions you can ask about the equipment you'll be using to learn how to kayak:

Do you have standard safety equipment available during all classes and trips?

Instructors should have, at a minimum, a first aid kit and evidence of current first aid training. Life-jackets are a must.

May I take a look at the fleet of boats?

They should look well-maintained and free of any evidence of shoddy repair practices. Duct tape patches are a bad sign. All cables and rudders (sea kayaks only) should work properly and be in good shape. Is there adequate flotation —sealed bulkheads fore and aft, or air bags—in the boats themselves?

Do you have emergency equipment such as spare paddles, bail buckets or pumps, and flares? Is there a wide enough variety of boats, helmets, life-jackets, etc. to meet the fit and performance needs of everyone in class?

Answers must be yes.

Other Safety Considerations

1) Wear shoes.
2) Protect yourself from sunburn.
3) Stay away from poison oak.
4) Secure your glasses—and anything else you don't want to lose—with a safety strap.

TRUE THRILLS

Here's how introductory kayaking stacks up in relation to the reward variables I've outlined for thrill sports. Because whitewater kayaking and sea kayaking offer such different experiences, both will be described.

Whitewater Kayaking

Speed

Whitewater kayaking, like whitewater rafting, is an infinitely variable speed sandwich. Each time you get on the river, you know only one thing for sure: You're in for several bursts of rapid action, each sandwiched between a couple of bobbing or cruising floats.

Focus

Again, infinitely variable, depending on the river and the flow. Rest assured you'll tend to focus on the here-and-now the first time you navigate your own boat through the hard part of a Class II or III rapid. Afterwards, when your instructor herds you and the rest of your class members over to an eddy pool so you can plan your route through the next rapid, don't be surprised if you find yourself earnestly searching the immediate past: "Just what exactly did I do right on that last one?" you'll say to yourself. "And what makes me think I can do it again?!" Finally, the lazy float down to take-out after the last rapid is a good time to envision the perfectly clean run that hides somewhere in your future.

Rest assured you'll tend to focus on the here-and-now the first time you navigate your own boat through the hard part of a Class II or III rapid.

Your view of the world

It's hard to describe a whitewater kayak run as anything but the ultimate definition of narrow and channeled. Still, there are significant variations within the channel. The river widens and narrows and gets steeper or flatter. Narrow and steep means more action. Wide and flat opens things up but tames the action.

Because a kayak feels like an extension of your body, a successful kayak run feels like you've merged—briefly but completely—with a different world.

How does it compare to REAL life?

You don't ride rapids in a river kayak. You flow with the whitewater. Because a kayak feels like an extension of your body, a successful kayak run feels like you've merged—briefly but completely—with a different world. If you run the same stretch of river in a raft you'll have fun, but it will feel more like you're just passing through.

How does it feel?

The first time you see an upcoming rapid from a kayak, you'll notice a strange puckering sensation at one spot along the bottom of your boat. That's when you widen your eyes real big in hopes of balancing out the whole system. A few quick digs of your paddle later, you're either laughing at the sky or thrashing blindly in the throes of a mid-rapid wet-exit.

SEA KAYAKING

Even in ocean swells or in the mild chop of a windy bay, sea kayaking has a deliberate beat, a steady gliding rhythm that can't be found in any other form of boating.

Speed

Sea kayakers rave about the mellow, utterly personal pace of their sport. Even in ocean swells or in the mild chop of a windy bay, sea kayaking has a deliberate beat, a steady gliding rhythm that can't be found in any other form of boating.

Focus

Contrary to popular belief, sea kayaking can rivet you in the present. Coastal cave or rock garden touring, for example, delivers sights and sounds that absolutely flood the moment. And it's the kind of here-and-now experience that isn't totally dominated by a requirement for decisive action. With no looming rapid to deal with, you are free to sop up the beauty of your surroundings.

But it's the other end of the time spectrum that truly distinguishes sea kayaking from any other adventure sport. With nothing but an endless expanse of ocean as far as the eye can see, you can drift six thousand years into the past in a heartbeat. Use the time to commune with the ancients who invented kayaks or contemplate your own navel. It doesn't matter. Time expands in all directions for sea kayakers.

With nothing but an endless expanse of ocean as far as the eye can see, you can drift six thousand years into the past in a heartbeat. Use the time to commune with the ancients who invented kayaks or contemplate your own navel.

Your view of the world

It's hard to beat sea kayaking for "horizon awareness." From your position in the middle of an ocean or bay, the rigid clutter and crowding of shore life magically disappears. It is replaced by 360 degrees of wide-open, natural, fluid beauty.

How does it compare to REAL life?

You definitely visit other worlds in a sea kayak, but it's more a function of time travel than bold new dimensions of space.

How does it feel?

Sea kayaking is one of the few adventure sports that can deliver a bona fide cardio-respiratory pump. Cruising along in an open expanse of water is great for working up a sweaty, sustained huff. The rotation of your arms and shoulders and the steady cadence of your own breathing is a physical delight.

RESOURCES FOR DOERS AND DREAMERS

If you're intrigued by river kayaking or sea kayaking, and want to find out more about it before actually doing it, consider any of the following resources.

Organizations

American Rivers, Inc.: 801 Pennsylvania Avenue S.E., Suite 203, Washington, D.C. 20003. (202) 547-6900. This is a national river conservation organization.

Friends of the River (F.O.R.): Fort Mason Center, Building C, San Francisco, California 94123. (415) 771-0440. This is a California river conservation group. Regular publication, *Headwaters,* includes some articles with a recreational focus.

California Kayak Friends (CKF): 14252 Culver Drive, Suite A-199, Irvine, California 92714. One of two large sea kayaking clubs in the state. Several hundred members in service area: Morro Bay to San Diego. Write for information.

Bay Area Sea Kayakers (BASK): 229 Courtwright Road, San Rafael, California 94901. The other big club. Several hundred members in the San Francisco Bay Area.

Trade Association of Sea Kayakers (TASK): P.O. Box 84144, Seattle, Washington. These folks have developed a series of two-page safety guidelines for their members: "Suggested Guidelines for Rental Operations," "A Guide to

Safe Paddling," and "Suggested Guidelines for Lessons." They'll help you separate the wheat from the chaff in the world of sea kayaking schools and outfitters.

Sierra Club: 730 Polk Street, San Francisco, California 94109. (415) 776-2211. Local chapters organize kayak pool sessions and river outings.

American Canoe Association: P.O. Box 1190, Newington, Virginia 22122. (703) 550-7523. Kayak instructor certification, regular publication: *American Whitewater Journal.* Articles of interest to all paddle sports enthusiasts.

Books and Magazines

California Whitewater, Jim Cassady and Fryar Calhoun. ($19.95.) Revised 1990. North Fork Press, Berkeley, California. This is the definitive text on California whitewater. Detailed maps, critical flow and gradient information, plus rapid by rapid descriptions of every runnable stretch of whitewater in the state.

The Basic Essentials of Kayaking Whitewater, Bill Kallner and Donna Jackson. ($4.95) 1990. ICS Books, Inc. This little book presents all the basics in a friendly style. Be sure to read the last page first in this one. That's where it tells you to learn kayaking from a professional instructor.

A Guide To The Best Whitewater in The State of California, Lars Holbeck and Chuck Stanley. Revised 1988. Friends of the River Books. Great kayaking stories from some of the most aggressive kayakers in the state. Geared to experts.

The Whitewater River Book, Ron Watters. 1984. Pacific Search Press. A well-illustrated guide to whitewater techniques, equipment, camping and safety. Rafts and kayaks.

California Coastal Access Guide, University of California Press. A must for ocean sea kayakers. This mile-by-mile guide to the California coastline is loaded with all kinds of information critical to safe, enjoyable ocean touring: beach access points, legality of camping, historical, cultural, and wildlife information.

Recreation Lakes of California, D.J. Dirksen and R.A. Reeves. Recreational Sales Publishing, Inc. Burbank, California. (818) 843-3616. For those who want to know the wheres and hows of sea kayaking on California's lakes.

The Basic Essentials of Sea Kayaking, Mike Wyatt. ($4.95) 1990 ICS Books, Inc. Basic information in a short, sweet style. Read page 10 first, under "When to buy." It's the only place in the book that mentions the need for professional instruction when you're just starting out.

Sea Kayaking, Derek Hutchinson. Includes information of interest to intermediate and advanced sea kayakers. Excellent line-drawing illustrations.

Seekers of The Horizon: Sea Kayaking Voyages from Around The World, Will Nordby. Globe Pequot Press, Chester, Connecticut.

Headwaters: The Newsletter of The Friends of the River, Fort Mason Center, Building C, San Francisco, California 94123.

Paddler Magazine: P.O. Box 697, Fallbrook, California 92028.

Paddler's News Bulletin: Sierra Club River Touring Section, 6014 College Avenue, Oakland, California 94618.

Currents: Newsletter of the National Organization of River Sports, P.O. Box 6847, Colorado Springs, Colorado 80904.

Paddle Sports Magazine: 1509 Seabright Avenue Suite B-1, Santa Cruz, California 95062. (408) 459-0425. New publication covers both whitewater and sea kayaking. Articles of interest to all paddle sports enthusiasts, beginner to advanced.

Sea Kayaker Magazine: 6327 Seaview Avenue N.W., Seattle, Washington 98107. (206) 789-1326. The premier magazine for the sport—a serious sea kayaking journal.

Canoe Magazine: 10526 N.E. 68th, Suite 3, Kirkland, Washington 98033. (206) 827-6363. Largest, most well-established publication for canoe and kayak enthusiasts.

"Yak-ity-Yak: Kayaking the West" (video). Rivers and Mountains. (800) 234-5522. Kayak runs throughout the West. Some rare footage on the new sport of river body-boarding.

"Paucartambo: Inca River I and II" (video). Brighton Video, New York, N.Y. Exciting adventure with leading edge kayakers on a long, hard stretch of river in South America.

Whitewater Tales of Terror, William Nealy. Menasha Ridge Press. Hilarious cartoon exposure to river culture.

Kayak: An Animated Manual of Intermediate and Advanced Whitewater Technique, William Nealy. Menasha Ridge Press. This highly entertaining cartoon-illustrated book carries valuable information about whitewater hydraulics that any river person should know.

Kayaks To Hell, William Nealy. Menasha Ridge Press. More cartoon river culture. Nealy's bent humor dazzles river people everywhere.

Observation Points

There are three good ways to get in on the excitement of a whitewater kayaking trip without actually taking the trip yourself:

- Go to any "put-in" site—where kayakers enter the river—and check out the buzz of excitement and anticipation in the group.
- Go to a place where you can watch kayakers shoot rapids. You'll hear howls of anticipation before the rapid and hoots of victory afterwards.
- Go to any "take-out" site—where kayakers exit the river—and check out the excited, but tired, yammering that goes on while kayaks and other gear are packed up and carried to the shuttle vehicle.

Here are some of the most popular and easily accessible whitewater observation locations in the state. You can find them on the whitewater rafting map on page 106.

Sandy Flat put-in: (Lower Kern) May through September. See #1 on map page 106.

Chili Bar put-in: (South Fork American) April through September. See #5 on map page 106.

Ewings rapid: (Upper Kern): Class II-III, April through mid-July. See #2 on map page 106.

Limestone rapid: (Upper Kern): Class IV, April through mid-July. See #12 on map page 106.

Banzai rapid: (Kings): Class III+, May through July. See #3 on map page 106.

Troublemaker rapid: (South Fork American): Class III +, April through September. See #5 on map page 106.

Ned's Gulch rapid: (Merced) Class IV, April through early-July. See #4 on map page 106.

Freight Train rapid: (Salmon) Class V, April through early-July. See #13 on map page 106.

Democrat Picnic area take-out: (Lower Kern), May through September. See #1 on map page 106.

Kernville Park take-out: (Upper Kern), April through mid-July. See #2 on map page 106.

If you want to observe kayaking instruction, call one of the schools in the resource guide and they will give you directions to their training area.

• Southern California sea kayaking options range from coastal and island touring to a whole slew of perfectly calm marinas and bays. Upper Newport Bay is a popular spot for those who want to watch birds and love nature.

• Popular sea kayaking spots in the Bay Area include the calm waters of Richardson Bay, the entire San Francisco Bay, Point Reyes National Seashore, plus an assortment of estuaries and marinas.

RESOURCES FOR DOERS

For updated reports on river flows and where to go:

The River Flow Hotline: (916) 322-3327. The recorded message is updated three times a week.

Pacific River Supply, El Sobrante: (510) 223-3675. Owners Jim Cassady and Mike Martell will be happy to tell you where to go. PRS also publishes a "Flow Update Information Sheet" that can be mailed or faxed.

California River Kayak Schools

California Canoe and Kayak (CCK): Owner Keith Miller operates out of three locations: Program and Reservation main number: (800) 366-9804. CCK introductory river kayak courses include: "Kayak River Basics:" two days with a graduation run on the Lower American River between Sunrise and Rossmore (Class I and II rapids); "Beginning Whitewater:" two days with a graduation run on South Fork of American River (Class II whitewater). Intermediate and advanced classes available. Locations: **Sacramento:** 8631 Folsom Boulevard, Sacramento, California 95826. (916) 381-6636. **Point Richmond:** 229 Tewksbury Avenue, Point Richmond, California 94801. (510) 234-0929. **Redwood City:** 1484 Oddstad Drive, Redwood City, California 94063. (415) 364-8918.

See #1(Sacramento), #7 (Point Richmond, Redwood City) on map page 274.

Otter Bar Lodge: Forks of Salmon, California 96031. (916) 462-4772. California Salmon.

Longer trips in kayaks. One of the best kayaking schools in the world. Instruction: beginning to advanced. Salmon River (California). Beautiful scenery. Owner Peter Sturgis.

See #5 on map page 274.

Sierra South: 11300 Kernville Road, Kernville, California 93238. (619) 376-3745. In business since 1985. Brother-sister team Tom Moore and Marriane Moore-DeChant, proprietors. Full service retail store on East bank of Kern River in Kernville. Kayak courses on The Upper Kern include "Beginner Kayaking 101," a two day course with graduation exercises on the Powerhouse Run on the Upper Kern, and "Kayak Sampler," a one day course that culminates in a short Class I run through the park next to the shop.

See #12 on map page 274.

Adventure's Edge: Arcata (707) 822-4673. Owner Steve O'Meara offers retail sales only. No lessons. Specialty is river kayaks and canoes. One of few kayaking resources in northern part of state.

See #4 on map page 274.

Wilderness Sports: 12401 Folsom Boulevard, Rancho Cordova, California 95742. (916) 985-3555. Charlie Fox and Alan Baty, owners. In business since April of 1991. Storefront at Nimbus Winery Mall. Two day basic class: first day on Lake Notoma, second day on the Lower American (Class II). Roll classes Wednesday nights at YMCA pool in Sacramento. Private lessons available.

See #1 on map page 274.

Sundance: 14894 Galice Road, Merlin, Oregon 97532. (503) 479-8508. In business 19 years, owner Judo Patterson draws most customers from California. Excellent school, one of the largest and most respected on West Coast. Advanced as well as beginning on Rogue River.

See #6 on map page 274.

The River Store: 1032 Lotus Road, Lotus, California 95651. (916) 626-3435. Whitewater kayak headquarters on the South Fork of the American. Owner Susan Debret does not have a lesson program but her store is a key part of the South Fork kayaking scene.

See #1 on map page 274.

CAL Adventures, U.C. Berkeley: 2301 Bancroft Avenue, Berkeley, California 94720. (510) 642-4001. Rick Spitler, coordinator. Bobby Dery, whitewater director. Beginning whitewater program starts at the UC Berkeley Aquatic center, and ends with a Class I and II run on the Lower American River between Coloma and Lotus.

See #7 on map page 274.

Outdoor Adventures, U.C. Davis: MU-Recreation, University of California, Davis, California 95616. (916) 752-1995. Dennis Johnson, director. Matthew Levin, kayaking coordinator. Beginning whitewater kayaking lessons include "Beginning One," a two-day course on the South Fork of the American between Coloma and Lotus (Class I and II whitewater); and "Beginning Two," a two-day course on the Gorge section of the South Fork of the American (Class II and III whitewater). Special roll class: two days, two hours each.

See #1 on map page 274.

Outdoors Unlimited Co-Op, UCSF: P.O. Box 0234-A, San Francisco, California 94143. (415) 476-2078. Steve Leonoudakis, director. Call or write for catalog detailing programs and classes.

See #7 on map page 274.

Adventure Outings: California State University, Chico: BMU 750, Chico, California 95929. (916) 898-4011. Rowland McNutt, coordinator. Four-day introductory whitewater kayaking course: first day in pool, second day on Sacramento river, third day on Feather River, fourth day is graduation on the Helena run of the Trinity River (four miles of Class II and III whitewater).

See #2 on map page 274.

Sierra Club, California: Many chapters of the Sierra Club offer roll classes at local pools. For a schedule of the roll classes nearest you call:

Angeles Chapter: (Los Angeles and Orange County): (213) 387-4287
San Diego Chapter: (619) 299-1744
San Francisco Bay Chapter: (510) 658-7470
Loma Prieta Chapter, Cupertino: (408) 734-3429
Redwood Empire Chapter, Santa Rosa: (707) 526-0940
Toyiyabe Chapter, Tahoe: (916) 587-0124
Mother Lode Chapter, Sacramento: (916) 587-0124. Modesto: (209) 523-7612.

California Sea Kayak Schools

Sea Trek Ocean Kayaking Center: 85 Liberty Ship Way, Sausalito, California 94965. (415) 488-1000. Owner Bob Licht, who opened shop in 1982, is considered the father of California sea kayaking. Sea kayaking lessons include: "Introduction to Sea Kayaking," "Wave Play," and "Open Bay." Private lessons, private groups, trips up to 50 people. Introductory lessons offered on seven-day Baja wilderness trips. Full service shop located in beautiful Schoonmaker Marina, Sausalito. Rentals and boat storage available.

See #7 on map page 274.

Southwind Sports Resource: 1088 Irvine Boulevard #212, Tustin, California 92680. (714) 730-4820: Doug Schwartz and Joanne Turner run the largest and most successful sea kayaking operation in Southern California. Complete range of lessons at coastal locations throughout the Southland include: "First Strokes," "Sea Legs," "Surf Zones," "Intensive Weekend," "Zen and The Art of Rock Garden Paddling," and "Roll Around." S.S.R. also organizes adventurous trips, some of which are open to beginners, to places like Topock Gorge on the Lower Colorado River. S.S.R. doesn't sell equipment but they'll help you pick out what's best for you. They have cross-referral arrangements with major equipment stores such as R.E.I. Co-Op, Sport Chalet, and A-16 Outfitters.

See #15 on map page 274.

California Canoe and Kayak (CCK): Owner Keith Miller operates out of three locations. Program and reservation main number: (800)

366-9804. CCK offers four separate one-day sea kayaking classes: "Beginning Sea Kayaking," "Intermediate Open Water," "Advanced Open Water," and "Surf Kayaking." Locations: **Sacramento:** 8631 Folsom Boulevard, Sacramento, California 95826. (916) 381-6636. **Point Richmond:** 229 Tewksbury Avenue, Point Richmond, California 94801. (510) 234-0929. **Redwood City:** 1484 Oddstad Drive, Redwood City, California 94063. (415) 364-8918.

See #1 (Sac), #7 (PR and RC) on map page 274.

Baja Expeditions: 2625 Garnet Avenue, San Diego, California 92109. (800) 843-6967. Owner Tim Means has been in business 16 years. His specialty is "teaching tours" in Baja California. The Espiritu Santo Island tour on the Sea of Cortez lasts nine days. You kayak around a 13-mile by 3-mile island, and camp at three different campsites. Espiritu Santo features desert scenery, cactus, jagged cliffs. Magdalena Bay tour is nine days of kayaking among grey whales on the Pacific side of Baja. Both are designed with the first-time kayaker in mind.

See #14 on map page 274.

Long Beach Water Sports: 730 East 4th Street, Long Beach, California 90802. (213) 432-0187. Andy Sninsky offers lessons and equipment. Although his specialty is day trips along the coast of Catalina in inflatable kayaks, he does offer a few basic closed-cockpit classes. His retail store offers sales and rentals as well.

See #15 on map page 274.

Earth Trek, Santa Ana: 23342 Madero, Suite B, Mission Viejo, California 92691. (800) 229-8735. Jerry Ashburn books trips, lessons and adventures for sea kayakers. Southwind Sports Resource are his sea kayak vendors.

See #15 on map page 274.

Monterey Bay Kayaks: 693 Del Monte Avenue, Monterey, California 93940. (408) 373-5357. Owners Jeffrey and Cass Schrock have been in business seven years. They offer sales, rentals, tours and lessons out of their 4,700 square foot retail store which is located right on Monterey Bay. "Basic Skills" is a 1-1/2 day course that is especially good at teaching raw beginners how to deal with stronger water conditions. "Rolling Class," "Surf Zone," and an intermediate/advanced class called "Racing Strokes" round out the lesson program. Guided tours for intermediates along beautiful Big Sur coastline.

See #8 on map page 274.

Environmental Travelling Companions (ETC.): Fort Mason,Building C, San Francisco, California 94123. (415) 474-7662. This group serves the general population, but their true mission—and it makes them unique—is to provide sea kayaking lessons and adventures to special populations, including physically handicapped individuals and groups. They also do whitewater rafting.

See #7 on map page 274.

Southwest Kayaks: 1331 Rosecrans Street, San Diego, California 92106. (619) 222-3616. Owners: Ed Gillette and Katie Kampe. Beginning instruction includes "Basic Sea Kayaking," and "Surf Survival." Intermediate instruction on weekend trip to La Bufadora, on the coast of Mexico between Tijuana and Ensenada. Camp one night on Todo Santos Island. Twenty different kayak trips to Baja are available to paddlers with basic skills.

See #14 on map page 274.

Force Ten: P.O. Box 167, Elk, California 95432. (707) 877-3505. Owner Steve Sinclair offers two services that are totally unique in the world of sea kayaking. His specialty is "K-2 Tours" along the wild and wooly Mendocino Coast. For $30 per hour (2-hour minimum) Sinclair will put you in the front seat of a two-person "K-2" kayak and take you on a tour of local sea caves, seal rookeries and bird rookeries. No experience necessary. Sinclair also offers a two-day action seminar called "Tactics for the Ocean Shoreline Explorer." This course is designed for those who already have a basic, flat-water lesson under their belts. Aggressive "Storm Surf Tours" for intermediates/advanced.

See #3 on map page 274.

Aquarius Adventures: 302 North Granados Avenue, Solana Beach, California 92075. (800) 328-5776. Bart Berry, owner. Primarily a rock-climbing school, Aquarius also does occasional group sea kayak lessons and is one of the few schools in the state that teaches closed-cockpit kayak surfing (private lessons only.)

See #14 on map page 274.

Kayak Tahoe: P.O. Box 11129, Tahoe Paradise, California 96155. (916) 544-2011. Owners Susan Lannoy and brother-in-law Steve Lannoy offer tours and lessons out of Camp Richardson in the Lake Tahoe area. Seasonal: June 1st to September 30th. Kokanee salmon tours available by reservation through October 12th.

See #10 on map page 274.

CAL Adventures: U.C. Berkeley: 2301 Bancroft Avenue, Berkeley, California 94720. (510) 642-4000. Rick Spitler, coordinator. Claudia Hossberg, director of sea kayaking. Sea kayaking basic, intermediate and advanced lessons. Overnight tours to various locations, most of which require basic skills as a prerequisite.

See #7 on map page 274.

UCSB Outdoor Recreation Program: Trailer 303-B, Robertson Gym, U.C. Santa Barbara, Santa Barbara, California 93106. (805) 893-3737. Wayne Horodowich, Director of Outdoor Recreation. This UCSB program has been around for 20 years, the sea kayak program for five. "Level I: Basic skills, two person rescues," "Level II: Advanced paddling, solo rescues," "Level III: Rock garden technique/navigation/overnight touring," "Surf Zone," and "Roll Class." Day tours (coastal and Channel Islands) available for qualified kayakers. Private lessons and group charters available.

See #13 on map page 274.

Outdoor Adventures: U.C. Davis: MU-Recreation, University of California, Davis, California 95616. (916) 752-1995. Dennis Johnson, director. Introductory sea kayaking courses include: one-day trips to Tomales Bay and Point Reyes, a Monterey Bay weekend, and a Point Reyes weekend.

See #1 on map page 274.

Outdoors Unlimited Co-Op, UCSF: P.O. Box 0234-A, San Francisco, California 94143. (415) 476-2078. Steve Leonoudakis, director. Call or write for catalog detailing programs and classes.

See #7 on map page 274.

CHAPTER ELEVEN

BEYOND THE FIRST THRILL

UP TO NOW YOU'VE BEEN READING ABOUT professionally supervised introductory rides or lessons that are carefully controlled by providers who have two goals in mind: The first is safety. The second is fun.

After you've taken one of the basic lessons or rides described in this book, you may find yourself wandering around in a daze, with a big grin plastered across your face. You may even find yourself daydreaming about future dances with earth, water or air.

Thrill sports are powerful. Some of you will find them addictive. It's very easy to get hooked on any one of these wacky things. If you do, you'll be tempted to drive yourself as quickly and completely as possible through all the stages of learning that separate you—a beginning "Skywalker"—from the "Jedi Masters" who shape and define your sport's outer edge.

Forget rides of passage or leaps of faith. You could be looking at a whole new lifestyle, or maybe even an obsession.

Obsession, or even simple exhilaration, puts you in the single most dangerous period in your thrill sport career. There is simply nothing like the combination of unbridled enthusiasm, basic skill, minimum experience and limited knowledge for making thrill sports as dangerous as they can possibly be.

This chapter, by sharing with you the normal safe paths of progression within the thrill sport that's calling your name, will give you a nodding acquaintance with perhaps the most deadly of the three biggest killers in thrill sports: intermediate syndrome.

Intermediate syndrome is a fancy term for unsafe, out-of-control progression from beginning to advanced stages. Intermediate syndrome was, is and will always be "the tendency of relatively inexperienced [pilots, boaters, divers or climbers] to become so overwhelmed by the exhilaration of [flying, boating, diving or climbing] that they forget or ignore their own skill limitations, established safety procedures and/or the limitations of state-of-the-art technique and equipment."

The problem, from a safety point of view, is that the further you get from your introductory experience, the more choices you must make, often without the assistance of someone who knows more than you do. You must assume responsibility to pick and choose from a wide array of options that represent your next step in the progression from beginner to advanced.

Granted, some sports—like skydiving and hot air ballooning—have clear cut paths of progression in the form of FAA certificates and pilot licenses. Still, unsafe progressions from basic licenses to advanced licenses are surprisingly common.

Others—like hang gliding and paragliding—have clear industry standards for training and progression. Most people follow them, although there is no law that says they have to. Unsafe intermediate progressions are easier to fall into in these sports because they are easier to get away with.

Still others, like whitewater rafting, kayaking and rock climbing, are wide open. Industry standards exist, but they are not clearly institutionalized or uniformly observed. You can pretty much take whatever chances you want as a rock climber or a boater, without having to produce any proof that you're up to the challenge.

The bottom line in all cases is this: It's up to you, and no one else, to make sure that you progress as safely as possible. What makes it hard is that you have to assume that responsibility in the face of powerful addictions like "airtime," "rapid fever," or "climber's euphoria."

Of the sports covered in this book, the following have both addictive powers and dangerous paths of progression. They also are affordable enough so that you can get into them for less than the price of a mid-sized motorcycle.

- Skydiving
- Rock climbing
- Whitewater boating (rafting and kayaking)
- Hang gliding
- Paragliding

If your thing is parasailing, ballooning or bungee jumping, you really don't have too far to go beyond repeated rides. Unless, of course, you're rich enough to buy your own balloon or boat, or crazy enough to be your own bungee engineer.

For each of the five potentially addictive—and affordable—thrill sports, here are:

Voice from the edge: Testimony of a top person in the sport about the addictive qualities of the sport (what's at stake for those who want to progress to higher levels.)

Telling it like it is: Common—often amusing—terminology that describes levels of participation and other phenomena within the sport. A thrill sport's "slang" also reveals the spirit and culture of its participants.

Idiot lights: The main warning signs of "intermediate syndrome."

Life preservers: Normal, safe paths of progression within the sport.

SKYDIVING

Voice from the edge:

Dan Poynter is a life-long skydiving addict and author of *Parachuting, The Skydiver's Handbook* and *The Parachute Manual: Volume II.* Poynter's parachute books are definitive in the world of skydiving.

"I was in my early twenties when I did my first skydive. For a long time I described the feeling as 'kind of like falling in love.' But then I realized you can say that about hang gliding and most other thrill sports.

"What really makes skydiving unique is that anyone can do it. It doesn't take any special skill to jump out of an airplane. But the instant you do it, you'll automatically feel superior to anyone who has never done it, which is almost everyone.

"If you go skydiving—just once—you'll probably be the only person on your block or in your office who has ever done it. And you'll know in your heart: There are those who skydive, and those who don't."

Telling it like it is:

The following terminology separates skydivers from non-divers, distinguishes levels of accomplishment within the sport, and describes equipment and phenomena unique to skydiving.

Whuffos: Inquisitive non-divers. As in: "Whuffo you do that?!"

Ground Hogs: All other non-divers.

Kikis: Extremely nervous first-timers. As in: "Ki-Ki-Rist, it's a long way down!"

Dirt Dive: Practicing a skydive on the ground.

60 Jump Commandos: Recently graduated students who think they're better than they really are.

100 Jump Wonders: Intermediate jumpers who think they're better than they really are.

Dirty Low Puller: Advanced jumper who likes to deploy his chute as low as possible.

Sky God: The best kind of skydiver there is.

Cheapos: Old-style, round parachutes.

Squares: Modern parafoil parachutes.

Augering in or frapping: Same as "bouncing." A fatal accident.

Idiot lights:

Basic skydiving training is well-regulated. There are four licenses (A,B,C and D) plus a pro rating. Once you earn your A license and start diving on your own, however, there are a number of warning signs that you're headed down a bad path.

- Jumping with an outdated reserve parachute.
- Failing to do a thorough pre-jump check of all your equipment.
- Rushing through re-pack of your main parachute.
- Breaking established rules for minimum deployment altitude.
- Doing "hook turns" on landing with minimal experience.
- Locking legs with another diver while under canopy so you can "downplane" (descend

faster with the canopy facing straight down) to as low an altitude as possible.

Life preservers:

If you just follow established rules—rules that have been around for more than 30 years—you'll be fine.

• Always pre-jump check all your equipment.

• Always pack your main parachute carefully.

• Have your reserve parachute repacked every three months.

• Follow deployment rules: A and B licensed skydivers are required to deploy their main canopy at no less than 2,500 feet above the ground.

ROCK CLIMBING

Voice from the edge:

John Fischer is an independent guide who has been climbing for 30 years and guiding for 22. A board member of the American Mountain Guides Association (AMGA), John pursues his addiction by climbing and guiding all over the world.

"I think rock climbing is infinitely appealing and interesting. No matter what your level of participation, you're constantly learning and facing new challenges. And rock climbing is always enjoyable—as long as you keep a healthy focus on why you're doing it.

"I do it because I have a great time moving over stone. I love traveling in the mountains. Climbing is instantly rewarding in a number of ways. There are so many aspects to it besides just climbing. There's geology, botany, photography, fitness and social aspects to climbing. If you do it internationally, there's the exposure to other cultures and languages.

"In some ways climbing is just a great excuse for adventure. I also love the unique competitive aspects of climbing. You don't really compete with other climbers. If you do that, you're missing the point. It's the competition with yourself, and with your route up the mountain, that truly matters in rock climbing."

Telling it like it is:

Rock climbing terminology is both blunt and richly descriptive. It's as straightforward and focused as the sport itself.

Bumblies: Beginners, usually unsupervised, who have no idea what they're doing. Bumblies jingle and jangle when they carry their equipment, loose, to the bottom of a climb.

Rogue: An instructor who operates illegally —one who doesn't have insurance or a permit to use a climbing area.

Idiots: People who climb with any combination of inadequate skill and inadequate protection.

Sewing Machine Leg: Violent shaking in your leg as a result of holding a bent-knee position too long.

Crag: A natural outdoor climbing area.

Face: A vertical part of a crag.

Slab: A less than vertical part of a crag.

Route: A specific way up a face, crag, or slab.

Free Soloing: Climbing without protection. OK up to Class III.

Third Classing: Free soloing a Class IV or Class V route without protection. If you do it before you're prepared to do it, you're an absolute "idiot."

Flashing: Climbing a route with no falls on

your first try.

Hang Dog: Traditional climber term for a sport climber who hangs on his protection while figuring out a move.

Red Pointing: Sport climber term for climbing a route successfully after working on it. Traditional climbers say that red pointing is what comes after hang dogging.

Hard man: Outdated name for a person who is addicted to rock climbing.

Hey, Man, Guide Service: Loose term for casual guide service. As in, "Hey, man, let's go climbing!"

Rock God: The best kind of climber there is.

Bronze Rock God: A climber who thinks he or she is the best kind of climber there is.

Rat tails: Excessively worn, unsafe climbing ropes.

Gear Freaks: Climbers who have lots of gear but very little idea of how to use it.

Gobey: A scabbed-over nick on your hand.

Flapper: Torn skin on your hand—the kind that flaps.

Taking the Big Ride: Another term for "cratering." A fatal fall.

Idiot lights:

• Competing with other climbers rather than the terrain. If you do that, you'll lose focus and not climb as well. The best competitive sport climbers are very friendly with one another during a competition. They know that their competition is the climb—not each other.

• Finding yourself stuck on a wall, not knowing what to do next. That means you're in over your head. If it happens a lot, you're headed in a bad direction.

• Relying on others to throw you a rope or

rescue you from a bad spot. If you're not self-reliant, you're not safe in rock climbing.

• Failing to plan your climb. If you don't have a contingency plan for anything that's likely to come up on your climb, you'll find yourself in dangerous positions.

• Failing to plan your descent. A perfect ascent can be ruined by a sloppy, frightening or poorly planned descent. Descents can be more dangerous than ascents—especially if you don't take them seriously.

• Getting sloppy with belay techniques. If you and your partner find yourself miscommunicating, leaving too much slack in the rope, or taking your brake hand off the rope, you're headed for trouble.

• Relying on gear instead of technique, skill and judgement. "Gear freaks" seem to think that extra gear will get them out of trouble—even if they don't really know how to use it.

• Failing to pre-climb check all your gear. Using gear that's excessively worn. One of the best ways to decide whether you want to climb with someone you've just met is to eyeball their gear, and watch how they use it.

Life preservers:

• Always keep in mind that your own skill and judgement is your first line of protection. Ropes, harnesses and anchors are second. Help from other climbers is third.

• Stay focused. Remember that safety, not ascent, is your first priority.

• Always remember that you are engaged in a potentially dangerous activity—that oversight, carelessness or neglect can cost you your life at any given point in your climbing career.

• Always play "What if—" with yourself. Envision worst case scenarios every time you climb. Have a plan to deal with them.

• Turn your pre-climb safety check into a routine. Do it the same way every time, and it will become habit. Have your climbing partner check your gear while you check his or hers.

• Cultivate self-awareness. Constantly monitor your own level of fatigue and concentration. Don't climb when you're beat or unfocused.

WHITEWATER BOATING

Voice from the edge:

Jim Cassady is co-owner of Pacific River Supply in El Sobrante and co-author of *California Whitewater*, the definitive text on California's rivers. Cassady has had a life-long love affair with water. It started when he was a kid growing up in Washington, D.C.

"Even as a kid I knew I had a thing about water. The ritual we used to prove our manhood was 'maul ball.' It's a real simple game: One kid has the ball and the other kids try to take it away. The goal, of course, is to keep it as long as possible. I wasn't very good. I rarely got the ball and when I did it was quickly wrenched away.

"In a swimming pool, however, I was invincible. I could get the ball in a heartbeat and no one could take it away.

"Years later, as 9th graders, we would rent open canoes that were meant for flat water. We'd paddle on the canals next to the Potomac River until we got out of sight, then sneak over to the rapids on the river itself. We were total idiots running rapids in those things. But we were also lucky. We escaped without any major bodily injuries.

"The magic of running whitewater totally

grabbed me. It was wet, exhilarating, refreshing, adventuresome and exciting. I felt like Huck Finn.

"In the early 70s, after seeing the movie *Deliverance*, my friend Erik Fair and I bought an open canoe together. Erik is one of the guys I played maul ball with as a kid. We set out to be river runners in our shiny new canoe. Unfortunately, my unusually large comfort zone in the water started getting us into trouble. Erik wisely bailed on river running and wound up in hang gliding where he felt safer. Meanwhile, I continued on without any professional guidance whatsoever.

"I lost the canoe one Memorial Day when I ran the Merced at 8,000 cfs without float bags. When I dumped over, the canoe immediately filled with water and headed downstream like a torpedo. I was lucky I didn't lose my life chasing after it. My whitewater addiction was so strong, however, that I immediately bought another canoe and continued in my reckless ways.

"Finally, I did something right. I signed up for a Sierra Club indoor pool kayak lesson. I was still hooked and fanatical, but I advanced my skills at a manageable pace. Most of my early kayak runs were in Class II and Class II+ water on the Powerhouse Run of the Upper Kern and the Electra Run of the Mokelumne. I advanced gradually to Class III, Class IV and finally Class V.

"Not long after I started running Class V water, I made a decision to back off from kayaking and concentrate on whitewater rafting. My love of rafting was growing, plus I had a growing mental fear of kayaking in Class V water.

"One incident clarified my decision. In February of 1980, I kayaked Rattlesnake Creek, a difficult Class V run that is only runnable when the weather is cold and wet. I didn't have any mishaps, but at the end of the run, I was thinking: 'Thank God that's over with—I'm glad I made it,' instead of 'Wow, what a wonderful and exhilarating run!'

"By that time I had learned an important lesson: when fear dominates exhilaration, it's time to back off—so that's what I did.

"My progression in river running was different from most. Most people progress from rafting to kayaking."

Telling it like it is:

Whitewater boating terminology reflects some of the unique aspects of "river culture."

Geeks: Basic term for bad beginning boaters (i.e.: stoned boaters who don't wear life jackets).

Hole Bait: Geeks who ride innertubes down rapids.

Rubber Duckies: Geeks who run rivers in cheap department store boats.

Thrashers: Careless intermediate boaters who get in over their heads.

Crash and Burn Artists: Careless advanced boaters who push the edge.

Ninja Boater: An aggressive but safe advanced boater.

Zen Boater: Advanced boater who uses flow to best advantage. The ultimate stylist—a river dancer.

Natural Selection at Work: Generic term for bad boating.

Bucket Boats: Non-self-bailers. OK on Class III whitewater.

Bailers: Self-bailing rafts. The only way to go on Class IV and V water.

South Forker: A river guide who is only qualified to lead trips down the South Fork of the American River (Class III). Considered dangerous when guiding on a different river.

Float N' Bloats: Commercial rafting trips on oar boats. So named because you don't have to paddle. All you have to do is float and eat.

River Bum or River Rat: Name for a person who is addicted to river running.

River Scum: Name for person who is addicted to river running *and* the casual, counterculture aspects of river life.

Getting Slimed: Capsizing your kayak in a rapid.

Air brace: What you do when you "seize" and hold your kayak paddle in the air rather than on the water—where it would brace against capsize.

Carping: People who are just learning the Eskimo roll have a habit of trying to come out of the water lips first, presumably so they can breathe again as quickly as possible. Kayak instructors call this "carping."

Ethan Winston's Rules of Whitewater Rafting:

- If you fall out of the raft, it's your fault.
- If you and one or more others fall out, it's the guide's fault.
- If the guide falls out, it's the crew's fault.
- Your guide is your God.
- God could use a few tips.

Idiot lights:

- Fear is the biggest idiot light in whitewater boating. When you feel fear instead of exhilaration at the end of a run, it's time to change things. Run less difficult water until your skills and techniques are developed enough to handle tougher water.

• Cold is the other big idiot light and it's more likely to sneak up on you when you're under the influence of fear. You run a real risk of losing your life if you aren't aware of the subtle warning signs of hypothermia. They are: loss of energy, slurred speech, disorientation. At advanced stages the symptom is obvious: uncontrollable shaking.

• If you run unfamiliar stretches of whitewater casually, you'll be less likely to scout from the river bank when you should. If you don't scout, you'll eventually run an unsafe route, or a rapid you should have portaged around. See "Fear" above.

Life preservers:

• Boat at your level of ability. Develop an awareness of what your ability level is and stick to rivers that fit it.

• Always carry water with you. You shouldn't drink river water. Dehydration can be a big problem in the hot Sierra sun.

• Wear or carry protection against hypothermia: Use wetsuits, paddle jackets and booties. Use synthetics like Polypropylene, not cotton.

• Always carry a gear checklist and always carry a spare paddle or oar.

• When in doubt, scout. Still in doubt, PORTAGE. If you can't see a runnable route through a rapid, or you can't see a downstream eddy you can catch in case of a spill, stop and scout the rapid from the river bank. If you still can't see a runnable route, portage.

HANG GLIDING

Voice from the edge:

Joe Greblo owns Windsports International, the oldest and arguably the best hang gliding school/shop in the Los Angeles area. Joe is a top-knotch competitive pilot, a conscientious businessman and an excellent teacher. In his 18-year relationship with the USHGA, he has helped develop many of hang gliding's safety and training standards. He's also totally addicted to hang gliding.

"Hang gliding satisfies much more than my simple need for fun and excitement. It dives right into my deep-rooted need for power and freedom—the things my dreams are made of. Hang gliding allows me to escape life's everyday conflicts and pressures at will. Taking on the challenges of the sky helps me overpower my fears and release my anxieties. For the minutes and hours I'm in the air, it's just me and my glider. Nothing else matters, and not a single outside pressure can bother me.

"I wish I could describe these feelings more completely. Such a description would surely include words like challenge, solitude, escape and accomplishment. Of course fun and excitement are definitely in there too—but you probably already knew that.

"I can tell you this much: Those of you who have had dreams of personal flight already know what I'm talking about. The feelings you get in your dreams are the same ones I have when I fly."

Telling it like it is:

Hang gliding terminology is both zany and serious. It reflects the unique blend of off-beat individualism and safety consciousness that pervades the hang gliding community.

Wuffos: Almost anyone: non-fliers, ignorant beginners, careless intermediates, advanced pilots who make a mistake.

Freezers or Seizers: Students who are so tense they can't move enough to control the glider.

Intermediate Syndrome: The disease which afflicts intermediate pilots who consistently fly in conditions they are not ready for.

The E Team: Lake Elsinore locals. Notorious for going way out of their way to live up to the out-of-control image of hang gliding.

Whack!: What roving bands of E-Teamers shriek to any pilot who drops the nose of his or her glider on landing.

Whack attack: A series of bad landings. Sends E-Teamers into a frenzy.

Jedi Master: The best kind of advanced hang glider pilot there is.

Billow Cruisers: Old style, low performance hang gliders.

Blade Wings: Modern, high performance hang gliders.

Death Trap: Old or beat glider that isn't airworthy.

Nailing the Core: Finding the center of a rising mass of hot air (thermal) and riding it all the way to the top.

Air junkie: Name for a hang glider pilot who is addicted to flying.

Air hog: The pilot who stays in the air the longest.

Mid-Air: Collision between two flying gliders.

Hang Check: Critical pre-flight check to confirm that you're hooked into your glider.

Diver: Aggressive term for a hang glider. Used

to scare wuffos. As in: "Wanna go divin' in my new diver, baby?"

P.I.O.'s: Pilot induced oscillations. Fancy term for "over-control."

Push out!: Hang gliding version of 'Aloha.' Means hello or goodbye. Refers to pushing out on the control bar in order to climb faster in a thermal.

Idiot lights:

If you hook up with a qualified instructor in a good school, you'll graduate with decent launch, approach and landing skills, and an awareness of safety issues and attitudes. However, you also may be afflicted with a blazing desire to learn as much as you can as quickly as you can. Watch for the following idiot lights as you progress:

• Thinking that safety rules and pilot rating limitations are too conservative for an exceptionally bright and aggressive quick learner such as yourself. If you fly in strong conditions before you're ready, or otherwise "push" the rules, you're more vulnerable than you can possibly know. Hang gliding's rules of progression are written in the form of a very specific pilot rating system. They were written for everyone—especially for those who think they don't need them.

• Believing that hang gliding is dangerous only for stupid pilots who make careless mistakes. The truth is that hang gliding, like any other form of aviation, is always dangerous. The only way to protect yourself from the dangers of hang gliding is to consistently recognize them and carefully address them each and every time you fly.

• Showing off. If you find yourself trying to impress other pilots or your instructor, you are creating your own risk. A classic example is the pilot who buys high-performance equipment before becoming a high performance pilot.

• Confusing flying skill with flying safety. Flying skill is just the easy half of flying safely. The other half is understanding flight theory, knowing how to read weather, developing good judgement, being aware of your own limitations and the limitations of your equipment, and behaving responsibly in all aspects of your flying. If you stop reading, watching, learning and listening, you should also stop flying.

• Forgetting or ignoring basic safety procedures. If you don't bother to pre-flight check your glider and do a hang-check to confirm hook-in just prior to launch, you're creating extra risk. There are some things you only get to do once in a hang glider. One is "forgetting" to hook in at a cliff-launch.

Life preservers:

Joe Greblo of Windsports International says it best:

"In hang gliding you are as safe as your training, your equipment and your judgement allows." Don't look any deeper. It's that simple.

Assuming that you've received good basic instruction, the real test of your ability to enjoy a long, safe career in sport aviation comes after you complete your lessons and start flying under your own supervision.

While it may seem reasonable to think that your level of safety would naturally increase as you develop more skills and gain more experience, that's simply not the case.

There are two sides to the equation: On the one hand, you are a pilot who is indeed becoming more skilled and experienced. But on the other hand, you are emerging into a realm where the conditions you fly in and the situations you encounter in the air are becoming increasingly complex and dangerous. Different launch and landing areas, more turbulent soaring conditions, more complex equipment, and the need for new flight plans and strategies are just some of the potential pitfalls that lie ahead.

Combine that with the indisputably addictive quality of soaring in a hang glider, and your almost incessant desire for air-time, and it's easy to understand why the danger level is high at the intermediate stages of progression.

Here are some ways to protect yourself:

• Constantly re-define the line: As you progress, routinely solicit the opinions of the instructor who trained you, and frequently review the USHGA pilot proficiency rating system. The lines of progression recommended by your instructor and the USHGA are far more reliable than the lines of progression recommended by fellow intermediate pilots who are dealing with addictions every bit as powerful as your own.

• Fill your toolbox. When you graduate from hang gliding school, you have just the basic tools in your toolbox. A good example is landing approach skills. As a recently graduated student, you only have experience executing landing approaches at expansive training landing areas in moderate training conditions. Your skills are not developed enough to handle smaller landing areas or approaches in turbulent soaring conditions. Full development of your approach and other skills comes after you graduate from hang gliding school.

When you graduate, ask your instructor for a specific list of the additional skills you need to develop or refine—and a timetable for you to develop them.

• Watch pilots who are more skilled and experienced than you. It's not uncommon during risky flying conditions to see many intermediate pilots launch while the more skilled and experienced pilots wait on the ground for conditions to improve. One definition of a Hang Four (advanced) pilot is: "A pilot who lets a Hang Three (intermediate) launch first."

• Minimize the variables. Try to develop one major skill area at a time. If it will take several flights to master a skill, make all of them in similar conditions. If you're trying to get a practical handle on your glider's "glide ratio," for instance, you don't have a chance if you take several flights in widely varied, turbulent conditions.

• Make only one change at a time. Launching a glider you've never flown before, at a site you've never flown before, in a harness you've never flown before, is courting disaster.

• Don't try to "keep up with the Joneses." As your skills increase, so will your desire to explore more of the incredible world of hang gliding. This often means visiting new places and making new friends. Don't try to keep up with the ones that are more skilled or more experienced than you. Always be aware of your own limitations and don't let social desire or pressure cause you to ignore them.

• Watch out for bad habits. As you get more experienced and comfortable in the air, you may find yourself making turns dangerously close to the ground, or transitioning into the prone flying position before you've completed your take-off run. Safe flying is an "every time" thing. If you get sloppy with a skill after mastering it, you're no better off than a pilot who is just learning it. It takes hard work to maintain your good, safe flying habits; they will disappear in a heartbeat if you ignore them.

• Practice basic skills at a training area from time to time. Some skills—particularly launch and landing skills—atrophy with lack of use. Ironically, they are the skills most important to safe flight. If you're not "current" in your launch and landing skills—which you won't be if you only fly once every two weeks—return to a training hill and brush up. There's absolutely no shame in it, and it shows good sense.

PARAGLIDING

Voice from the outside:

I want to handle this one.

The addictive powers of paragliding are similar to those of hang gliding. Also, all the "idiot lights" and "life preservers" listed under hang gliding apply to paragliding as well. As in hang gliding, paragliding skills are a *very small* part of the safety picture compared to judgement and overall airmanship.

From a "career" safety perspective, there are two key differences between hang gliders and paragliders: First, it is ridiculously easy to learn how to launch and land a paraglider. They are soft, slow and require virtually no speed control. Second, paragliders are—in my opinion—ill-suited for flight in turbulent air. Of all the things you can fly, paragliders have the least speed, the worst glide performance, and the least structural capability to maintain shape in turbulent air. You can soar in a paraglider, of course, and rather easily.

The problem is that the combination of "easy

learn," "easy soar" and "easy collapse" don't mix well with the addictive powers of the sport. The bottom line is that you will be strongly tempted to fly a paraglider in turbulent conditions well before you accumulate enough experience to do it with an acceptable degree of safety.

If you can resist that temptation, fine. If you can't, you're in far worse shape than you would be in a hang glider.

Hang gliders are semi-hard airfoils. Their shape is defined by aluminum spars and ribs. Paragliders are soft bundles of cloth. They only become airfoils when filled with air. Moderate turbulence that a hang glider can handle without any problem whatsoever can cause full or partial collapse of a paragliding canopy.

It all adds up to this: The penalty for premature progression into soaring conditions is far more severe in a paraglider than in a hang glider. Canopy collapses, partial or full, are fairly routine in soaring conditions. Often they can be dealt with rather simply—*if* you have a paraglider that is stable enough for your level of ability, and *if* you are experienced enough not to "freak out" when half your wing wads into a ball of cloth, and *if* you know when to abandon "re-inflation" procedures so that you can deploy your emergency parachute. Otherwise, you're in big trouble.

It's that simple.

Don't get me wrong. Paragliders are great—a true dose of air magic. They can offer safe, fun personal flight. The mere fact that they're backpackable makes them the most convenient sport airfoil around.

But paragliders also give you an incredibly easy means to hurt or kill yourself in turbulent air. As always, the choice is yours.

Telling it like it is:

Much of the terminology used by paraglider pilots was "R and D'd" (ripped off and duplicated) from hang gliding. The following terms, however, are specific to paragliding.

Canopy Collapse: Deflation of all or part of a wing. Some collapses are done on purpose, others are a result of turbulence.

Big Ears or Pulling Ears: Collapsing both tips of the wing on purpose. Used to increase speed and rate of descent.

Horseshoe: Collapsing the middle front of the wing on purpose. Another way to increase speed and rate of descent.

Front Collapse or A-Riser Collapse: Collapsing the front of the wing on purpose. Causes you to drop like a stone.

Full Stall: Collapsing the rear edge of the wing on purpose. Should only be done on landing or over water.

Rocket: A rocket-deployed emergency reserve canopy.

Building a wall: Inflating the wing, then letting it settle gently back on the ground. This is how pilots prepare for a launch.

Parapente: French term for paragliding.

Pair of panties: American version of French term for paragliding.

Panty hoser: Diane McKenzie's term for her paragliding husband, Rob—who is Canadian.

Air sport of the 90's: How paraglider pilots view their sport.

Death sport of the 90's: How hang glider pilots view paragliding.

Rock wing: What paraglider pilots call hang gliders.

Rock jockey: What paraglider pilots call hang glider pilots.

Dope on a rope: What hang glider pilots call paraglider pilots.

Parapounding: Paragliding equivalent of the macho hang gliding term "hang diving."

Idiot lights:

Same as hang gliding with the following additions:

- If you allow yourself to be deluded or lulled into complacency by the ease of launching and landing a paraglider—and you take your delusions and complacency into the wild blue yonder—you are an accident waiting to happen.

Life preservers:

Same as hang gliding with the following additions:

- Practice controlling your paraglider on the ground. Purposely inflate, collapse and re-inflate your canopy on the ground in every way imaginable. That will help you develop skills and quick reactions that you can use in turbulent air where all kinds of collapses can happen suddenly and unexpectedly.
- Constantly remind yourself of the fact that it takes an advanced paraglider pilot to fly in wind conditions that intermediate hang glider pilots handle with relative ease.
- Realize that advanced instruction—the kind you need before taking on moderate to severe turbulence—is even more necessary in paragliding than it is in hang gliding. You have to know how to deal with collapses, spins and the limited speed and glide performance of your wing.

Big Ride/ Ultimate Leap

Yow. What rides. What leaps. I'm hooked!

But now it's time to take out, pack up and head home.

It's hard to imagine how researching and writing a book could be any more fun. Not many authors get to hurl themselves through time and space as thoroughly as I did during the preparation of this manuscript. It was hard, exacting work, but—like they say—*someone* had to do it!

Thrill sports expose us to the natural environment in unique and dramatic ways. Each of the rides of passage and leaps of faith covered in this book immerses us in—or merges us with—earth, water or air. Each distorts time, space and gravity in its own special way.

Perhaps because of our special connection with the power and beauty of nature, most of us who pursue risk sports are committed to the preservation of the environment. River people constantly battle to save wild rivers so they can continue to commune with nature from their rafts and kayaks. Air people have nightmares about losing their precious few launch and landing areas to development. Rock people face land-use conflicts and permit problems at every turn.

Unfotunately, we in thrill sports constantly lose sites—either to development or to fear of litigation. The Livermore area in Northern California is all but lost to hot air ballooning because of development, and the Del Mar ballooning area in Southern California is under duress from nervous landowners. Understandably, they don't want to face a flurry of lawsuits if a basket full of hot air balloonists crashes and burns on their property.

On another front, one of the best hang gliding schools in the state (Mission Soaring) can no longer teach for profit at one of the best training hills in the state (Ed Levin Park in San Jose) despite a 15-year legacy of safe operation.

Which brings me to my deepest thought.

Nearly everyone in the world of high-risk sports is—on one level or another—appreciative of the grim irony in the words "risk management."

To us, risk management means accepting responsibility for ourselves so we can have a good time. To us, risk management means looking risk in the eye and doing our level best to minimize it while we enthusiastically pursue the special rewards of sky, water or rock. To us, risk management means consistently behaving in a way that proves we are willing to assume full responsibility for our lives, and accept the consequences of our actions.

But that's not what risk management means to "them." To them, risk management means eliminating, or severely curtailing, any activity that could conceivably result in a flurry of lawsuits. In this country, of course, you can get sued for anything from failing to scoop up after your dog to owning a piece of property that some poor hang glider pilot crashes into.

From a classic "risk management" point of view, your most reasonable response is to get rid of the dog and not let the hang glider pilot anywhere near your property.

Listen. Thrill sports are an endangered species in this country. We lose when the environment loses to development, and we lose every time a lawyer invokes his or her understanding of risk management without fully appreciating ours.

But you can help. Now that you've read this book, you're a card-carrying thrill sport participant—if not by deed, then at least in your dreams.

Spread the word. Tell the people you know and love that maybe these "rides of passage" and "leaps of faith" aren't so crazy after all. Set them straight when they say "If the bungee breaks, you're dead," or when they ask: "Doesn't the wind control a hang glider?" Tell them they heard wrong if they heard that it's "real hard" to "escape" from an upside-down kayak or that rock climbers die when they miss a step.

Tell them that river runners need rivers, not dams; that air people need places to launch and land; and that too many rock climbing schools have thrown in the towel in the face of liability concerns. Tell them that you know for a fact that thrill sport participants have heartfelt reasons for treasuring the environment, and that they are superior to most Americans when it comes to accepting responsibility for their own safety.

Look those suckers in the eye and tell them what I'm about to tell you—something that went "klunk" in the night as I was dreaming my dreams about this book:

Tell them that the big "ride of passage" is the one we all take on planet earth, and that the ultimate "leap of faith" is in ourselves.

INDEX

Acknowledgements

I'd like to sincerely thank *everyone* who shared their knowledge and experience with me during the preparation of this manuscript. Special thanks are in order for the experts: those who provided a bulk of the information pertaining to their sport; those who served as chapter editors; and those who donated a "ride of passage" or "leap of faith" so that I'd know what I was talking about when it came time to write. Chapter by chapter they are:

"Who, Me?!"—Jessie M. Fair, my momma.

Bungee Jumping—John and Peter Kockleman, Bungee Adventures. John Wilkinson, Total Rebound. Martin Zemitis.

Rock Climbing—Peter Mayfield, CityRock Gym. Tom and Theresa Anderson, Adventure-16 Outfitters, Costa Mesa. Amelia Rudolph and the Project Banda Loop Dance Troop.

Whitewater Rafting—Jim Cassady, Pacific River Supply.

Hot Air Ballooning—Brent Stockwell and Christine Kalakuka, Balloon Excelsior. Roger Barker, Cameron Balloons. Alan and Cindi Ehrgott, Coloma Country Inn.

Parasailing—Dan Poynter, Para Publishing. Ed Diruscio and Mike Perrin, Newport Parasail. Mike Trudeau, Island Cruzer Boats.

Skydiving—Gary Douris, Freeflight Enterprises. Don Balch, Skydiving Adventures.

Hang Gliding—Rob and Diane McKenzie, High Adventure Hang Gliding. Joe Greblo, Windsports International.

Paragliding—Ken deRussy and Bonnie Nelson, Hang Glider/Paraglider Emporium. Wills Wing, Inc.

Kayaking—Tom Moore, Sierra South. Joanne Turner and Doug Schwartz, Southwind Sports Resource. Eric Fournier, California Canoe and Kayak.

Beyond the First Thrill—competent thrill sport providers everywhere.

Big Ride/Ultimate Leap—environmentalists and professional therapists everywhere.

Thanks to Karen Voight of The Voight Fitness and Dance Center for her autographed poster, "The Power. The Grace." And thanks to the "No Fear Dangerous Sports Gear" company of Carlsbad, California for their hot line of "Thrill Sport" T-shirts.

For simply being there, I'd like to thank Maggie Rowe, Sandy Fair, Rick and Susie Zimbelman, Dean and Sue Tanji, The Abracadabra Sliders, Jan and Joe Aldendifer, Scott Fair, Linda Fair Ratcliffe, Al Fair and Kerry Delk.

Finally, extra special thanks to Foghorn Press—Ann-Marie, Vicki and Dave— for the basic idea and for making it happen.

About the Author

While teaching hang gliding to hundreds of students between 1980 and 1988, Erik Fair learned that the two keys to personal safety in any thrill sport are: 1) picking the sport, and the level of involvement, that is right for you; and 2) relentless risk management in the name of exceptional fun.

Fair's first book, *Right Stuff for New Hang Glider Pilots,* sold over 8,000 copies, even though there are less than 8,000 active hang glider pilots in the United States. His articles on thrill sports, recreation and fitness topics have appeared in *The Los Angeles Times, California City Sports, SELF Magazine, Orange Coast Magazine,* and *Soaring, Hang Gliding, Men's Fitness* and *Runways* magazines.

Fair won the prestigious A.O.P.A (Aircraft Owners and Pilots Association) 1991 Max Karant Award for Excellence in Aviation Jouralism. He is a proficient beginner-level participant in each of the nine thrill sports covered in this book.